Sculpture

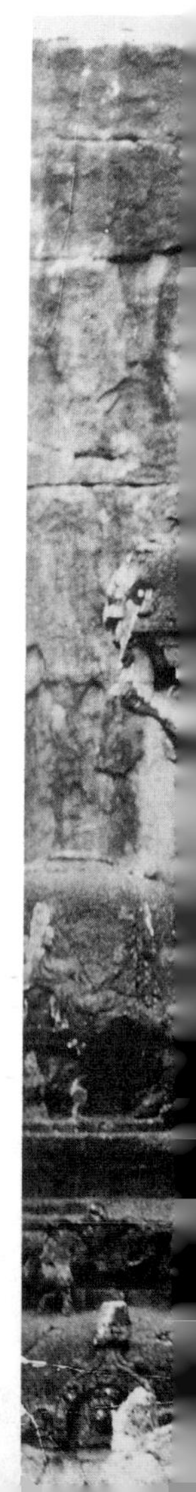

Sculpture

Philip Rawson

PENN

University of Pennsylvania Press

Philadelphia

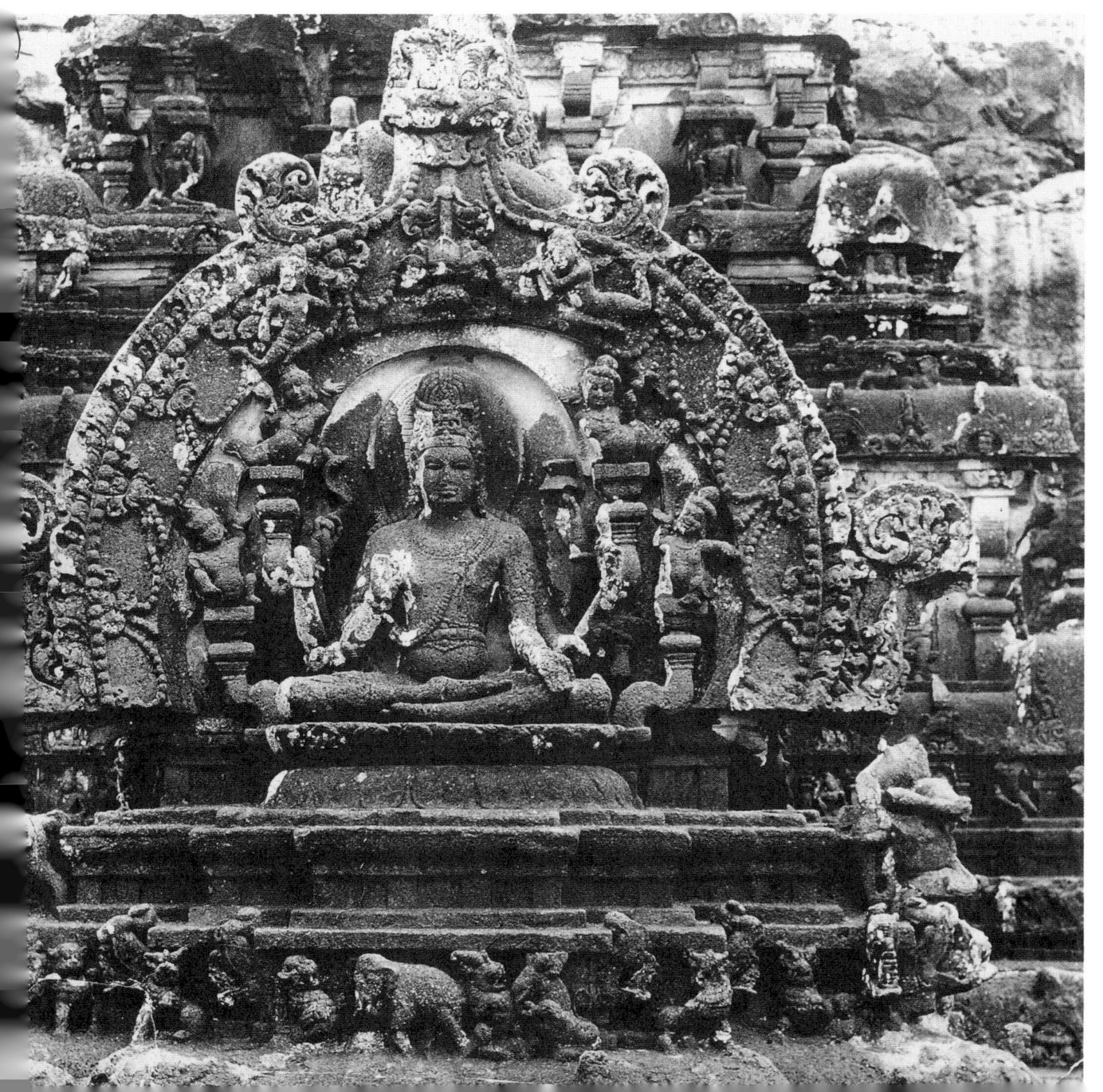

PUBLICATION OF THIS VOLUME WAS GENEROUSLY SUPPORTED BY

FUNDS FROM PROFESSOR AND MRS. MARTIN MEYERSON

10   9   8   7   6   5   4   3   2   1

Published by
University of Pennsylvania Press
Philadelphia, Pennsylvania 19104-6097

Library of Congress Cataloging-in Publication Data
Rawson, Philip S.
    Sculpture / Philip Rawson.
        p.   cm.
    Includes index.
    ISBN 0-8122-8258-2 (cloth : alk. paper)
    1. Sculpture.   I. Title.
NB60.R36   1997
731'.028—dc20   96-28432
                                         CIP

Design: Carl Gross

Frontispiece: Shiva in glory, Kailashanatha Temple, Ellora, India, rockcut, ca. 900 A.D.

Contents

List of Illustrations

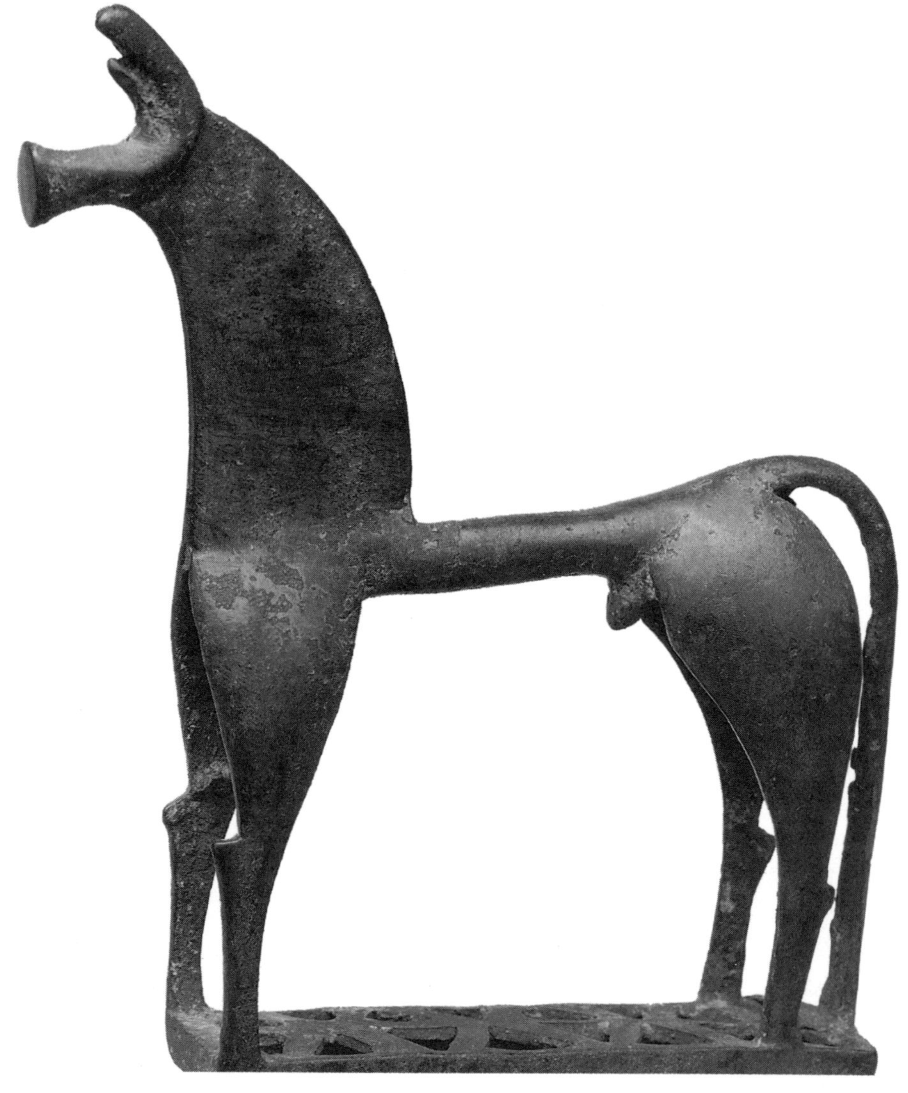

1. Statuette of a horse, Cyclades, bronze, eighth century B.C. Virtually a three-dimensional sign for vital energy. (Courtesy The Metropolitan Museum of Art, Rogers Fund, 1921 [21.88.24].)

1
Introduction

The Book

This book is about sculpture as a worldwide language in which many different thoughts and insights can be expressed. It is not an art history, presenting sculptures chronologically to connect them with contemporary events, though art historical information is quoted here when necessary. Nor is it a book about theories of art. It aims rather to define its own terms by describing sculptural qualities that people can recognize once they realize where, how, and for what they should look. The language of sculpture has had distinct dialects, widely separate in space and time. All sculptors, however, have needed to use at least some part of the range of "terms" available for expression in three-dimensional shape. Like all developed human languages, sculpture conveys the contents of people's minds, combining and above all articulating inner sensations, feeling, emotion, ideas, not remaining content with reporting information on and itemizing detail about external, publicly accepted "facts." In exploring the subject I hope to distinguish two levels of sculptural technique—the material and the formally structural—and to suggest lines of thought for people who make sculpture as well as for those who want to appreciate it fully and perhaps describe it accurately. In passing, people may come across clues to what makes individual works good or less good, or reveals them as fakes.

We live in a world that sets little store by lively sculpture, in comparison with other worlds whose cities and countryside were populated with sculptures that kept alive intensely felt meanings for whole societies. Despite our present human numbers we produce few sculptures and of limited kinds, and these we tend to isolate in museums or special display areas. Currents of skepticism, religious intolerance, and economic pressure have narrowed our interests and skills.

Twentieth-Century Changes

Until recently artists and scholars misinterpreted the aim of Classical Greek sculpture as being to describe as accurately as possible the details of human anatomy within an established framework of ideal proportions. To succeed at this task was to achieve "beauty." Sculpture was thought to consist of imitating and assembling the most beautiful anatomical parts chosen from different beautiful people, none of whom individually would be perfectly beautiful. This idea originated with the first-century-A.D. Roman writer Pliny the Elder. Renaissance sculptors were thought to have revived such an approach, and eighteenth-century Italianate Classicism ossified it, with modifications. Against this background assumption, few sculptures from other traditions were thought to have much value, especially those like the Indian, which followed their own, very different criteria of beauty. In the nineteenth century the Gothic style was admitted to the canon, but onto lower slopes of the peaks occupied by Classical and post-Renaissance sculpture. "Primitive" sculpture still had no place at all.

During the twentieth century we have become able to take a radically different approach. We have learned to accept all sculptural thought as interesting, no matter what its origins. We recognize that only during certain phases of Western art did sculptors actually press far to match each visible and scientifically named part of the human anatomy with a sculptural shape. Most world traditions did parallel with elements of shape the major parts of the human body to which their spoken languages gave names—arm, thigh, eye, cheek, and so on—but this was usually done as the basis for metaphorical matching, as we shall see. In this book I shall use the term *beautiful* to refer not to the Classical anatomical ideal but, as one would in discussing music, to expressive wealth, fine development, and articulation.

In recent decades we have been able to see and appreciate a wide range of the world's sculpture, either at first hand in museums or at second hand through reproduction in art publications. We have learned to accept and read sculptural thought in many dialects of the language of sculpture for two main reasons. First, between about 1880 and 1920 two generations of Western artists began to admire previously unacceptable tribal arts and assimilate elements into their own styles. Among these artists were Paul Gauguin, Ernst Kirchner, Paul Klee, Amedeo Modigliani, Picasso, and many Surrealists. During the first two decades of this century they began to explore seriously arts that had not been previously admired, an investigation that arose not from any anthropological interest or knowledge but purely for the sake of the impact of these works' formal expression. At first, these artists either made virtual copies of "primitive" works of Oceanic and African sculpture or built actual imported pieces into fantasy assemblages. Then, on the basis of this initial experience, sculptors such as Constantin Brancusi began developing formal methods of their own. The term *primitive* is misleading because many of the works so called represent pinnacles of development in their own long-established traditions. Here I shall use the term *tribal*. To explore the formal aspect of these sculptures gave Western artists and public insight into the nature of sculptural language. But the twentieth-century "modern" masters saw tribal arts initially as an aid in disintegrating and dismantling the stale conventions of Western academic sculpture, particularly the "aesthetic cuirass," that set of standard sub-Classical shapes of the front torso musculature which had hardened into a kind of body armor.

The works of tribal art were accessible to artists as a consequence of Western imperialist adventuring around the world and the resulting need to know something of the peoples the West colonized and administered. Traders and administrators first appropriated the artworks of peoples they

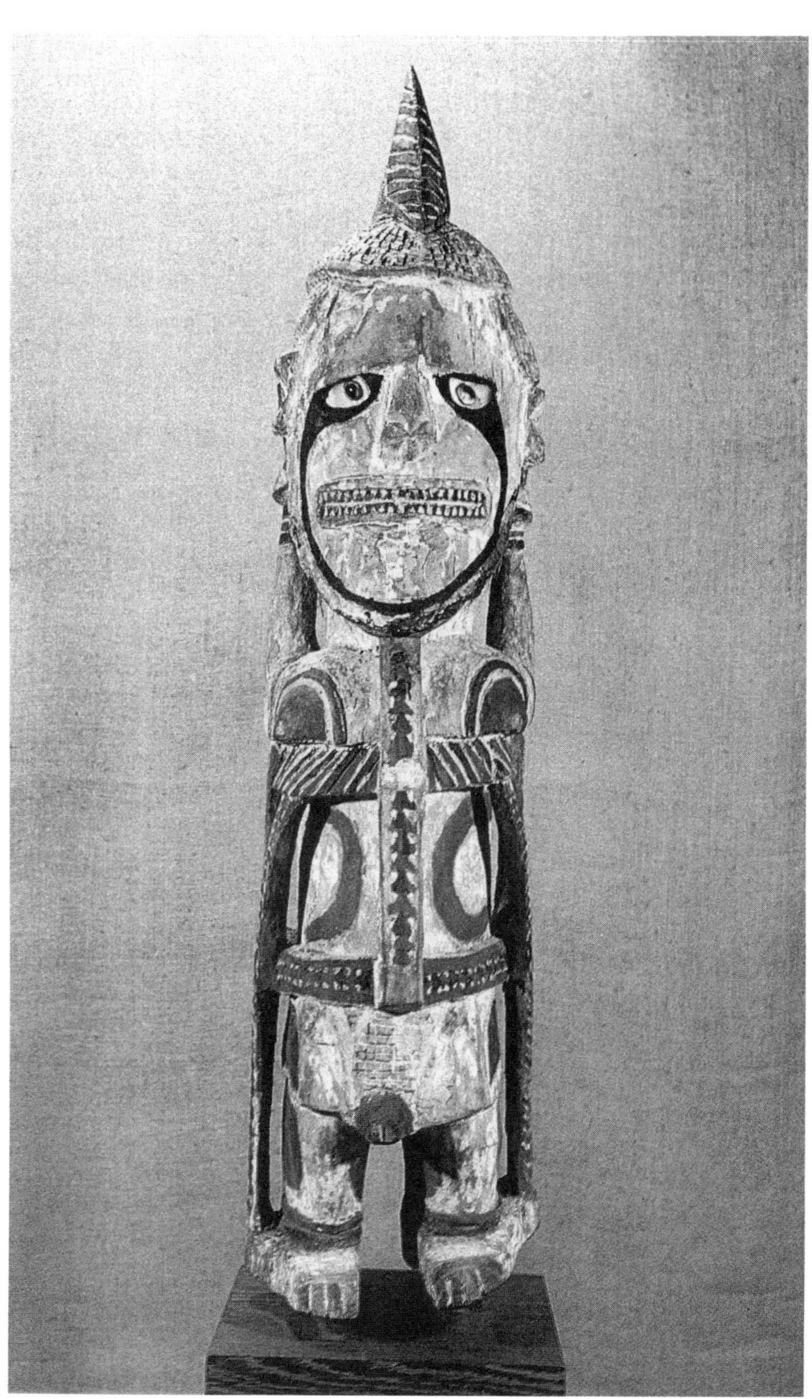

2. Uli figure, New Ireland, painted wood, late nineteenth century. A seminal sculpture for the twentieth-century revolution in sculptural language. (Owned and portrayed by E. L. Kirchner in 1915.)

called "primitive" on the assumption that they represented the mentality prevailing at primitive stages of human evolution. Only a few anthropologists took the works seriously for the sake of their content of meaning. Most Westerners met these artworks isolated in museums and collections, removed from the original contexts that gave them that meaning. So Westerners were able to read only what they called the "significant form," divorced from what that form signified to its maker. Our Western belief in the validity of "abstract art" leading to "pure" aesthetic experience may well be a direct result of this divorce.

The second reason we have learned to accept and read a plurality of expression in scultural thought is that at the time of this artistic exploration, the ideas of depth psychology were spreading across the Western world, especially the Freudian notion of the presence in each individual of the subconscious and its functions. (Jung's wider conception of the *un*conscious took longer to arrive.) Westerners began to recognize an equation between the personal subconscious and the "primitive." In addition, they came to assume that, to become truly creative, a person needed to bypass the conscious, conventional ego and make contact with his or her subconscious. Hence exploring the formal language of "Primitive" arts was considered as an important mode of access for both artist and public to the rich subconscious and "primitive" levels of the individual mind.

Our present-day ideas about the unconscious functions of the psyche are broader and deeper than they once were, and we now realize even more clearly how the meanings that an artistic language precipitates derive from levels of mental operation beyond the direct reach of ordinary consciousness. At these levels, people who differ in the surface culture of their everyday lives may nevertheless have a great deal in common. This view justifies our belief that we do perceive something valuable and meaningful, and therefore not wholly culture-specific, in the expressive shapes of tribal arts.

Chinese calligraphic artists use a term that translates roughly as "the meaning beyond the text" of a handwritten document. Even though the text may be a familiar poem or hackneyed piece of prose, the active handscript adds to the convergent sense of the text through its qualities of touch, speed and continuity, divergent overtones of dancelike gesture, visual reference to the shapes of things not mentioned in the text, plus nuances of emotional tone. Sculptured shapes similarly convey their own "meanings beyond the text" in particular ways, as halos of unconscious formal references. These are available within the matching activity of the minds of both sculptor and observer, which can be tapped and set resonating by inflections of shape.

Since sculpture is essentially three-dimensional, it is not possible to appreciate fully its real qualities of shape from flat, two-dimensional photographs, although the best photographs can be helpful, as can studying two or more reproductions of the same piece. This book, of course, contains two-dimensional pictures, which can only hint at the three-dimensional realities from which they are abstracted. Readers should make every effort to visit and study actual sculptures, including plaster casts (not copies by other people) of historical works that give a truthful three-dimensional impression. At the same time readers should cultivate their sense of three-dimensional reality in everyday life. We all need to do this because so many of us spend our lives boxed between flat, rectangular surfaces at home and in the street. Few of the objects we are able to touch and handle "speak" to our hands and bodies in terms of three-dimensional movement, offering softness and hardness, changing textures, sets of grips and pressures, sliding transitions, and welcoming nonmechanical curvatures. The bulk of our experience of art is two-dimensional, coming to us through two-dimensional design and the flat-screen technology of camera and television. So it is not surprising that many people now think of art as primarily painting and miss out on the whole realm of experience that sculpture offers. In some great ages of sculpture the case was quite the reverse; painting was thought of as the lesser art.

Sculpture Defined

Strictly speaking, the term *sculpture* means carving, but nowadays we use it for almost any method of translating a mass of material from one area of significance to another, from plain thing to meaningful shape and arrangement. All such processes involve reaching final surfaces in space, either by building out toward them in modeling or cutting back to them in carving. Most of the world's good sculpture does not treat space as an abstract, featureless emptiness into which each piece is "dropped," so to speak. Instead it shapes and generates its own inner spatial content along with its environment, by articulating rhythmically closed and open volumes, solids and voids for the visitor to scan and respond to. Sculpture and visitor are present to each other in a way quite unlike the other arts. Each piece offers structured shapes *of* space as well as *in* space. A relief by Donatello, for example, defines its spatial image almost totally, but a major outdoor piece—in a park, say—may work by focusing the open environment around and into itself.

Essentially a sculpture is an inert lump of matter, and artistically illiterate or culturally hostile barbarians may treat it as such. They have melted down bronze masterpieces for coinage or cannon, used superb stone carvings as landfill. Only when we learn how to question a lump for its shapes and their meaning do we begin to treat it as a sculpture. Art history can help the visitor here by suggesting what questions to ask and providing the sheer information needed to understand the sculpture's references. By this I do not mean that we need to translate art, which is not history, into the alien terms of verbalized history recounting "fact," but that we need to understand each piece in its own terms. These can, with some Western works, include historical references, but usually the "meaning beyond the text" remains outside the scope of history as such. We may, however, need to know basic facts such as the material used and perhaps even how it was worked, since both of these can have symbolic fields of reference: gold, jade, or concrete, for example. It will help to know what kind of dance a mask was worn for, or why particular features of a figure are stressed, such as a massive, strong right arm in early Mesopotamian dynastic sculpture.

Two Levels of Skill

A sculptor needs the craft skills to work the chosen materials, and sometimes also physical strength, but these are only the preliminaries to the real business of shaping and arranging, which belongs to a different level of skill and which in ancient and medieval times was the aspect designated "art." During the creation of a sculpture, the artist must be able to make contact intuitively with his or her own inner matrixes of formal relationship, to articulate convergent, divergent, and implied meanings into formal coherence. The visitor has to do the reverse, opening up his or her inner region of responses, deeper than merely recognizing standard facts, to allow the shapes to locate and connect with a whole range of matches beyond the scope of conscious will. With sculpture these memory matches and responses belong to the realm of three-dimensional experience, which is why it is necessary to nourish it as fully as possible in ordinary living. Through this aesthetic way of responding, as distinct from the utilitarian, different people are bound to find different meanings in a single work.

Analogy and Response

For both the artist to find and the visitor to respond to such correspondences depends on an important faculty of the human mind: analogy. Our active minds are busy continually scanning our registered experience and in effect crystallizing lower and higher orders of similarity into what we call forms. To recognize that two instances share a common form at some level constitutes an analogy. Obvious and familiar analogies connect everyday objects, enabling us to recognize a chair we have never seen before as a chair in form, function, and name. If it is an artistically made chair, its shapes may also stimulate analogy correspondences with shapes from other regions of experience: bowed and leafy armrests and front legs, feet like an eagle's triumphantly gripping an orb. When a work sets our inner recognitions resonating also at levels even deeper than this, it produces that mysterious feeling of supernatural but also blissfully familiar wholeness which is one of the chief rewards of the aesthetic encounter. Unless we are interested in the arts we can lose touch with great stretches of our own genuine experience. To repossess them can be of immense personal and psychological benefit.

A sculptor makes shapes that refer both to his or her own and to the visitor's inner range of active analogy linkages, not only between accepted everyday objects but between subsidiary parts, qualities, and functions of objects that may seem to have nothing to do with each other ordinarily.

These analogy links or correspondences that give meanings beyond the text operate through static visual resemblances as well as through similar properties of energy and movement that shapes seem to display: for example, an oblique affinity between a person falling spread-eagled and a leafy branch whipping the surface of a lake; between a fold of flesh and a ripe fruit squeezed to bursting; between fish and a girl's long eyes that suggest sideways glances like silvery flickers in a dark pool. These mobile qualities all must be conveyed by the artist's shapes, which can never be anything but stationary.

Each analogous form linkage seems to include echoes of feeling and emotion, which are also set resonating by the sculptor's shapes. An entire piece, therefore, can set up a complex of responses integrated by the overall image. It is sometimes wrongly assumed that artist and visitor should each experience a strong and specific emotion while making or responding to a work, which the artist is supposed to communicate. But this cannot be so, since any actual emotion—fear, desire, hatred—fills the whole mind and body, blotting out all else. Certainly television drama entertainment does rely on chains of images, often in closeup, that show men and women undergoing exaggerated standard emotions; but this is not real art's way. Art invites us to experience or taste echoes and resonances of form and feeling woven skillfully together, not necessarily all at once but over a period of time long enough for us to contact and reconcile them. To put it crudely, sculptures mean what they look like and make the observer feel. Everything a sculptor does is there to be interpreted; nothing, no emotional attitude or intention, however good or careless, however unconscious of it the artist may have been, can be hidden or discounted.

Most important of all is the consideration that the normal consequence of undergoing a real feeling is to act on it in some way. In an artistic context it is obviously necessary to refrain from action. Members of a theater audience know they are not supposed to dash up to the stage either to grapple with the actor who is in the role of a murderer or to kiss the seductive leading lady. That would be to misread artistic expression as a signal for action. By staying in their seats, audience members are driven back into themselves to taste their own emotive responses based on their previous experiences of life and art. This is virtually a definition of the aesthetic experience as distinct from the lived. We are signaled to realize the distinction by the symbolism of the artistic situation: proscenium or stage, gallery or plinth. In certain circumstances the very strangeness of a piece standing in our everyday environment, such as a sculpture of a woodland monster set up in a glade, can shock precisely because it has no such distinctive warning symbolism.

Decoration

All these factors put a new complexion on what we used to deride as "mere decoration." Good decoration or ornament is intended to amplify the aesthetic range and depth of a piece, to display its inner meaning, and is not a pointless extra simply tacked on. The basic meaning of the words *decoration* and *ornament* is "fitting out" or "equipping" something or someone with whatever is necessary to fulfill an intended role: a soldier with weapons, a room with appropriate furniture, a temple with icons, a cathedral church with prophets and saints—and a sculpture with subsidiary shapes that bear on its focal meaning. When our century rejected banal and excessive decoration, it threw out the baby with the bathwater. Modernist sculptors of all persuasions, but especially assemblage artists, took pride in stripping a piece down to its barest whole-image, and either banishing subsidiary shapes altogether or completing the lesser levels of interest by leaving them to chance (as César did with crushed automobile bodies) without considering them part of the formal invention.

Taken all together the factors just discussed should reveal how misleading is the old critic's cliché that a work shows how an artist "sees" the things apparently represented. Art is making, not recording. Artists compose coherent collections of shapes that are designed to promote images in the minds of viewers, which is where any image has to exist; it only arises there in response to what the sculptor has provided for the visitor to "read" and understand as a coherent if unverbalizable meaning. This means that each work has to awaken into resonance and to coordinate experiences and feelings which are stored in the mind of each viewer, but which may be inaccessible to him or her save in the presence of the work.

Form and Shape

The intermediary in this process is the stock of "forms" that the minds of sculptor and viewer hold in common, which explains why sculpture can be called a language of human communication. While "form" is a mental perception, the physical realities that carry forms from creative mind and hand to receptive eye, hand, and mind I call "shapes." Forms are not things, although things, parts, and clusters of things may convey forms. In geometry we accept that no actual thing can *be* one of the ideal forms with which geometry works. We accept that physical shapes of cardboard, metal, or plastic can convey the idea of the ideal circle, cube, cone, or whatever, which constitute the meaning by reference of the shapes as we meet them in a particular context. Each physical shape in a sculpture, along with its material properties and its context of other shapes, needs to evoke its own formal analogues from the mental stock of the viewer—not only those already in familiar pragmatic design use, such as the recognized "ideal" forms, but also those that the viewer may never have realized that his or her mind contains and has no names for. In fact it is with this last kind of form that the arts primarily deal. Some forms are more comprehensive and general than others, more remote from the infinite variety of live experience and its moving shapes through time. But all forms exist to set up connections and differentiations among our experiences, and the aim of sculpture, like any other art, is to synthesize structures of shape that refer to structures of analogical form within our lived human experience, static and moving. Sculpture especially evokes and combines echoes of fact and feeling that may have no connection in our everyday commonsense world.

Mental Modeling

Sculpture can develop our abilities to think in three-dimensional form and to imagine as well as realize corresponding three-dimensional shapes. These abilities have a great importance for everyday life that is not recognized often enough in our contemporary societies, which tend to treat this art as a minority interest that the majority do not need to bother with. We can view sculpture as fostering a special kind of "literacy," the value and pleasures of which the sculpturally illiterate never experience. It is probable that, just as the verbally literate know and understand more of the world and human mind than do the illiterate, so the sculpturally literate see and understand more of the three-dimensional world, through the mind's three-dimensional formal models of it, than do the sculpturally illiterate.

Model is a key word. The three-dimensional modeling faculty is vital in all kinds of life activities, from architecture, engineering, and the topological sciences to the solving of many everyday problems. Sculptural literacy can enable one to hold and combine in the imagination formal images of complex three-dimensional realities, which one can then symbolize and project as physical shapes. The difference between sculptural and technical three-dimensional modeling involves "abstraction," a term that has become so much entangled in art discourse as to lose its clarity.

Abstraction

An abstraction is not a physical thing; it is a mental image of a common form of a particular order shared by and "taken off from" (the definition of the Latin word *abstractum*) a range of phenomena, excluding as different anything that belongs to other categories of the same order of form. Thus a physical work of art cannot itself be *abstract*; it may exhibit shapes, such as thin straight edges outlining flat, featureless surfaces, which prompt the visitor to read them as referring to shapes of a single geometrical order. The sciences use signs or symbols with physical shapes that refer purely by convention to similarly conventional categories of formal character and relation. The visual *Gestalten* of such signs or symbols do not have to resemble, in their overall shapes, what they mean. In the visual arts, however, it is expressly by their *Gestalten* that shapes carry their meanings from one human mind to another. Some may be so commonly used as to become conventional—for example, the familiar eye-nose-mouth formula for a face. But artists may develop other *Gestalten* which have no obvious conventional meaning, and which the visitor approaches with an open mind ready to read into them what he or she has it in him or her to read.

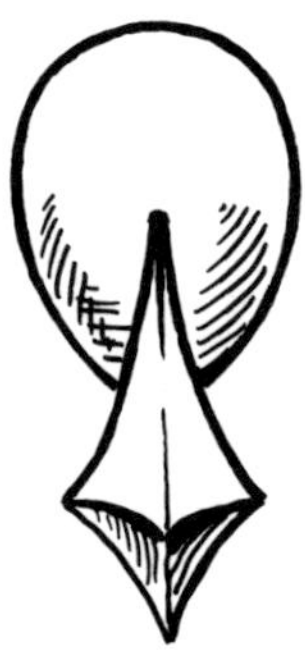

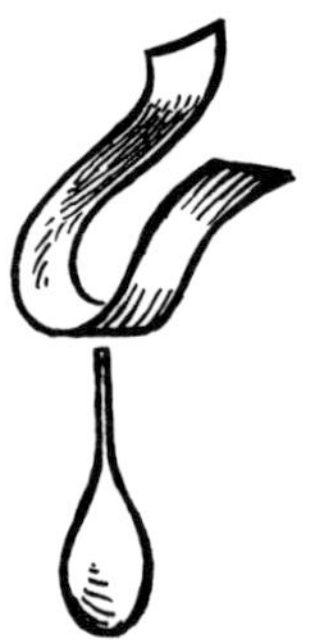

Figure 1.
Pairs of contrasted
form and shape.

Whereas scientific categories of formal abstraction refer exclusively to characteristics in terms of which they are categorized as identical (for example, number, income bracket), the forms of visual art refer inclusively to ranges of concrete experience from what would normally be regarded as separate orders of fact. Each sculptural shape can refer by analogies to forms of more than one order at the same time, combining and overlapping them to produce metaphorical combinations that add both life and variety to the forms and fresh possibilities of response to the experience of sculptor and visitor. A sculpture may exhibit qualities other than three-dimensional shape that have the value of forms. Among these are the colors and physical properties of materials, as well as the traces of human action on them. These qualities impart that evocative richness characteristic of human languages which distinguishes them from scientific sign systems.

It is vital, though, that we, sculptors and visitors alike, recognize scales of distinction among the forms we respond to, which challenge our sense of order, and that we learn to carry on the kind of internal conversation in terms of three-dimensional form, in which our skill for outward expression is rooted.

Structure and Language

It is generally accepted today that we understand and even perceive the structures of our worlds primarily through the symbolic language structures we apply to them, mathematical as well as verbal. Structuralist theory has described how spoken languages operate by stipulating a wide variety of differences, oppositions, and contrasts—and hence similarity groups—and attaching word-signs to them. These signs are conventional and need no longer have much immediate similarity to what they designate. Although the three-dimensional signs that the language of sculpture uses do retain some direct resemblance to what we use them to mean, here too the principle of setting up distinctions is fundamental, and we need to establish basic formal differences, oppositions, and contrasts—and from them relations—among our three-dimensional shapes before we can "say" anything sculpturally interesting with them. Other languages also employ developed sets of rules and signs for modulating, interrelating, and reconciling their basic sets of distinctions to make propositions both varied and coherent. Sculpture uses its own connections and layouts across three-dimensional space to similar effect. A sculptural language gains its strength initially from the strength and value of the basic sets of distinctions which it asserts, then balances out, combines, and reconciles in the structure of each work. Strong and clear distinctions of basic form were precisely the qualities that had been lost under the smooth, naturalistic surfaces of nineteenth-century "beautiful body" sculpture; the revelation of tribal sculpture brought home to early twentieth-century artists the importance of vividly distinct form and shape as the basis of sculptural thought. Nevertheless, we know that languages have their limits.

We all have direct experiences that are quite unconnected with available linguistic terms, and at which we can only hint in words. There may also be several different ways of phrasing the same elusive feeling, experience, or thought.

Forms and Feeling

The Euclidian forms mentioned earlier serve Euclidian geometry as maximum degrees of three-dimensional difference and contrast between basic units of volume. For some practical purposes we may analyze more complex three-dimensional shapes in terms of combinations of and variations on these regular solids. Realized alone as individual physical shapes, however, they have limited sculptural interest: they are overfamiliar, they are relatively featureless, and they refer to a range of instances much too vast to connect up the host of analogical and feeling references that are the essence of broadly human, as distinct from narrowly logical, experience. When artist-sculptors have realized Euclidian forms strictly, as the twentieth-century Russian avant-garde did, it has been for the sake of the emotional overtones the shapes carried at that time: scientific clarity, democratic neutrality, and moral purity. Some of the traditional modes of the type of sculpture I define later as "radical shaping" may operate with sets of fundamental form distinctly different from the geometrical, such as the African. Any mode may work those variations and combinations of shape, which are the essence of sculptural thinking, by employing its own set of basic differentiated forms.

In any given mode, basic forms, recognizable and repeatable as shape, are the ground of communication between sculptor and visitor, differentiating intelligible three-dimensional "sound" from haphazard "noise." It is a fallacy to assume that creative artists either must or can continually invent totally new fundamental forms. What they do invent are fresh inflections, combinations, connections, and aggregates of shape in new contexts, as poets operate with familiar syllables, phonemes, and word structure, musicians with standard note-scales and chords. In art a basic S-curve, for example, may be interpreted as the spinal contour of a twisting animal or the stem of a plant, according to the context of other shapes among which it is placed or to which it is linked. Whether all the basic forms are derived only from past experience, recorded on the mind's "blank page," or are somehow implicit and archetypal in the evolved human constitution, is a question not yet answered. The artist has to operate as though all levels and stretches of form beyond the basic are far wider and deeper than the categories of systematic logic, as we shall see.

In our daily lives we do encounter varied spreads of shape in different contexts that imbue them with feeling-tone. And we may learn to recognize among them characteristic forms that make "sense" of them. It is our experience of our art as "language" that enables us to comprehend three-dimensional forms and structures along with their fields of reference at the levels of both fact and feeling. Some cultures recognize and name distinct forms in places where we might normally see none, though we can learn to recognize them if we learn to share the experience on which they are based. Inuit people recognize and have names for different forms of falling and lying snow that other people are not familiar with. Certain African tribal people who are passionately devoted to dancing give names to specific qualities of shape their dancers try to achieve in the hollows between their erector spinae muscles or to the interplay between the ends of their shoulderblades.

Tenor and Topic

In an earlier book on drawing I proposed an important distinction within any artistic image between two elements I call "tenor" and "topic." The tenor is the overall object or set of objects the work depicts, its overt iconography; the topic is the specific set of arranged shapes by means of which the tenor is presented. The tenor works like the poles of a tent to deploy and hold together the fabric of artistic expression. The topic is the "meaning beyond the text." This distinction explains the extraordinary differences between the many versions of a familiar tenor, for example, mother and child, or heroic horseman.

The point of the tenor is to provide a numinous focus for the whole work, a context for distinctive elaborations of its parts, and a basic coherence to underlie complex variations of shape. Tenor poses a real challenge to the contemporary sculptor as we emerge from the era of utterly conventional tenors—female nudes, bust portraits, and tabletops. These were still needed even by the Cubists to anchor their novel and experimental execution in the contexts of both real life and accepted art. Even in the first decades of the twentieth century, however, there were sculptors who also developed original methods but felt that the tenor constituted a major part of the sculptor's invention for any piece because it was so important as stimulus for the topic development. This was equally true for Renaissance artists such as Botticelli and Michelangelo, who found their tenors in mythological literature. Among sculptors of the twentieth century who adopted or evolved such stimulating tenors were Auguste Rodin, Jacques Lipchitz, and Constantin Brancusi. They married the symbolism of their tenors intimately with their topic-methods of shaping.

Two Modes of Sculpture

Sculptors approach the tenor in two distinct ways that are closely connected to the distinction between two fundamental modes of sculpture. I call these modes "radical shaping" and "assemblage," the latter being technically the much quicker and easier approach. The radical shaping sculptor tends naturally to start with a chosen tenor and work out the topic shapes in a single integral material (occasionally more than one). Every part of the material needs to participate somehow in the reading of the whole piece. The traditional kinds of modeling, molding, and carv-

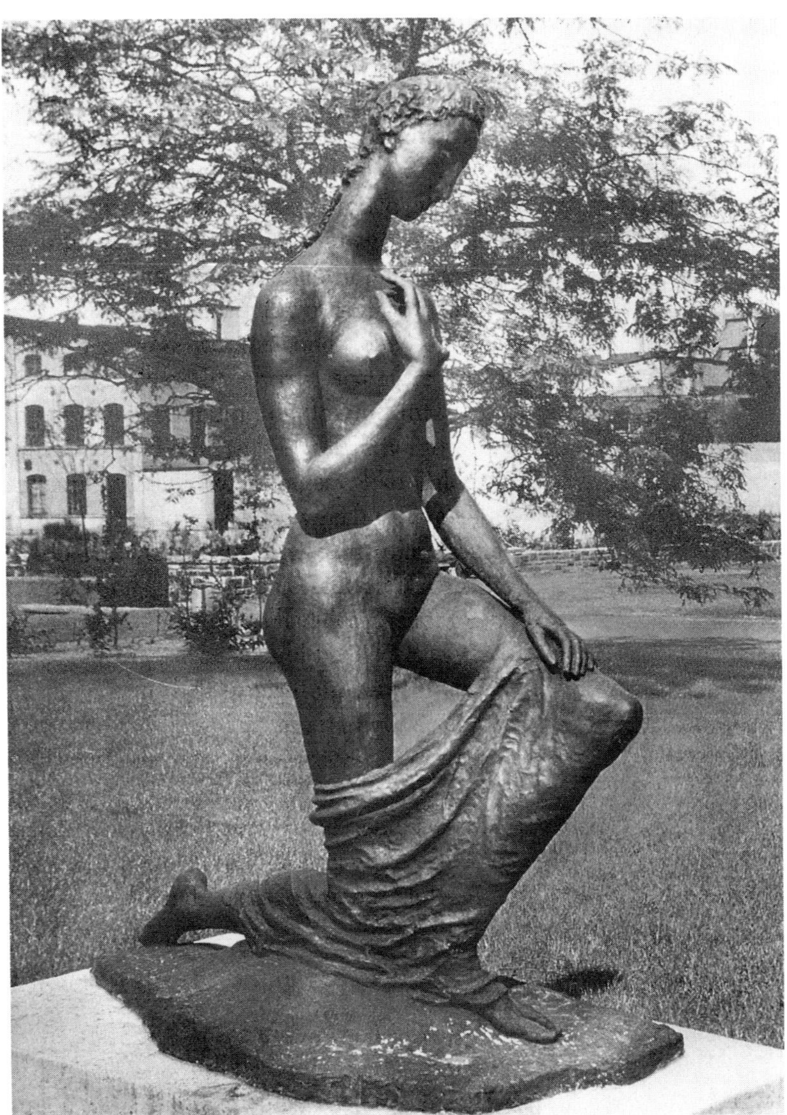

3. Wilhelm Lehmbruck, *Kneeling Woman*, bronze, 1911. One of the first great twentieth-century works in which the Classical spirit and tradition were modified by twentieth-century formal language. (Wilhelm Lehmbruck Museum, Duisberg, Germany; Foto Moser, Rembrandt Verlag, Berlin, no. 79.)

ing are usually done in this mode. It is more demanding technically than assemblage because every part of the visible surface calls for active shaping and balancing out against every other. Some sculptors in this mode have taken as tenor extremely unfamiliar aspects of the world, such as greatly enlarged segments of, for example, body parts or plant material, or combinations of shape from different orders of reality, as when Alberto Giacometti presents a lifelike hand within an otherwise largely geometric structure in one of his earlier Surrealist-influenced pieces.

The assemblage sculptor fixes together or arranges objects that already exist so as to give rise to an image, often suggestively figural, but which may by its title imply a remote tenor—so remote, in fact, that many people may have difficulty in glimpsing it. Although the process depends on the physical combination of existing objects, sculptors may still have planned their assemblages in advance, either as drawings or maquettes (small preparatory models).

Full-fledged assemblage art probably originated in tribal societies as a permanent derivation from the custom of the ceremonial (and so temporary) decking out of the heads and bodies of dancers with magically symbolic materials and objects, such as colored pigment, feathers, bones, quills, teeth, and shells. These lifted the dancer to a fresh symbolic level through the interpretations the society put on the objects assembled, which were then incorporated into masks and images. Some assemblage artists today build into a body image of some kind components manufactured for another purpose, such as steel pipe, and strict Constructivists require their components to have a definite industrial function, not just look as if they do. Some sculptors make objects specifically intended to be assembled, such as furniture spars or carved or cast fragments; others compose assemblages from objects found in nature, with "natural" qualities, or from city garbage, such as bits of wrecked cars or burned homes. These objects carry with them connotations and symbolic values springing from both their original functions and the hazards to which they have been subjected to produce their present shapes. Sculptors have used and can use anything whatever, including working machines, projected transparencies or film, tanks of water, live creatures, and printed texts. The topic-working of such art may result more from the artist's contextual placement of the piece than from any active shaping.

Tenor

A sculptor may adopt a tenor in response to the specific demands of a patron or to follow current conventions (still a powerful force in the contemporary art world). In the past, dominant rulers used to demand of their sculptors images reflecting their force and prowess. Religions still require their central imagery to be presented with maximum doctrinal accuracy and emotional conviction. Bourgeois patrons still choose tenors that flatter their sense of status, reflect their enjoyment of high living, and symbolise "success." Politicians naturally expect tenors to exalt the principles for which they stand. It is at the level of tenor only that the patron's control and consequent social criticism can be fully exercised. Except in the most severe tyrannies, true topic is beyond the reach of explicit argument, since it depends so completely on personal responses to subsidiary expressive shaping. Tenor and topic fully match each other only when the commissioning authority and artist are in accord, or when the artist is his or her own patron.

As a language of feeling, sculpture needs a focus if it is to be at all clear.

It speaks primarily of how the artist feels about something: topic about tenor. Even in ordinary life unfocused expression of generalized feeling is not usually interesting. A sculptor who has no other tenor may fall into emotive self-portraiture, which rarely has any continuing interest beyond that of historical document.

Here questions of moral assessment become relevant, even though some people deny vigorously that morality in the ordinary sense has anything to do with art. We can, however, recognize that sculptors treat particular tenors with attitudes we are bound to respond to and which they reveal in their topic shaping. They may express oppressive cruelty, as so much Stalinist sculpture did, or, at the opposite pole, respect or tenderness, as so much life-enhancing and spiritually valuable sculpture does.

Symbolism

Both tenor and topic operate at their own levels of symbolism, tenor through the meanings of objects, topic through those of shape, connection, and what we might call the "musical" leading of forms. The term *symbolism* may need clarifying, because for the time being criticism and history seem to be passing through a phase of extreme reductionism. This approach interprets the arts as doing nothing much more than pointing at the "plain facts" of the artist's life and times, in the belief that these are the "real meaning" of the works. This view is the opposite of the actual process of artistic creation, which is dedicated to distilling and synthesizing within human experience a sense of meaning and unity that has nothing to do with concepts imposed later by historicism. The artist has only his or her own experience of living at a given place and time as basic material out of which to work; therefore the historian may be interested in looking into the art for its value as a documentary source. But no artist works with the intention of providing documentary source material for historians, as a journalist might. If the historicist position were true, the historicist would always be able accurately to read back from a work whose provenance and historical background were totally unknown the contemporary circumstances under which it was made; this has never been accomplished.

The point of a symbol of any kind is that it focuses and connects regions of feeling and sense that are otherwise not connected, perhaps unthinkable save through the intermediacy of the symbol. It is the symbol that lifts them to the level of "reality." Every recognized object, person, or shape can be read on two levels (at least): as part of the structure of the common, communal world to which one would normally react appropriately, or as standing symbolically for a complex of connected experiences to which it is the only key, and which is accessible only when one abandons normal-life reactions for the sake of inwardly exploring the complex. We need to develop the capacity to read and use things as symbols, just as with any other mode of communication, such as mathematical symbols. Artistic symbols, however, have no fixed canon that we can memorize.

Viewers can only rely on their human capacity for refraining from pragmatic action and taking aesthetic experiences as symbolic.

Sculpture's physical components deal symbolically with things that cannot be seen. They use a formal imagery of visible and tangible shape to explore thoughts and feelings; we are never expected just to react to the tenors of sculpture as if they are real people or things standing around in our own space. This is why works that are narrowly naturalistic—waxwork portraits, say—and do no more than record outer facts of physiognomy and dress are so uninteresting. They fail to reveal themselves as focal points for the gathering and precipitation of the analogies and feeling-echoes of true topic-shaping. They therefore establish no real communication between "speaking" sculptor and responding visitor.

4. Colombian art, gold pendant, tenth to sixteenth century. Probably worn to invoke, by its energetically gesturing shapes, the protection of supernatural power. (The Metropolitan Museum of Art, Gift of H. L. Bache Foundation, 1969.)

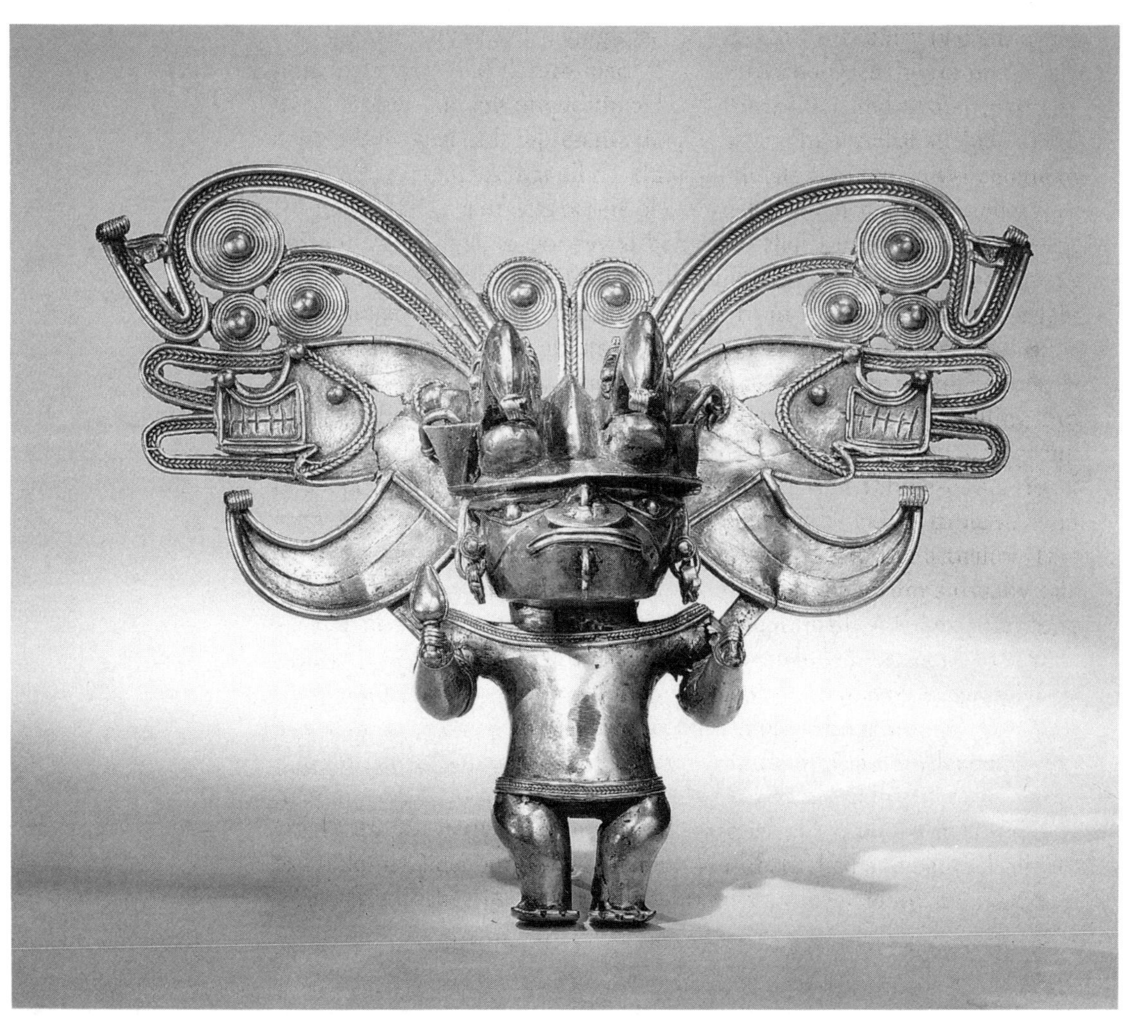

The overwhelming majority of sculptures take as tenor the living body in one guise or another—usually human, but sometimes animal with implied human reference. Our own bodies are what we know most intimately, through the store of memories of our own and other people's postures, gestures, and actions, which are associated with what we felt them to mean. By evoking our inner mimetic responses, body images speak to us in a particularly personal way, and sculptural images are capable of seeming to "act" even more emphatically and with stronger focus than a dancing body. Apparently "abstract" pieces, such as Anthony Caro's or Eduardo Chillida's, gain their depth of significance by referring us inward to our sympathetic responses to weight, support, balance, and stress. Body image can thus unify distinctive expressive shapes. And it may well be important that a shape looks like "a leg" that acts *so*, a "pair of arms" gesturing *so*, a "head" that is positioned *so*. The poet Dante, who knew Giotto, wrote that an artist who intends to paint a figure must first *be* it. Conversely, the visitor who wants to "understand" a sculpture should first feel his or her way into *being* it inwardly.

The prevailing norm of bodily proportion is one factor that must always be taken into account with any body image. Any variation of or departure from this norm is bound to play a part in the reading of an image. One of the principal features of early modernist twentieth-century art, and a consequence of the interest in tribal arts, is the way in which it freed itself from the need to follow the standard and accepted proportions of the "factual" structure of the human body. Until about 1915 all Western artists were subject to the post-Renaissance academic principle, based on drawing from the model, which conditioned the way everyone saw art. Both the public and conservative critics considered any deviation from the norm as representing at worst a physical deformity, at best an expressive distortion.

Tribal and other "exotic" arts have their own visual body norms which their artists respect. But these norms are not, of course, our norms, so they can still seem "unnatural" to us. Of course, their very "unnaturalness" may have contributed to their intended meaning. In the Western-influenced world the vast quantity of photographic images carried by magazine advertising and television has fixed extremely rigid norms in the popular mind, against which sculptors and public alike measure what body images mean: we adhere strictly to them, take them as givens which we then modify, or react violently against them. One of Picasso's principal services to art is that by his example he freed artists both to use shapes referring to, yet fragmented from, parts of the body image—without any requirement that they add up to a whole-body norm—and to assemble highly nonresembling shapes into body images. Fragmentation, unless the sculptor is careful, can give the impression of executing an act of sadistic butchery on the tenor, and nonresembling shapes can seem merely arbitrary. Fragmentation in space works only at the visual level.

At the tactile level we need to make sure that our transitions from shape to shape are both continuous and coherent, even though they may not follow the formal layout of the whole-body image. Jean Arp's full three-dimensional work shows this level of coherence clearly.

Indian Metaphor

Late medieval Sanskrit texts from India include descriptions of how the body image can focus analogies from other realms of experience, creating a dense poetic imagery of metaphor. The implications of the advice to sculptors in these texts lead us to recognize how metaphorical references of similar kinds are expressed in the nonnaturalistic body shapes of sculptures from many other traditions, though without surviving texts to help us we have to rely on our analogy intuitions to sense what those references may be.

As well as giving an overall proportional grid, based on a module measured on the face from hairline to chin and having twelve equal subdivisions, the texts suggest that each part of the body should be shaped so as to resemble some other object that has a strong poetical resonance in the Indian cultural context. The bodies were usually those of divine persons and so should never display bones, muscles, or veins. Indian culture experienced the body as being inwardly inflated with "breaths" (*pranas*) and expressed this sculpturally through almost total convexity. Females and males obviously differ in some proportions and physical features. Here is a list of the principal parts of the body and their poetic shape analogues.

Face	resembles overall an egg or a betel leaf
Forehead	over the brows resembles a compound bow, able to shoot arrowlike glances from the eyes
Eyebrows	like willow or nim leaves, rising like such leaves disturbed by the wind
Eyes	shaped like fishes or wagtail birds, both of which move quickly, or like lotus leaves, or when wide open like water lilies
Ears	like the letter क, the insides of sea shells, or crouching vultures
Nose	like the perfumed sesame flower with nostrils inflated like the flowers of the long-bean, or like the beak of the parrot, bird of love, with nostrils drawn taut
Lips	like the bright red bimba fruit, or shaped like the banduli (snapdragon) flower, visited and pressed slightly open by bees searching for its sweetness
Chin	like the hard stone in soft, ripe mango fruit

Figure 2. After Abanindranath Tagore, *Some Notes on Indian Artistic Anatomy* (fig. 9).

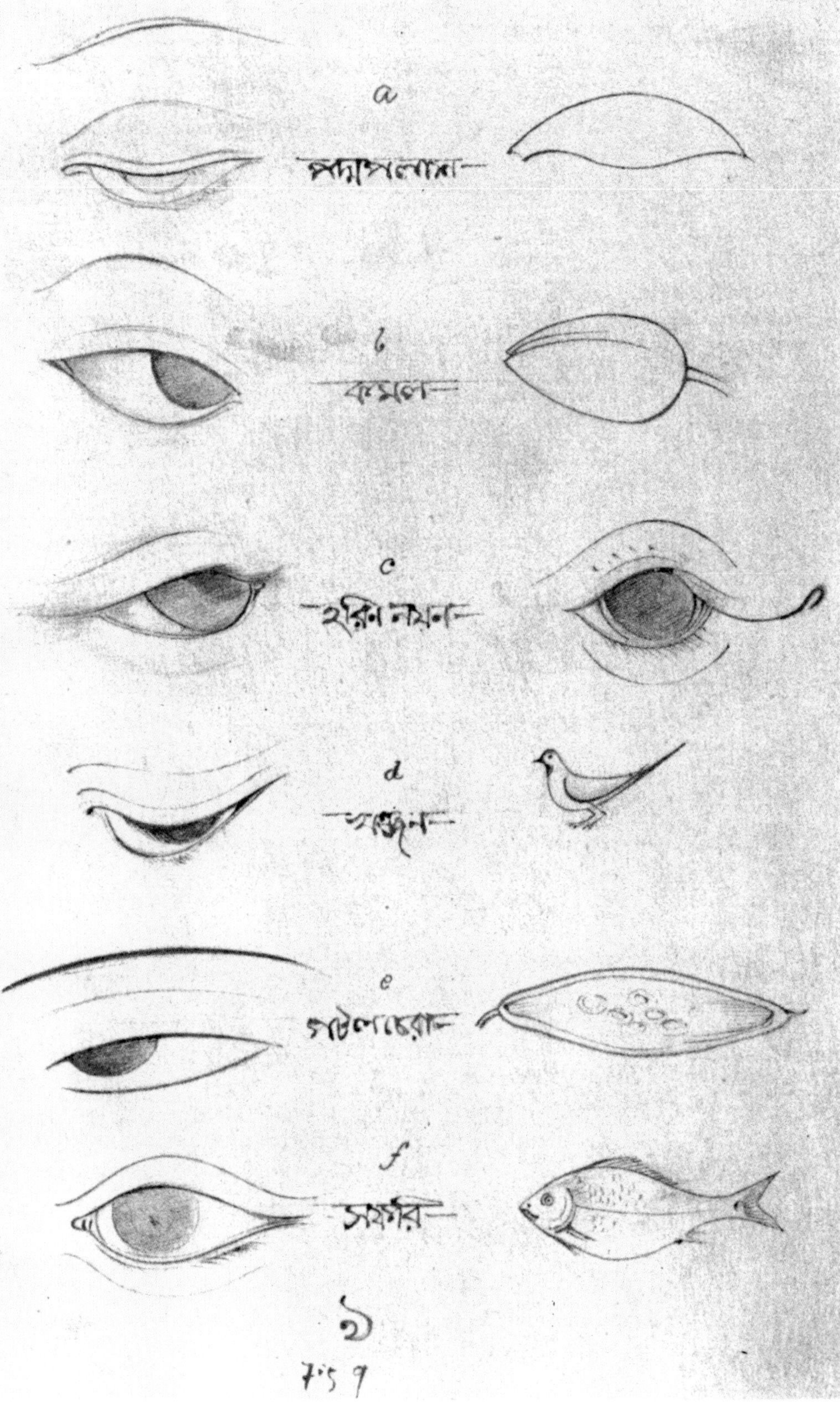

a
পদ্মপলাশ
b
কমল
c
হরিণ নয়ন
d
কপোত
e
গুটলাচেরা
f
সফরী
৭
7.59

Neck	like the conch shell with its slight surface creases and the powerful sound it can produce when blown
Trunk of body	like the face of a sacred cow, or the torso of a lion
Waist	of a woman, like the waist of a double drum
Breasts	of a woman, like deep cups
Shoulders	like the forehead and trunk of an elephant, running down into the upper arm
Forearms	like young plantain trees
Hands	like long flower buds with fingers like opening petals, or the pods of peas
Hips	of women, in plan like a great wheel with its axis
Thighs	like the trunks of full-grown plantain trees; of women, with their hips, like the trunks of young elephants
Kneecaps	like crabshells
Shins	with their calves like fish full of roe
Feet	insteps arched like seashells

These descriptions give us some clues to the many other kinds of three-dimensional analogues from the surrounding world of nature and city we should look for in reading the works of other cultures, as well as how we might increase the poetic content of our own body images. In practice, if we try to devise sets of forms that are markedly distinct and apply them to parts of what can be recognized and treated as a body, however unnaturalistic, these forms are virtually bound to evoke metaphorical resonances of some kind, although they may not be so immediate and concrete as those the Indian tradition schematized.

Power and Life

One final speculative point about the implications of what sculpture may accomplish bears mention. When we describe a piece as being powerful, energetic, impressive, and vital, these words of appreciation are not merely casual. They have behind them a history and serious intent with which we can connect, if we consider the implication of each: "full of power," "imbued with energy," "applying its impress," "displaying life." These words all imply an active force working through the sculptural expression. We tend to think that this force is no more than the sculptor's "personality," which may be partly the case, but is not the whole story.

Earlier ages identified this force with a transpersonal energy: not exactly communal but present and acting to create and change the world from somewhere beyond the control of either person or community. The best general word for it is *spirit*, which implies air moving invisibly. Spirit works through sexual activity to create children; it animates the environment of earth, sky, forest, and sea. Until the end of the nineteenth century almost every sculptor felt him or herself to be "inspired," that is, imbued with spirit, when the work went well. In the twentieth century, too, many sculptors have had a similar feeling, even though they may not have believed in any transcendent principle. The origin of the term *genius* refers not to something a person possesses but to a spirit that may sometimes possess a person.

Sculptures have been perceived since the earliest times and all over the world as providing bodies or dwellings for spirit-beings or forces. In Oceania ancestral spirits have been given humanoid shapes and set up in and outside villages to watch over events. In other regions they have been accommodated in family shrines. Spirits of more general power have been called up—or down—to take possession of dancers at rituals, and the masks that we so much admire were part of the apparatus of possession, treated as sacred objects in themselves. It is probable that many of the earliest clay figurines from the Balkans, the Middle East, and Mesoamerica were also made to precipitate spiritual energies (as we know many more recent tribal sculptures were) and so fertilize the ground or fortify a community. Indeed to invest any image with strong form and radiant color seems to have been meant to translate it from the banal here-and-now into the realm of spirit.

Sculptures in resistant stone or bronze make permanent and enduring the spiritual energy they contain or the intention to which they bear witness, as with the great dynastic works of the early Middle East. On medieval Christian cathedrals the sculptures are intended to testify to the permanent presence of the sacred persons who constitute and support the Church of God until the end of time. Innumerable examples could be cited to make the point that to set up a sculpture is always a highly significant action, which imbues a place or event with the specific power the piece embodies.

Particular shapes have been and still are used to express inner energy or power. Two-dimensional graphic emblems have been inscribed for many thousands of years on caves, stones, and houses and painted or tattooed on people's bodies as amulets. Among them are triangles, spirals, and labyrinths. Modern artists have often reclaimed these to add force to the topics of their works, but for sculpture the emblems have deeper implications. Again we can look back in time for the roots of such signs.

First are eye shapes. Many different peoples have painted or carved eyes on objects such as boats and weapons to animate them. Maori tikis and Hawaiian fiber and feather war gods have huge eye-rings of cut shell, and virtually all tribal carved figures or masks have exaggerated eye shapes to demonstrate the presence of an indwelling spirit looking out. Often shapes of nose and mouth are connected with eyes into a diagrammatic image of the male and female sexual organs: ancestry is sexual. The early twentieth-century painter Paul Klee said that "pictures look at you." There are possible reasons for this effect in biological signaling, but regardless of the explanation, the way to make any sculpture effective is to give it pronounced eyes.

Second, spirals and labyrinths refer to the mysterious region of spirit in general and add power to objects on which they are inscribed. In many regions of the world, arts based on complex spiraling have flourished.

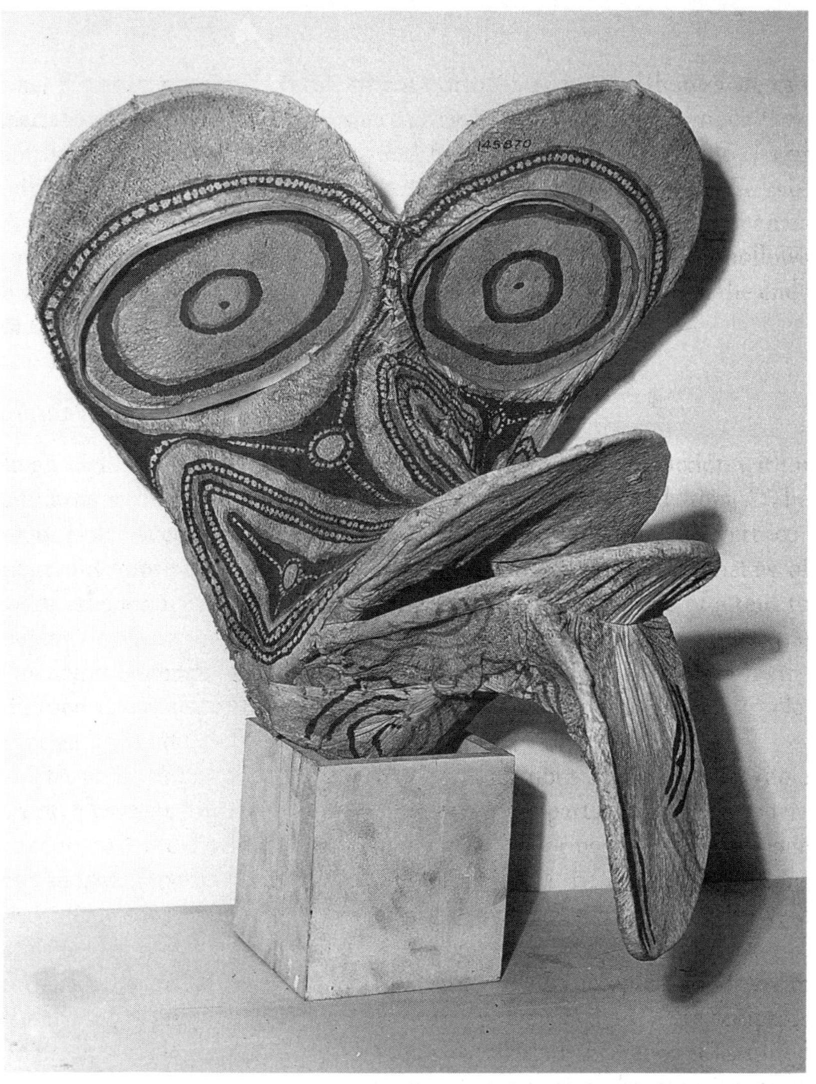

5. Baining tribe mask, Gazelle Peninsula, New Britain, bark cloth (nineteenth century?). Its maximal projection into actual three-dimensional space symbolizes its spiritual vigor. (Photograph courtesy the Field Museum of Natural History, A91289, Chicago.)

Wooden sculptures in Oceania were often carved with spiral designs, perhaps added as panels on both sides of a head. In ancient China huge ritual bronze vessels were cast with eyed masks executed as elaborate spiral and hook designs in relief. Heads with hair seem to have been regarded almost worldwide as the focus of power for the human and spiritual body, and so have been painted or sculpted with spirals. Some tribal peoples have kept the actual heads of revered ancestors or powerful enemies, and virtually everywhere people decorate their own living heads with crests, hairdos, hats, feathers, and crowns to emphasize their power and status, and to celebrate holidays. These features are adopted in sculpture.

Another shape, the downward-pointing triangle, has historically been used to symbolize the female generative power, since the shape resembles the frontal aspect of the external female genitals. Even apparently realistic figure sculptures may wear a version of this emblem at the proper place.

Most of the emblems and signs discussed so far have customary recognized values. Other elaborate shapes that artists build into sculpture also seem meant to convey spiritual energy. The great undulating waves that the carvers of the Parthenon pediment and Michelangelo sent rolling through the surfaces of torsos; the endlessly varied streams and whorls of drapery ("robes of glory") that Gothic, Baroque, and Rococo sculptors sent billowing mysteriously; the fantastic bumps and hollows that Rodin set working in his active nudes—all seem intended to infuse into their tenors a comparable spiritual force represented by the energy and variety of the formal invention. However we may interpret such "life" or "spirit," this idea certainly disposes of the common cliché that such artists "see the world" like that. In fact, they create an imaginative construct that is emphatically *not* visible in the ordinary world to anyone.

We must ask how any sculpture can express such "life" or "power," since no sculpture is essentially more than that inert lump of material that the artistically illiterate cannot interpret. Reading is the key, and an

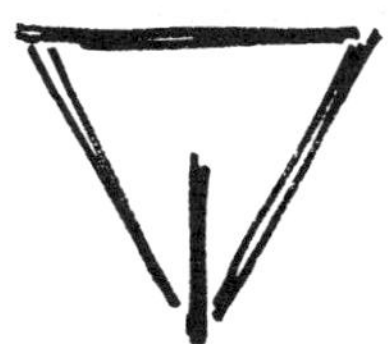

Figure 3.
Female triangle.

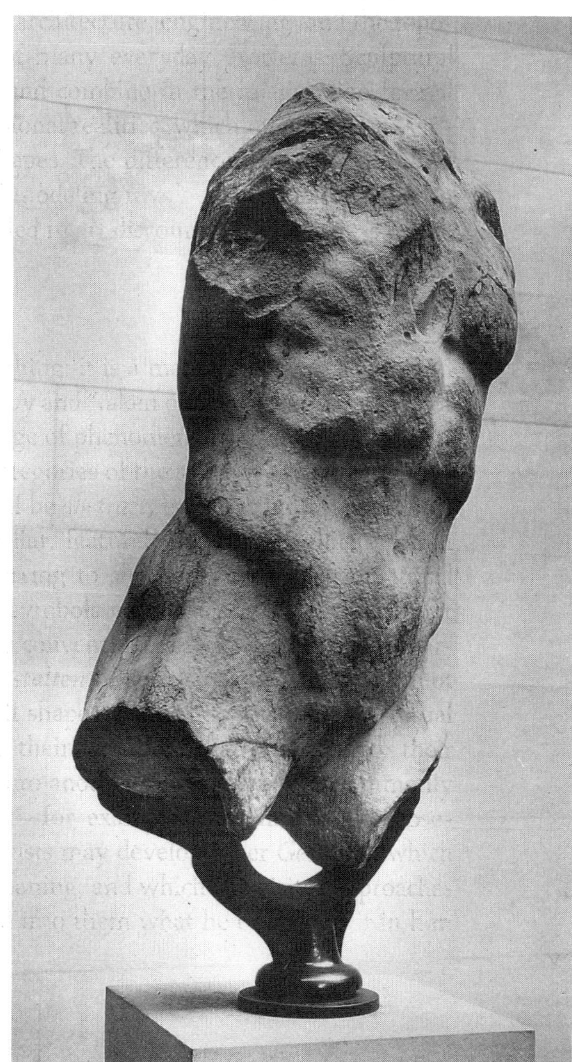

6. Torso of Hermes, marble, from West pediment of the Parthenon, Athens, ca. 435 B.C. Waves of undulating and coherent three-dimensional surface convey a sense of the god's superhuman energy. (Reproduced by courtesy of the Trustees of the British Museum.)

inert piece of material can only "borrow" its "life" from the active life of the person who reads it. We humans attend to our world by a process of continually scanning, matching, and conflating our perceptions. We read text by scanning rows of letters, and to read a sculpture means to scan it along tracks of attention that the sculptor has built into it. It is the mobility of our scanning, picking up and connecting the runs and sequences of varied shape and direction according to which the artist has worked the material, that brings a sculpture to life. Its shapes then become a kind of permanently present music that the sculptor has composed and the visitor can follow. This is one reason why variation and coherence in a sculpted shape are both interesting and necessary. Unless we read them as sequences, even the most various and beautiful arrays of realized form may lie dead in the stone. Sculptured shapes of all kinds as well as their articulation and spacing are rooted in linear scanning, however "eternal" these works may be supposed to seem.

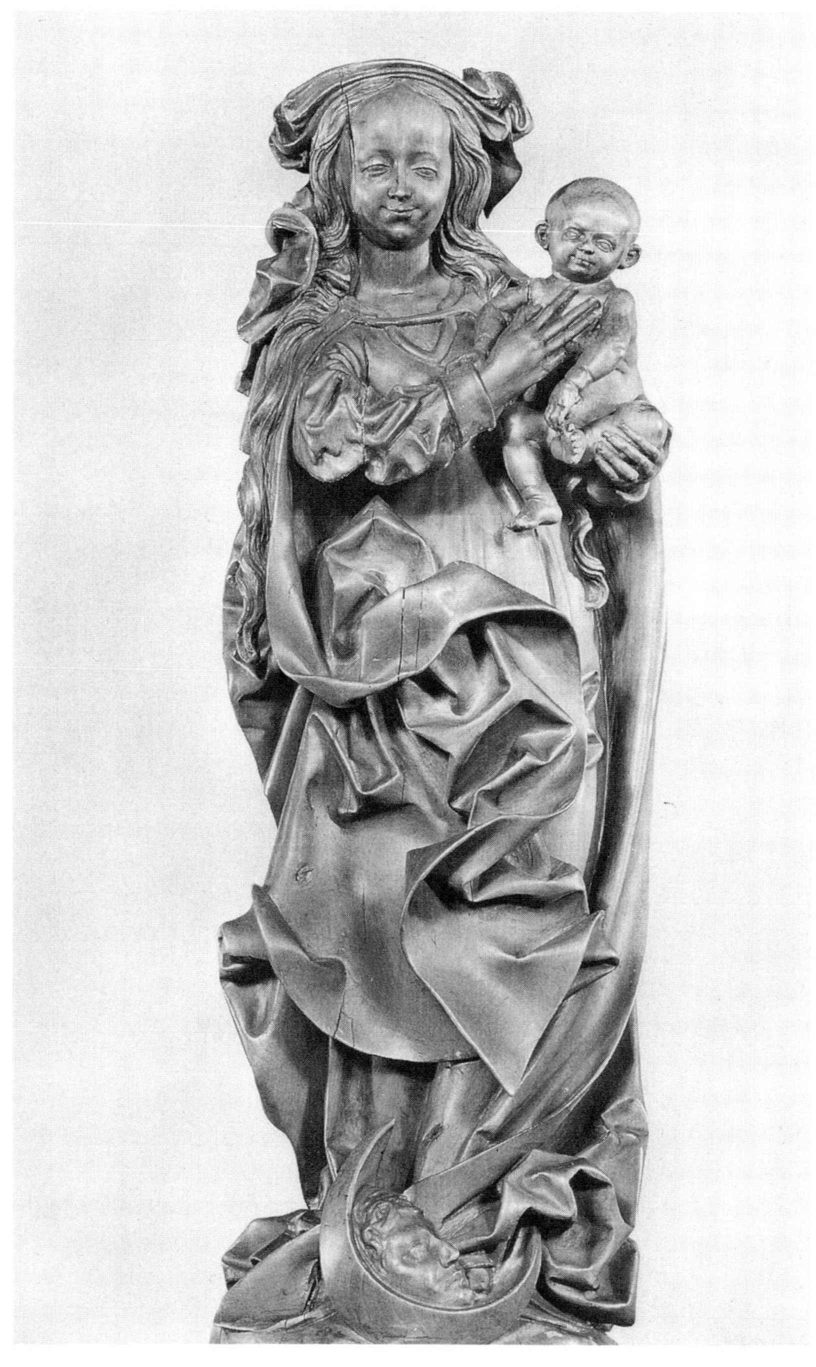

7. Veit Stoss (ca. 1447–1533), *Virgin and Child*, boxwood, early sixteenth century. By formal development and rhythmic complexity resembling fugal music, this carver of colossal altarpieces concentrated a sense of celestial glory into a tiny image expressing and meant for private adoration. (Courtesy the Trustees of the Victoria and Albert Museum.)

2
Processes and Materials

Permanence and Transience

The material for any sculpture has usually been chosen for a variety of symbolic reasons, but especially to embody thoughts and feelings so as to convey these to visitors over a period of time, perhaps very long indeed. A few mechanical assemblage sculptors, the best known being Jean Tinguely, have chosen out of calculated ironic perversity to construct pieces that destroy themselves in front of spectators as a "happening." Materials differ in their permanence and resistance to decay, as well as in their appearance and color. The sculptor's choice of material is largely governed by the purpose for which the work is to be made. Some works may even be meant to be disposed of almost at once after a ceremony. The skill and density of formal invention that go into the work may reinforce its effect of permanence as well as its expressive power.

The most durable materials are the most physically resistant and the most difficult and expensive to work with, especially by hand. Stones such as diorite and granite, for example, have been chosen expressly for the symbolic value of these properties for images of royal and state power (Sumer, Egypt, Mount Rushmore), and to provide "eternal" dwellings for the spirits of dead royalty in the tomb. Such images survive long after the power and significance of the patrons have passed away; this fact may add an element of pathos to the meaning of the work for us, which was certainly never part of its original intention. Other stones and bronze have been used widely as personal memorials for the spirit and achievements of the dead, and often bear inscribed text praising the person.

Icons that mark out a sacred site and provide a dwelling for the sanctifying spirit or deity may be carved in the living rock, in the stone of a preexisting structure, or in some other durable or valuable material such as bronze, gold, or ivory (for example, the chryselephantine statue of Athena Parthenos), to be installed in a shrine. A shrine itself, built of stone or wood, may be carved with figures and ornament that demonstrate and distribute its indwelling powers, perhaps by recording the legends and events associated with holy persons.

Some materials, such as gold, jade, and certain woods, have symbolic value that is rooted in their traditional magical properties; this supplements the imagery into which they are worked. Sculptures may also be made in impermanent materials such as straw and paper, especially to be

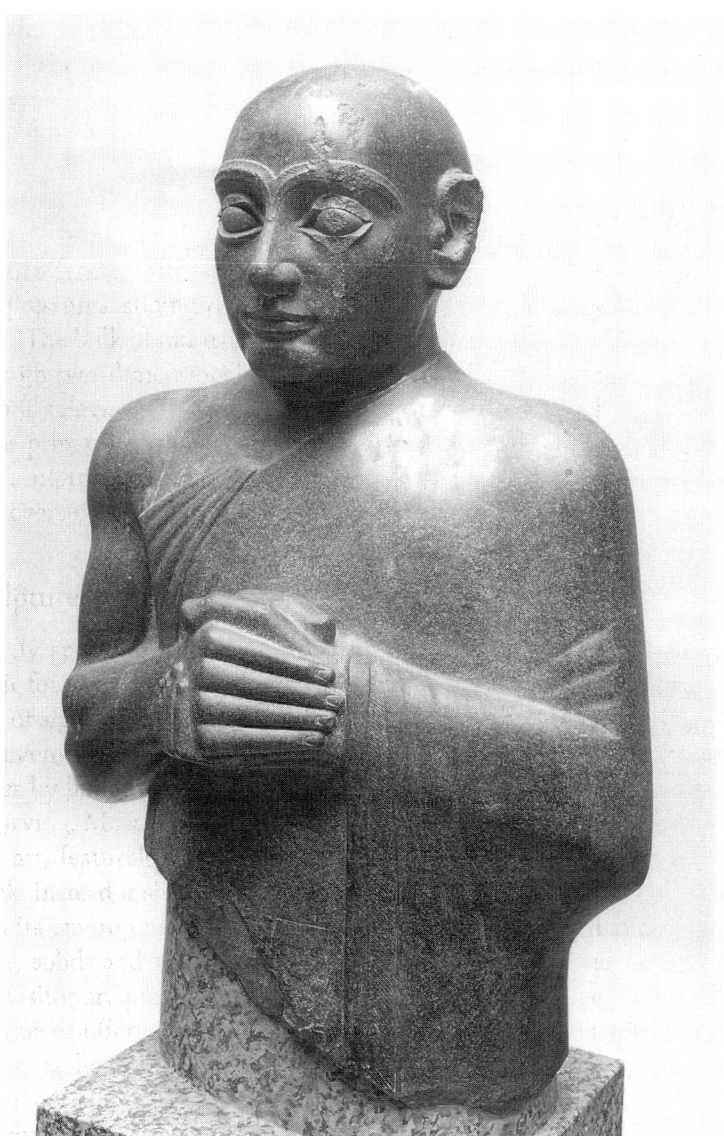

8. Sumerian ruler (incorrectly restored at neck), diorite, ca. 2200 B.C. Carved
only by bruising and abrasion in one of the hardest known stones, it aggregates an extraordinary variety of distinct formal ideas. (Copyright British
Museum.)

destroyed on some ritual occasion such as an annual festival or a funeral,
being thrown into water, say, or burned.

From the eighteenth century through our own era of rationalism and
swiftly changing vogues that ignore the spiritual dimension, sculptures
have come to be conceived as interesting but transient historical propositions. Artists in pursuit of prestige and fame have adopted materials that

are in fashion: polished marble and its plaster imitations during Classicist revivals; bronze for its Roman and Renaissance overtones as well as its intrinsic value as coinage; iron, junk, and fiberglass for their implications about our urban throwaway societies.

Types of Process

In practice, processes and materials are inseparable, though similar processes, such as chiseling or grinding, can be used to work different materials. Broadly speaking, radical shaping involves four different classes of process, while a fifth process is used for assemblage and includes all sorts of standard and familiar setting out and fixing methods. Many other books have described every process and material in detail; here I shall discuss the implications of processes and materials for the second level of sculptural skill; formal invention, expression, and articulation.

The first class of processes I call "modeling," which the artist applies to intrinsically amorphous materials that are built up and shaped by pressing and squeezing. The second class is "molding," which involves producing hollow shapes into which the sculptor presses or pours other materials which then become hard. The third class is "wasting," which involves cutting away waste from a material already hard, to leave the intended shape standing free. The fourth class is usually called "forming," which refers to bending or compressing a body of material that already has a shape into another shape. The fifth class, assemblage, typically involves arranging objects to stand on the floor or hang from wall or ceiling surfaces, and stacking, sticking, welding, wiring, looping, stitching, or slotting together components that already exist, and maybe illuminating them with a light system.

The distinction between modeling and carving has often been discussed. Modeling builds the image from nothing, whereas carving takes away excess material enveloping an image that may seem already there, "hidden" inside. These two methods illustrate how sculptural procedures have often been taken as fundamental metaphors for processes of Creation by God. Metaphors, depending as they do on analogies, work both ways; and sculptural processes have gained special value and dignity from association with these metaphors. Philosophical traditions may later hide the physical side of such creation metaphors in abstract terms.

Modeling

Modeling uses materials that can be shaped and attached by pressure; we call them malleable or ductile. The first group of materials is the most tactile, since they are worked with direct hand or finger pressure, pinching, squeezing, pulling, and pressing to add. This makes them especially suitable for Expressionist techniques that register feeling by immediate signs or strokes. The materials used include clay, wax, plasticine, and the thixotropic plastics that soften as they are kneaded.

Clay is the oldest traditional modeling material. It is dug from the earth, and so has strong symbolic value as coming from the maternal support of all life. Metaphors for Creation use clay's properties to characterize the primary chaotic matter capable of receiving any form from the hand of God. Clay can be mixed with water and used in different states of wetness: middle-wet for most modeling, when it easily takes and keeps a shape. If the sculptor wants to work on a piece for a long time, the clay is kept moist under damp cloths and plastic sheeting to avoid the hardening and cracking that would occur if it dried out. Fully dry clay is fairly hard but brittle, and can be damaged. When halfway dry, in the state called green-hard or leather-hard, clay can be scraped, cut, or stuck together with wetter clay. When a piece is absolutely dry it can be fired into terra-cotta or ceramic, but the mass must be hollowed out first to make the surface about equally thick all over, which will keep it from splitting under heat. If a large piece has been modeled solid, it can be cut in half with a wire when it is green-hard, scraped out inside carefully, then stuck together again with wet clay.

Most major bronze sculptures start out as clay models before they are molded. Large masses of wet clay are heavy and soft and may need support, especially any projections, so an armature of metal pipe, rod, wire, wire netting, or wood is necessary; the wet clay is added on top. Many twentieth-century sculptors have added only sparse pinched and chopped lumps and smears of clay, leaving parts of the armature uncovered or barely covered; when cast in bronze the rough and ragged effect can be powerful. The virtue of clay is that it offers to the sculptor in search of variety a language of pinches, wet pulls, double-handed squeezes, scratches, stabs, cuts, deeply pressed holes, even physical blows delivered by parts of the sculptor's body. These are shapes unique to clay. An interesting challenge is to find shape equivalents in clay for natural phenomena such as water or clouds.

Clay can be wetted down to a fluid condition, what ceramists call a "slip." It can then be poured into a mold. If the mold is made of absorbent material, it will suck out the water and leave an even thickness of drier clay inside, which is taken out, dried completely, and fired into ceramic.

Other modeling materials worked with the hands and fingers include clays mixed with glues that set hard when they dry, and plasticine which is mixed with glycerine (not water) so that it does not dry but remains workable for months without hardening or needing to be kept moist. The thixotropic plastics may be hardened by heating only to a moderate temperature in a domestic oven. Perhaps the oldest traditional modeling material is wax, either beeswax or, nowadays, paraffin wax.

Wax softens when warmed in the hand. Mixed with a solvent such as turpentine and sometimes with tallow and rosin, it makes an excellent modeling material that is highly durable as long as it is kept cool. It is essential to one of the molding processes called "lost wax," but it has been used particularly for small sketch models. During the Renaissance and Baroque eras, wax was used to make the original models for large molded bronze castings. We know, for example, that Donatello's late reliefs, now on the pulpits in San Lorenzo, Florence, traveled from city to city with the artist, still in the wax state on frames, before they were finished and finally cast.

One can work all these modeling materials with wooden, metal, or plastic tools that are specially shaped to smoothe, press, cut, and scrape, and one can warm metal spatulas to shape wax. Good tools that one has used for a long time get to feel like extensions of one's own hands and fingers.

Another way of hand-building a model, which also allows some tactile shaping, as either final product or preparation for molding, is too much neglected today, though it has immense possibilities. First the sculptor builds an armature of metal pipe, rod, wire, and net—possibly also burlap soaked in the modeling material. Onto this are applied layers of one of the setting substances, such as plaster or cement, and each layer must harden before the next is applied. (These substances can also be used for molding.)

Plasters and cements are derived from rocks and clays by calcining (burning). When mixed with water, they slowly combine with it chemically to return to a condition like that of the original rock. Plaster of paris is derived from alabaster, fat lime from limestone or shells, and cement also from limestone ground and mixed with clay. They are all sold as powders that are then mixed with water to an appropriate consistency. Cement is mixed with sharp sand, fine or coarse, in a proportion of about one part cement to three parts sand. Cement also should be mixed with an accelerator/hardener in the water, which makes it waterproof (and so excellent for outside work) and speeds its setting up to a few hours. Plaster of paris hardens fairly quickly, in about twenty to thirty minutes. Fat lime—the basis of stucco—is calcium hydroxide; mixed with water, it dries out to a fairly weak, chalklike hardness; over the months and years, however, it absorbs carbonic acid gas from the atmosphere and the outside layer hardens into limestone. The best Italian stucco was mixed with powdered volcanic pumice containing free silica, which combined with the calcium to form hard and strong calcium silicate.

Once the plaster or cement has been mixed, it is applied with a metal tool, a trowel, a special plasterer's tool or a strong, round-ended kitchen knife. The material is mixed to a consistency that suits the work; but one cannot apply very much bulk at once, as it falls off easily—cement especially. With cement it is best to brush some polyvinyl acetate (PVA) emulsion onto a surface that has already set to hold the next layer. After they have set, any of these materials can be carved just like stone.

Plaster of paris is not very tough or weather-resistant, so it needs to be kept indoors, though it can be hardened by soaking in limewater or solutions of borax or bicarbonate of soda. The cement mix described will last superbly outdoors, and, being water- and frost-resistant, it will not flake or allow its metal armature to rust away. Plaster of paris is often used for producing preliminary positive mold casts from major pieces modeled in clay and intended to be cast in bronze. At the plaster stage the artist can carry out finishing work by cutting and scraping, or building up with fresh plaster. One can go on troweling and tooling all of these media as long as they continue to respond prior to setting or final casting.

Being basically stone, plasters and cement are naturally associated in our minds with buildings and their permanence, especially concrete, which is the commonest building material in all our modern cities. For this reason some people feel uncomfortable about using it in a "fine art" context, but it is capable of being worked, polished, and colored to all sorts of attractive surfaces that it alone can give.

There are now many commercially manufactured modeling substances, including the thixotropic plastics, and clays that harden permanently when dry due to an adhesive with which they are mixed. One of the most useful combinations, especially for larger pieces, is the standard fiberglass/filler mix sold for making products such as boat hulls and surfboards, and for repairing automobile bodies. With its natural smooth finish, this mixture has overtones of sleekness and modernity. In a sense it is a present-day version of an old Far Eastern technique of modeling in layers with sawdust and powdered clay mixed with lacquer juice from a tree (*Rhus vernifera*) applied over fabric stiffened with the same lacquer.

Molding and Casting

Molding is a kind of natural offshoot from modeling, in that it also uses malleable materials, but the process is more complex and requires more time and special skills. It involves making hollow negative or reverse shapes called molds into which the sculptor presses malleable materials or pours fluid setting substances, which then give positive or convex replicas. Molds are made either by hollowing them directly out of some material such as stone, wood, or clay, or by applying a malleable or setting substance to the surface of an existing piece. The mold must not stick to either the positive original or the replica, so they should be dusted or wiped with soap, wax, or oil.

The first of the two techniques is ancient, but it also appeals strongly to modern sculptors and has considerable potential. In the ancient Middle East small seals were made by cutting intaglio (hollow) designs into the faces of stones. These would then be pressed onto moist clay or soft wax and would leave a raised impression of the design. A clay impression could be fired hard to be preserved. Scholars have speculated that this procedure might lie behind Plato's highly influential notion that the things of the world are impressed onto matter by a higher order of transcendent archetypes or ideas—a notion still important among us. Also in the ancient world artistic intaglio designs were cut into stone, wood, or clay molds and had positives taken from them. An opposed pair of such positives can be stuck together with wet clay, dried, and fired to produce a hollow, fully round piece. In many parts of the world intaglio decorative designs have been cut, say, in hard wood and used to replicate many versions. Jewellers have applied this technique, pressing sheets of soft metal such as gold into carved depressions, and decorative additions to much larger pieces meant to be cast solid have been carved into the faces of big negative molds, resulting in raised features. The ancient Chinese worked their ritual bronzes in this manner.

Many modern artists use intaglio methods to produce reliefs. They carve hollow shapes into the face of a sheet of wet clay, then pour into them a fluid setting material such as plaster. Georges Braque used this method. Other artists, such as Eduardo Paolozzi, have pressed natural objects or fragments of man-made objects into sheets of clay, cast from them plates of soft metal, then assembled these into humanoid images.

The term *casting* means filling a hollow mold with some material that will set and harden. Any of the setting materials already mentioned—plaster, cement, and several plastics—can be used for casting. To cast positive versions of pieces previously modeled or carved, hollow molds are made by applying a setting material, which hardens into exact negative versions of the original surfaces. These are then filled with fresh setting material. At each stage the positives and negatives must be checked to ensure they are not sticking to each other.

The simplest kind of mold for casting is a single-valve mold: it is made from an original that has only one front face, such as a shallow relief. The original must not have undercuts, which would prevent pulling the mold and original apart without damage. Many of the world's finest relief sculptures have been cast in this manner; they are recognizable by the way all their side surfaces slope away from the eye without curling back under. The sculptor should shape them in this way, although a slight degree of undercutting is possible if the negative mold used is an elastic rubber, either natural latex or a synthetic rubber that is mixed with a catalyst. Latex can take literally months to dry and set if it is at all thick, but it becomes wonderfully strong and so many casts can be taken from it, whereas the synthetic may set in less than a day but is less strong. Several quick-setting elastic plastic materials are on the market, some of which can be hardened in the stove.

To cast a fully three-dimensional piece, two options are available: the waste mold or the piece mold. The artist can build around the sculpture a waste mold that encloses it entirely. The best material for such a mold is plaster of paris. A wall is built either all around the halfway contour or around an area of, say, the back, against which the first investment stops as it is built up. When that is set, the wall is taken away, the face of the investment is treated to prevent sticking, and a second investment is built up against the rest of the piece, up to where the wall was, and it is left to set. If the original piece is in clay, the wall may be made by pressing strips of metal a short way in along one edge and pulling them out carefully when the time comes. If the original is fragile or sensitive, such as a human body, or of a hard substance, a wall of clay is built by just sticking it to the surface. The point is to be able to get the original out without damaging the mold. If the original is of soft clay, the two parts of the mold are separated (using lots of water) and the clay is dug out. If the original is hard, neither part of the mold should have any undercuts. This may be unavoidable, so a piece mold would be preferable. When a mold is made, a pouring hole must be left at the top; or if the whole mold is small enough to turn upside-down, the casting material is poured in through what was the base.

Before the setting material is poured, the empty interior of the mold should be treated with one of the antistick substances; then the parts of the mold are mated and tied together firmly. Next the setting material is poured, and to avoid bubbles, the mold might be rocked now and then. Significant leaks should also be avoided.

When the casting material has set, the sculptor starts to chisel off the outer negative mold; great care must be taken not to damage the cast inside. Never, for example, should the chisel travel across a small prominence such as a nose, always toward it. This method is called "waste molding" because the mold is destroyed as the cast is released. If the final cast is damaged or has blemishes, they are usually reparable with some of the casting material.

Piece molding is so called because instead of just two sections of negative investment, several are made, each of which individually includes no undercuts at all. The original must be studied carefully to determine where each successive stretch of wall should be built. The sculptor builds the mold piece by piece along behind each new stretch of wall, and as each piece dries he or she removes the stretch of wall against it and cuts nicks into the facade to provide locating keys for the next pieces. Antistick treatment is applied to the face of each piece.

When the whole original is invested and all the mold sections are hard, the outer casing is dismantled, which leaves the original intact. To make a cast, the interior of the pieces are sprayed or brushed with an antistick treatment, the pieces are assembled, bound together, and perhaps treated with antistick spray on the outside, then enclosed in an extra layer of plaster. The negative is then filled as before.

When the cast inside is set, the outer negative mold is dismantled piece by piece. With the resulting positive cast, the mold can be assembled again to make more casts. This technique is particularly important for casting a succession of ceramic pieces in slip. The assembled molds are normally small enough to be lifted so the sculptor can swill the slip around the interior until the mold (usually plaster) has drawn out the water from the slip to leave a deposit of clay thick enough to be fired as the final piece.

Molding has its own metaphorical overtones. We sometimes say of a person that he is "from the same mold" as his father or mother, or that her character was "molded" by her early environment. But it is interesting that we do not seriously think even of inanimate objects, let alone people or events, as being repeated identical versions from the same mold. Only in scientific generalizations do we come across a tendency to treat entities as identical, though at the level of human experience we know that nothing ever happens twice exactly the same.

Mold casting in bronze and other metals has always been thought of as the ultimate version of the technique. Disregarding its other qualities, bronze has always had an intrinsically high financial value, and most sculptors feel their modeled pieces reach their best potential in metal. Patrons tend to like bronze best, as well. The broad principles of making the molds are similar, but different materials are needed both for making originals and for building investments.

The best-known type of bronze casting is *cire perdue*, or lost wax. It is based on the principle that wax can be modeled easily and then be melted out of the mold. Small pieces can be created out of solid wax, but big pieces need to be made first in a heat-resistant clay, then coated in a fine layer of wax. The wax is then invested with a heat-resistant clay mold, either waste or piece; the wax is melted out and the metal is melted and poured into the space previously occupied by the wax. There are, however, many problems in dealing with a casting material at such high and dangerous temperatures.

First, the original model, if it is too big to be made in solid wax, needs to have a number of thin iron rods stuck into it and left protruding. These hold the outer mold in constant relation to the clay original after its coating of wax has melted away. Second, a set of little wax rods are fixed into the wax layer at points where bubbles of air or gas might need to escape to allow the hot metal to run into the whole wax space. If the piece is very big, some thicker wax rods connecting with the pouring hole at the top may be necessary. The wax surface is finished only broadly, since all bronzes need to be chiseled and polished after casting, partly at least to get rid of the iron rods and any seams. The heat-resistant clay is applied all over the original, with the pouring hole at the top open and the little wax rods emerging at the top, so that when their wax melts out they leave clear gas vent holes. The whole mass is then left to dry thoroughly. Bronze can be cast into a flat intaglio mold of clay, but that too has to be thoroughly dry.

The next stage is heating the mass of mold and model to a high enough temperature to drive off the water of chemical crystallization from the clay. This process melts out the wax, and otherwise the clay mold will shatter when the molten bronze hits it. Meanwhile the bronze—basically copper and tin, perhaps some lead—is melted in a pouring crucible. When the bronze is fully fluid it can be slowly poured in through the pouring hole to occupy the whole wax space. The bronze thickness will be the same as that of the original wax layer. When the bronze and mold parts have cooled, the outer mold may be broken away and the cast trimmed, patched, and polished. The fired clay core may stay inside or be chipped out. If the piece is large an iron frame may be fitted inside to support the weight of hollow bronze.

One other extremely difficult but interesting method can be used for bronze casting. It entails making a careful piece mold of clay around a wax-covered core, and dismantling it while it is still green-hard. Each section of the piece mold is then incised with its own area of an intaglio design and fired. After the assembled fired pieces are fixed in place, and

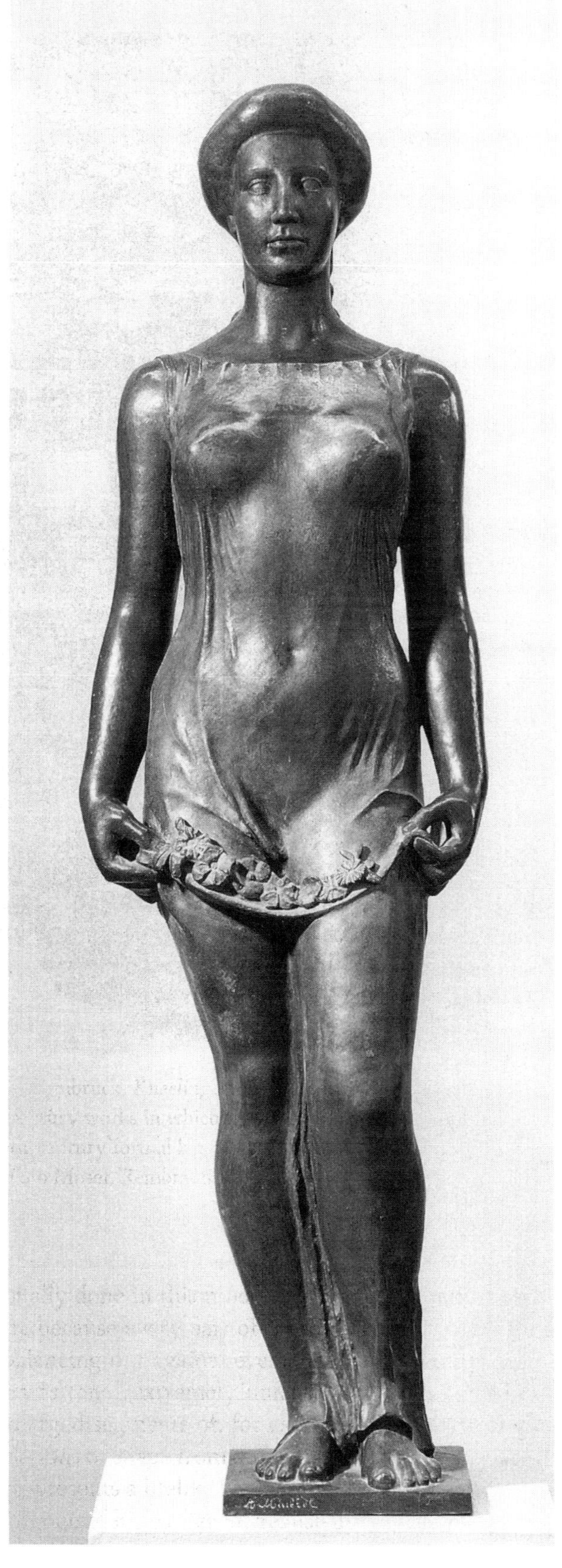

9. Aristide Maillol, *Flora*, bronze, life-size, ca. 1911. A contemporary image of an ancient ideal of flowering female beauty. (Kunstmuseum Winterthur, presented by Lisa Jäggli-Hahnloser and Prof. Hans Hahnloser.)

the bronze is cast as described earlier, the result is a positive cast with the design raised on its surface. The ancient Chinese were experts in this technique during the two thousand years B.C.

To take a bronze cast of a piece that already exists in a hard material, say plaster, a sculptor can either make a negative mold and cast a wax piece from it, or, if it is big, take an ordinary piece-molded cast from it in clay, if necessary scrape that down a little, coat it with wax, and then carry out the lost-wax process.

One other mode of casting, which is most useful for large pieces, is sand molding. It is a job for trained professionals who use bolted steel frames and special casting sand that hardens after being moistened. Contemporary sculptors making very large pieces for sand casting often build up the bulk of their original with shaped slices of lightweight polystyrene and then model the final surface with plaster.

One rather rare type of casting is to cover living people or actual objects with a layer of plaster of fairly regular thickness bonded with fabric. The sculptor cuts the plaster "overcoat" into sections to remove it, then reassembles it as a positive. George Segal has used this method. It produces a rough surface and a body image naturally thicker than life.

Many contemporary assemblage artists use molding to produce components either as plaster casts preliminary to bronzes cast from assembled plasters or as direct bronzes from objects jointed maybe with plaster. The originals for the molds may be unusual or startling objects, such as clots of cooked spaghetti, tangles of knotted ropes, or lumps of meat and bone.

Wasting

Wasting involves cutting away parts of a material, either a sheet with shears or a mass with carving tools. In the 1930s carving in stone was still widely believed to be the ultimate sculptural technique, which every real sculptor needed to master; wood came second. This idea was probably a holdover from the days when Greek and Roman marble carvings were believed to be the greatest possible masterpieces. Few contemporary sculptors carve, and those who do mainly use power tools. Carving does have one major advantage in generating beautifully integrated formal structures of solid and void: it naturally requires the artist to think first of the masses of material to be cut away as shaped volumes of space. Carvers working in established traditions usually follow clear-cut routine stages, each of which is completed before the next is begun. First, standard shapes of the main waste are cut away from the whole block; then lesser voids are defined, leaving the intended protuberant solid volumes standing between them. Only at the end are these volumes given their final surface shapes. As well as simplifying the whole procedure, this ensures that the design and qualities of a sacred image are accurately repeated. Generally speaking, the first stage of waste removal is far more important than a simple elimination of unwanted material: it shapes the voids that frame and participate in the main image.

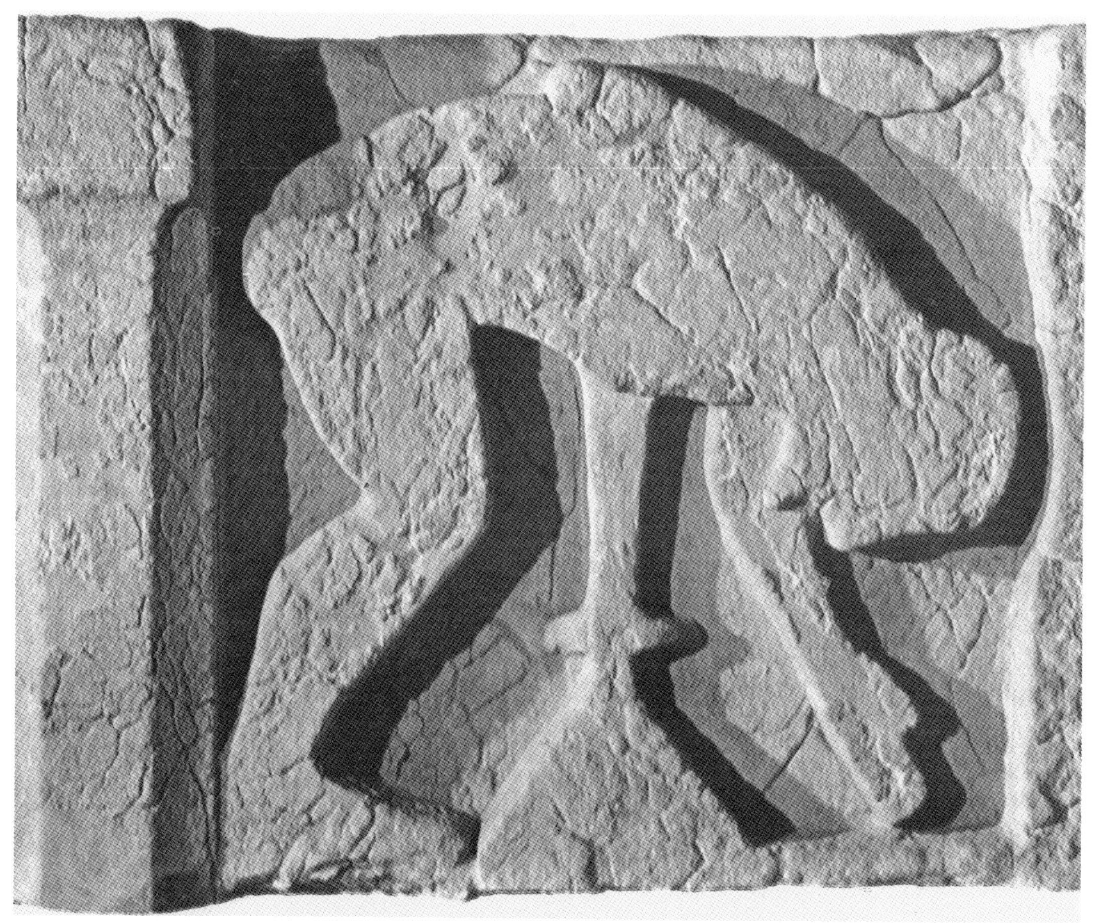

10. Suicide of Telemon, Temple of Hera, Paestum, Italy, marble, fifth century B.C.
This work illustrates an early stage in carving relief when clear shapes of void spaces
are first cut out. (Courtesy Museo Archeologico Nazionale, Paestum.)

Cutting flat shapes from sheets of paper, cardboard, wood, metal, or any other material can be a challenging artistic process, since it depends on the sculptor's skill in developing varied and interesting convex-concave contours. The few purely technical problems arise mainly in the process of assembling several layers of flat shapes, either directly against each other or spaced apart at precisely calculated distances. The spacing needs to be done with small blocks or rods cut carefully to length and stuck or welded in position.

The shape of a block intended for carving can be important. Of course, it is possible to cut the waste away so drastically that the original shape of the block ceases to have any value at all, but this is by no means a good thing. The faces of the block can have a primary spatial significance by setting up directional references that serve as built-in axes for the image. In Western sculpture, even in the pieces most baroque in their twists, the block has usually been squared off cubically, roughly at least, and treated as having one primary face with a top and bottom, two sides, with or without a defined back. Western design in general has dealt with space primarily in terms of right-angled axes. This approach owes its prevalence to the fact that many sculptures were intended for architectural locations, and it is particularly evident in the greatest Archaic Greek sculptures, in medieval European and Renaissance carvings, and even in the way Michelangelo attacked his blocks from the front, releasing the image within. Modeling has none of this implicit spatial reference, though modelers may assimilate this approach and build with a cubic sense.

Wood may be similarly squared off before carving. In tribal arts it is clear from the character of the image that the wood was usually left in the round log (sometimes in the flat plank), and that the sculptor compensated by giving each piece a marked frontal face-forward, even when it was intended as a dance mask, which would be seen from all sides. Other carved materials, such as ivory or tooth, often preserve clear evidence of their original shape, which may contribute an important symbolic element to their meaning.

Stone and wood have special symbolic values of their own. Stone is dug from the quarry or found as a boulder, in both cases viewed as being a part of the eternal earth. One of the purposes of carving images in stone is to eternalize them, displaying their unchanging value and timeless significance. The harder the stone (such as diorite, granite, or jade), the more difficult it is to carve and the higher is that value set. Stone is also used as prime building material in the Mediterranean and tropical areas of the Americas, with the intent to root the structure to the earth and so symbolically to modify the terrain itself.

Wood evokes the nature of the forest and is a substance still containing evidence of life in its grain. It is not surprising that it was the natural choice of carving material for peoples whose own life was closely bound up with forests, for example, in Africa, Oceania, and medieval Germany. Some woods are extremely hard, such as tropical lignum vitae and

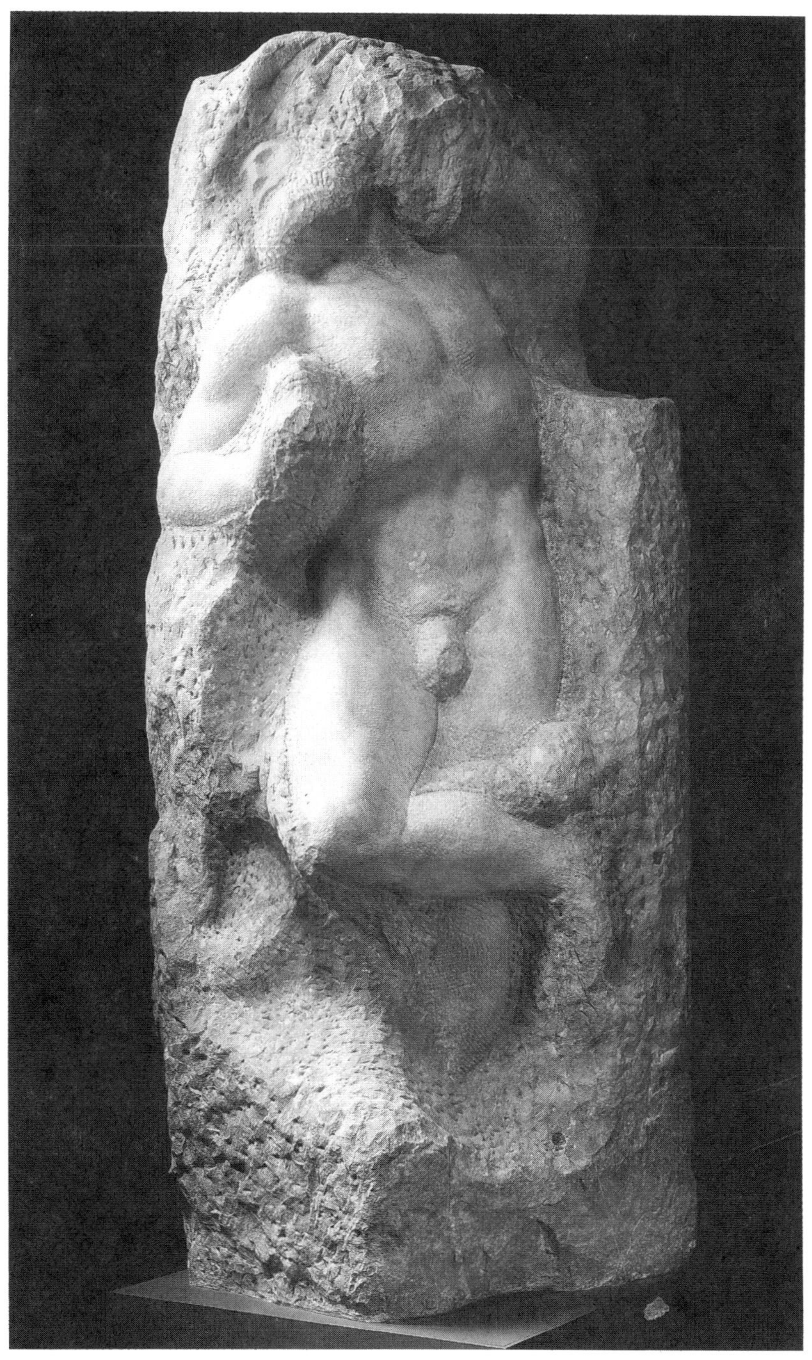

11. Michelangelo, *Prisoner (Prigione)*, Florence, marble, ca. 1516–19. This unfinished sculpture reveals the claw-chisel working by which Michelangelo reached
the final surface runs of his impossibly and wholly tensed musculatures, which for
him symbolized the ideal of spiritual striving. (Courtesy Galleria dell'Accademia;
Alinari/Art Resource, New York.)

heart of oak, but in general wood is far more easily and quickly carved than stone; West African baobab, often used for masks, is especially soft. Nowadays we choose our woods for the sake of their color and the interest of their grain.

Carving any material requires tools for three principal tasks. First, to remove the main bulk of waste, hammers, strong chisels, axes, adzes, and drills are used; for stone also perhaps plug and feathers, which are pairs of points that are stuck into rows of drill holes; the plugs are driven between them in sequence until the waste stone splits away. Rows of drill holes outlining the waste are still visible on some of Michelangelo's unfinished works. Second, the preliminary shaping of the main image requires a variety of different chisels, points, and gouges, which leave distinctive traces on the surface of the image. Many sculptors like to leave their work at this stage, intending the chisel-stroke to convey immediate feeling, as does the Expressionist brushstroke. Third are the tools and materials to smoothe and polish the surface, including files, rifflers, and abrasives. Different grades of material and the sculptor's aesthetic intention will emphasize one or other of these tasks. Very hard stones, for example, may resist chisels so powerfully that they can be carved only by the third set of techniques, using drills and abrasion with crystalline stones or powders; consequently the sculptor may choose to modify the shape of the original block as little as possible. At the opposite pole, soft woods can be chopped almost to the final surface, using tools appropriate to the first stage, and then finished fairly quickly, as many African carvers did. Archaic Greek figures in marble, which is soft when fresh, were worked almost to the end with the point-chisel, and then finished with a great deal of abrasion.

One final wasting process is polishing, which is achieved with ever finer abrasives by hand-held abrasive block, or with rotary drills and abrasive heads. Metals can attain a high gloss; Brancusi is one of many sculptors who have made a special feature of polishing to a brilliant sheen some of their shapes cast in metal from plaster originals. The surface is worked to an extremely close finish to start with, otherwise the final polishing can leave patches of the surface untouched. The effect is to emphasize the integrity and continuity of the surface by producing a continuous line or area of light reflection, which brings out the final shape with particular clarity. Stone is another material that is polished. The ancient Egyptians worked huge pieces of the hardest stones such as diorite and granite to a high gloss, as did the Sumerians and Achaemenid Persians, probably using many hours of slave hand-labor. The Chinese polished jade and other colorful hard stones, and the ancient Indians even polished sandstone.

Sculptors often polish woods, usually finishing with a light waxing. This process brings out the fluid grain, which enhances the three-dimensional shapes as well as condensing the surface so that the natural color shows. Most contemporary sculptors use power tools with abrasive heads for final poishing, and some use scouring heads, which leave highly visible traces as part of the surface effect.

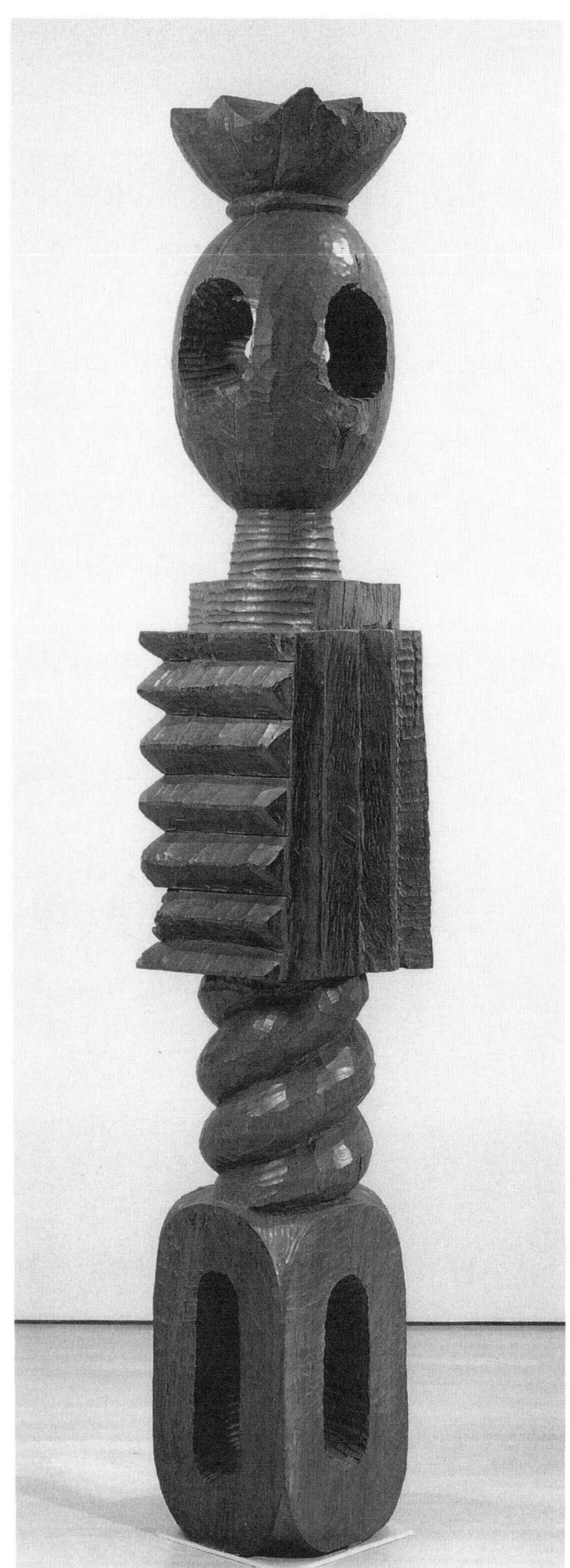

12. Constantin Brancusi, *The Spirit of Buddha* (*King of Kings*), wood, approx. ten feet high, early 1930s. Inspired by African carvings, the generalized shapes of this piece present the image of an inner spiritual condition with which the viewer may identify. (Solomon R. Guggenheim Museum; photograph by David Heald, copyright © the Solomon R. Guggenheim Foundation, New York. Copyright © 1995 Artists Rights Society, New York/ADAGP, Paris.)

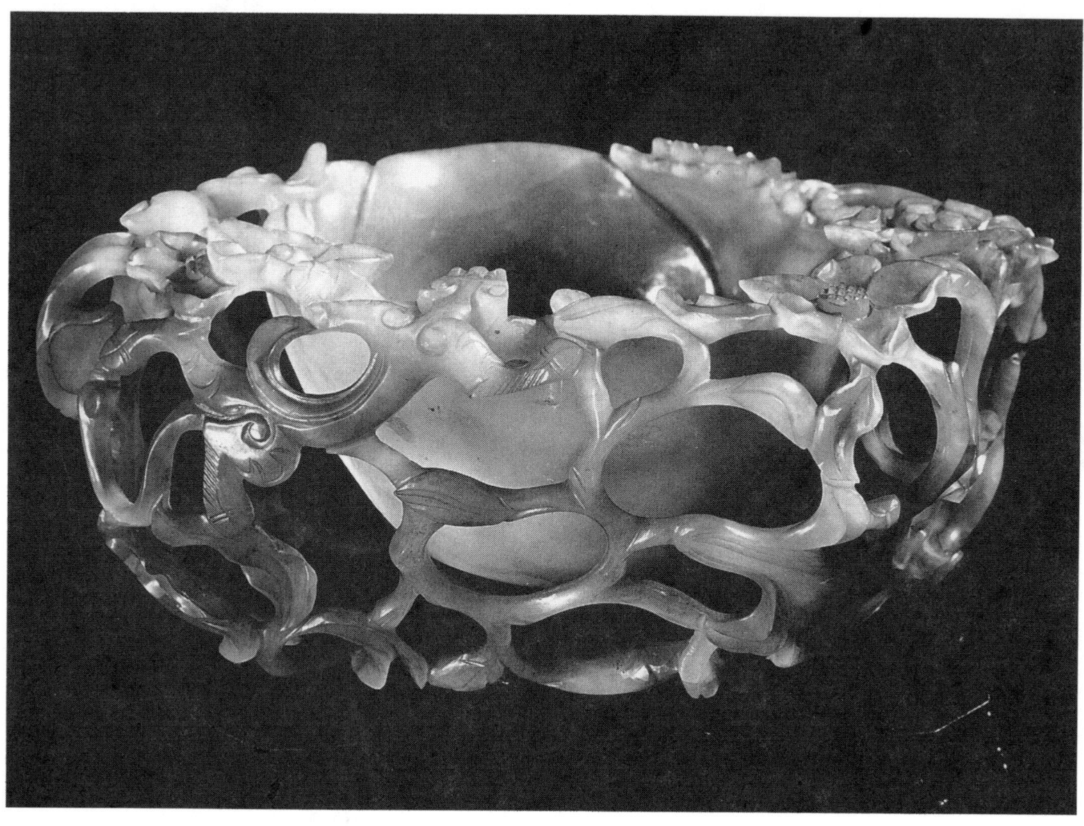

13. Chinese water-dipper for writing brush, jade, seventeenth century. The complex of fluid shapes left standing by grinding away the hard boulder moves freely through space and reminds the user of the Chinese imagery of continuously flowing time. (Courtesy Oriental Museum, University of Durham, England.)

Forming

The fourth class of shaping processes, called "forming," involves using pressure and beating to modify the shape of a piece of material that will respond when either cold or hot. Wooden branches or cane take a permanent bend if they are steam-heated and cooled in shape. Some metals are malleable when cold and will readily beat into shape; gold is the best known, and it also welds easily by simple pressure. Sheets of some soft metals, such as copper, can be "raised" into sculpture by beating them up from the back into shaped protrusions. Copper "work-hardens," that is to say it turns hard and brittle if it is stretched too far; so the parts being worked must be heated from time to time with a blowlamp to resoften the metal. Pieces of copper sheet are hammered into negative molds and soldered together along their edges to make hollow positive shapes. All metal sheet "raised" from the back may also be finished with punch or chisel from the front.

Perhaps the best-known forming technique is wrought iron forging. The sculptor heats iron billet or bar until it is red or white hot, then beats it into shape with a heavy hammer on an anvil while holding it with long pincers. White-hot pieces can be pressure-welded together permanently by hammering. When cold, most iron will rust (unless it is exceptionally pure) and this can give an interesting effect. The basic shapes that iron takes most readily are plates and rods, straight or curved, so most iron sculptures are compounded out of worked versions of these, pressure-welded or true-welded in place. They thus belong partly to the category of assemblages.

Assemblage

Assemblage consists of setting out or fixing together separate components, either specially made for the purpose or as found in nature, in the domestic environment, or among city garbage. Virtually any method or scheme of arrangement that seems to work and any components whatever can be used. When making the piece, the artist may need to take into account the shapes of the things put together, or may simply treat them as given. A chair placed over a splash of milk on a floor may need to be carefully placed to take account of the shape of the splash, whereas rows of glasses can be arranged without much reference to their actual shapes. If the artist uses projected transparencies (diapositives), he or she may need to take into account not only their image-shapes but also their image-sizes in relation to each other and to the viewer. Scale is always highly significant. Many artists include written or printed text, and its scale in relation to all the other components can be important, as it will determine roughly where the visitor stands in relation to the rest of the piece to read it.

The kinds of fixing involved depend on the materials chosen for assembly. For wood and certain metals that can be shaped, the sculptor may cut careful joints or flatten and drill faces so that they meet and can be bolted or screwed tightly together. Metals are welded or soldered, or connected with twist wire, whereas wood is pegged, nailed, screwed, or glued; modern glues can fix most materials together. Fabric may be stitched or glued, whether it is used free-floating or as a stuffable, shaped sack-form. Any additional graphic elements, such as floor or wall lines, need to be well protected with fixative or medium if they are to stay fresh. Unusual components may need to be treated specially, such as animal fats, mud, rope, or colored powder in heaps.

Broadly speaking, the physical techniques used by assemblage artists are those of familiar handicrafts. These methods themselves may be included into a piece's field of symbolic reference. Whereas some crafts—those of the woodworker or ironsmith, for example—have been used as metaphors for divine creative processes or fundamental philosophical ideas, the process of assemblage probably has not, perhaps because it depends too much on arranging what already exists.

Paper is an easily available material that is too often ignored or denigrated because it is used by school children and is fragile. Paper can be used in sheets (stuck, folded, or cut into shapes) or pulped into papier-mâché. The Japanese game of origami is well known and has established routines for folding paper into shapes such as birds, boats, and so on. It is also possible to build up hollow volumes quickly by sticking strips together so as to form a shell over some openwork base such as wire net or a basket. Papier-mâché is made by soaking and mashing paper to pulp, then adding glue. The resulting substance can be used to model three-dimensional shapes very freely, though if the model is large, it may need an armature. When dry, papier-mâché is easy to paint and light to carry.

The Pointing Frame

Before we leave the discussion of materials and techniques one other technical device to consider is the pointing frame, which is normally used as an aid in stone sculpture and has had a substantial effect on some people's ideas about sculpture for two or three centuries. The frame seems to have been invented in Italy in the sixteenth century and is still widely used in a simplified form, though not often acknowledged. It consists of a three-dimensional rectangular framework whose members are marked off with measured sets of numbers. Each pair of vertical and horizontal members carries at least one horizontal bar also marked off with matching numbers. The bars are free to slide along between their supporting frame members, and across each of them is attached transversely a rod, also bearing numbers, which can be slid in and out, and fixed, either by a clamp or a screw. Its tip reaches into the space within the frame to define a position within the three-dimensional axial grid. A live model, or the small version of an intended sculpture, can be placed within the frame, and the tips of the rods can be maneuvered along the constantly repositioned bars to touch principal hump and hollow "points" across and up and down the original, their positions in the frame being recorded as a set of three numbers. The material to be worked is then placed within the frame, and its surface developed to reach the points identified by their numbers. If the original is to be enlarged, the measurements are multiplied and adjusted proportionately. If the new piece is to be built of modeling material, the process is easy. But if it is to be cut from a block of stone, then the "points" have to be measured into the stone as the depths of drill holes, and the waste then cut back to the drill depths. Italian marble workers became especially expert at this last version of the technique, and were often employed during the eighteenth and nineteenth centuries by academy sculptors to produce marble versions of their own smaller clay originals.

3
Color in Sculpture

Types of Coloring

Coloring is inevitably an element in the overall effect of any sculpture, even if we are not conscious of it. There are three principal ways to treat color on sculpture, each having a different effect. First, a process of grinding and polishing brings out the self-color, or natural hue of the material itself, which is normally full of variations, sometimes mottled or striated, and has a depth that surface coloring rarely achieves. In casting concrete or plaster, for example, dry, good-quality pigment powder can be mixed into the dry concrete or plaster before the water is added. Chemically treating bronze with chloride and acid washes can alter the surface into a greenish blue material. Second, the surface can be stained using a transparent liquid tint that penetrates slightly into the surface of the material before it dries and does allow a depth of reflection to the color, making it seem almost like a self-color. Third, the surface can be painted with opaque color—either with a single overall pigment, which has the effect of flattening and equalizing the light-reflecting properties of all the shapes, especially if the pigment is mixed with white, or with mixtures of pigment and colored lacquers applied using painterly techniques to enhance or define surface shapes. Crayons or pastels are used on the surface in a similar way.

Part of the revolution in sculpture that took place in the early decades of this century was a change in sculptors' attitudes to color. Although during the nineteenth century a few sculptures were colored in a lifelike way, they were not taken seriously. During the late eighteenth and early nineteenth centuries, professionals and amateurs had modeled portraits and domestic scenes in colored wax, and both Switzerland and France were home to small museums containing wax effigies of famous people and historical scenes. The one Marie Tussaud established in London about 1835 has become the most famous. Her notion of the maximally lifelike waxwork in full color was derived from her youthful work taking casts from the faces of the decapitated heads of distinguished people guillotined under the Reign of Terror during the French Revolution. There can be little doubt that literal, tinted, but lifeless reproduction without any topic-language of being and feeling inevitably has a gruesome quality. Waxworks may fascinate, but few can be taken seriously as art.

White

Sculpture that was regarded as "High Art" in the nineteenth century was created under the influence of a Classicism that imitated the overall appearance of imperial Roman statues dug up during the Renaissance and later, which had lost all their applied color and so were polished marble-white. Revered Italian masters such as Michelangelo and Bernini had followed this example. In the 1750s the first great German art historian, Johann Winckelmann, began to spread his influential doctrine that such Classicism was the only valid sculptural mode. As his writings penetrated into the courts of Europe, collectors began to scrub all their sculptures white and reject the brilliant opaque colors in which many previous Baroque and Rococo work had been painted. We can see the influence of Winckelmann arriving at South German Roman Catholic churches then in the process of construction (for example, at the abbey church of Salem) by a clear switch in style and color of the interior from multicolored activity to mock-Classical white. Thereafter through the nineteenth century, Salon sculptures laying claim to serious prestige were executed in symbolically white polished Italian marble, and successful sculptors employed Italian marble carvers to produce finished pieces from the sculptor's own designs and original models, often quite small, using the pointing frame.

Surface Unity and Bronze

For the most part, we read the three-dimensional shapes of sculpture visually, by their highlights plus modeling and cast shadows under illumination (though our hands should be used more than they are). So there is a good deal to be said for preserving as clearly as possible the unity of the surface as it appears when illuminated. The Classical tradition of integral bronze surface coloring survives, and casters still try for subtle and attractive finishes. Untreated bronze has a yellowish red gloss. When attacked by atmospheric gases or buried in the earth, bronze may acquire a bluish green patina. Casters have developed ranges of lacquers and chemical washes, including chlorides and various acids, to produce beautifully variegated verdigris incrustations and patina colors deliberately, but often they keep their methods secret. Plutarch, in his essay "On the Pythian Responses," describes visiting a temple containing fine Classical bronzes patinated not the usual green but a wonderful deep blue, the secret of which remains lost.

In Ming China and in Europe in the eighteenth century, forgers of faked ancient bronzes used to bury new pieces in dunghills, which produced speedy corrosion effects. Once a treatment has had its desired effect, the metal may then be oiled or lacquered to prevent further unwanted changes. Steel and iron rust naturally, and rust too can be halted at a given stage; iron can also be patinated with a damson flush using muriatic acid.

Another way of coloring a sculpture without breaking the integrity of the surface is to paint it all over with a single flat color, which may be particularly effective if its overtones are at variance with the feel of the material, such as pale blue or pink on a heavy steel girder or ragged scrap iron construction.

Material Color

During the early decades of the twentieth century, partly as a result of a growing interest in archaeologically excavated sculptures that had lost their color, artists began to take a special interest in the "natural" colors of inorganic materials, some of which, like jade and finely veined stones, were seen as symbolic in themselves. Earlier in this century, before the damaging effects of atmospheric pollution, the bare carved and architectural stone of some medieval cathedrals was still strongly colored: pink sandstone at Strasbourg, pink, white, and black at Venice. Throughout the Byzantine and early medieval ages in Europe, finely veined agates and other stones had been valued almost as highly as gems. Charlemagne's chapel at Aix-la-Chapelle, for example, was lined with beautifully sliced and polished stone. In the 1930s sculptors in Britain, such as Henry Moore and Barbara Hepworth, began to polish the surfaces of their pieces to bring out the inherent layered and veined quality of the material, a practice that remains a valid sculptural option.

Applied Color

In fact, genuine Classical Greek and Roman sculptures had not always lacked local colors when they were first installed. Sometimes their bodies had been stained or painted pinkish brown, and clothing had been painted with colors like those in Roman wall paintings at, for example, Pompeii (where the figures had been conceived as primarily sculptural, anyway). Three-dimensional figures also used to have the whites and irises of their eyes either painted or inlaid with shell, no doubt to give them "life"; Plutarch recounts a legend that the shell inlays fell out of the eyes of the statue of a great man at the moment when he died far away.

All through the European Middle Ages, Christian churches had been elaborately painted in strong outlines with distinct local tints—sometimes virtually all over on the interior, and on their main sculptural compositions on the exterior, as well. Flesh was painted in flesh color, garments in standard bright hues, lips, eyes, and embroidery in their own hues, and radiant halos in gold, partly to differentiate philosophically their substances, but also to create for visitors an image of the heavenly splendor to be found only within the Church.

Indian, Chinese, and Mesoamerican sculptures and their entire temples were often similarly painted with distinguishing and stimulating local colors. If a material surface was rough, it could be prepared for painting with layers of fine lime and glue. Many cultures have regarded colored sculpture as the highest kind of art because of its actual three-dimensional modeling, and have looked on the two-dimensional modeling in pure painting as only a compensation for the lack of the third, spatial, dimension.

Successive layers of repainting on European medieval wood carvings, especially those applied during the nineteenth century, spoiled the sculptural qualities of many fine old pieces, sometimes even to the extent of relocating the eyes in faces according to tastes current at the time. Modern museums now remove what they can of such repaint. The original coloring was applied by members of a skilled craft guild, who must have worked according to techniques far more sophisticated than simply laying on flat tints. It is likely that the art of the medieval painter of sculptures enhanced the design and modeling of a piece. Certainly their technical heirs, the painters of later Baroque and Rococo sculpture, used color in particularly interesting ways: for example, painting the channels not necessarily darker than but even a different light color from the crests of volumes, or using a green to contrast with a pinkish white rubbed over the crests with the palm of the hand.

Color Programs

We tend to think of sculpture in terms of separate figures, and color them as such. But many Baroque and Rococo churches were filled with unified programs of colored sculpture. The color might develop from dense and dark by the door, to brilliant light colors, white, and gold at the east-end altar, to suggest the increasing intensity of light the nearer one approaches the "source." Such programs are specifically Christian, but there is no reason why contemporary secular sculptors, installation artists especially, should not develop programs of their own on similar lines.

Color Modeling

One method of modeling with color that was probably invented in the European Middle Ages is still in use today, especially for small popular ceramic figurines. It is derived from one of the sculptor's tonal drawing methods (discussed in Chapter 9). Wherever the rounded modeling turns away and recedes from the eye, it is reinforced with a darkening of the local color, leaving the more prominent faces of the volumes standing out in lighter tone. This emulates the effect of polish and highlight as color.

Modern Color

Only with the early twentieth-century discovery of tribal arts—many of which are highly colored—did adventurous secular sculptors begin to experiment with color in reaction against conventional white Classicism of the Salon. They began applying sets of hard tints, such as red, black, white, and blue, to select parts of an entire composition, leaving the rest in the natural color of the material—stone, wood, or bronze. Other sculptors developed the idea of coloring the strongly marked Cubist facets of their works with sequences of varied bright colors, reminiscent of the layout of colors on the costume of the Harlequin, then so fashionable a subject among French artists. This mode is still popular with some American ceramic sculptors, who use brilliant ceramic glaze colors. Pop sculptors have used either colored plastics or have painted their assemblage components in vivid arbitrary colors.

The colors in fired glazes are permanent, and since they are a kind of glass enamel, they can have a special transparent brilliance which comes from complex internal reflections among their layers of crystalline particles. Particularly among the Chinese, sculptors have inlaid the surfaces of bronze pieces with designs in enamel, and many twentieth-century sculptors have experimented with applying areas of enamel color to bronzes, notably in the former Yugoslavia.

Because sculptures exist primarily as shaped material surfaces, all the ways in which color can be applied change the interrelationships between surface shapes, not only along each single stretch but between one surface and its neighbors. In imagining and applying colors the sculptor must take into account the effects of areas and combinations of color on plastic values. A certain color in a group, for instance, may seem to flatten one surface in relation to others or make it stand out from the rest of the composition. Thus careful use of color can bring out a particular feature that might otherwise be lost.

Illumination

To read the shapes of a sculpture, we rely on illumination to define them. In this connection, too, color can either baffle or accentuate our perceptions and readings. Too light and flat a color can destroy shape-readings, and too dark a color can reduce the significance of shadow nuances; either can impair the formal invention. Good sculptors aim to produce a specific luminous and sculptural "color" by leading and conducting their surfaces in relation to the kind of light in which they normally work and in which they expect their pieces to be seen. Aristide Maillol, for instance, said that he always strove for a "blonde" effect across his surfaces, which were illuminated by the Mediterranean sky under which he mostly worked; Rodin, working much farther north, clearly did not work under similar lighting conditions. Under strong sunlight, emphatic "hump and hollow" modeling in a Rodin bronze can appear as a rash of light flares and shadow spots; so the smoothly inflected skins of medieval Indian stone figure-cutting were expressly created to avoid their surfaces being interrupted and fragmented by harsh patches of shadow from the fierce Indian sun. Museum curators should recognize the influence illumination may have exerted at the point of creation and take care not to over or under dramatize particular pieces through lighting.

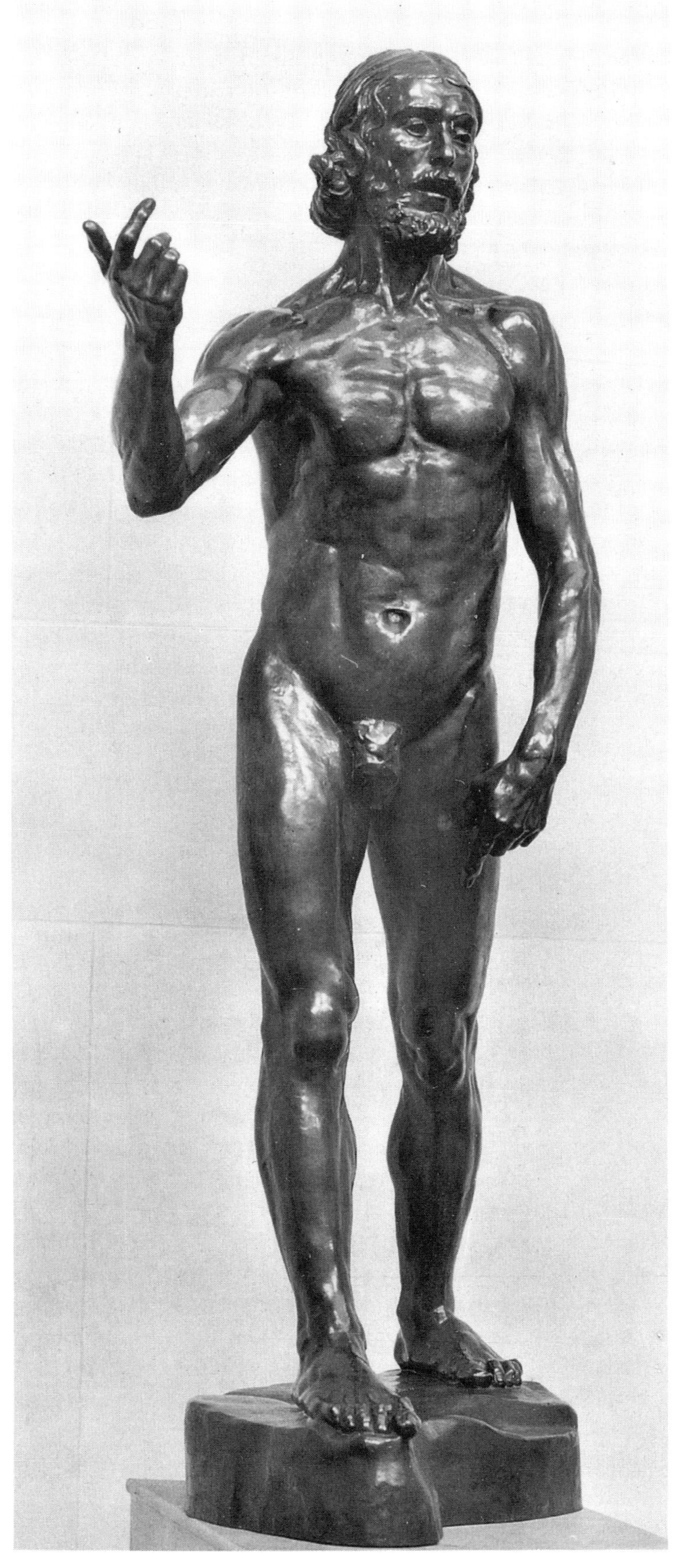

14. Auguste Rodin, *St. John the Baptist*, bronze, life-size, 1880. The energy of the figure is conveyed by realistically incompatible bodily positions and exaggeration of "humps and hollows" (Rodin's words). (Courtesy The Tate Gallery, London.)

Sculptural "Color"

What I call sculptural "color" is a matter primarily of the complexity and subtlety with which the convex and concave curvatures of a sculpture's surfaces are inflected, along with the way their given materials and textures are worked. Here I refer not only to isolated surfaces, but to surfaces in groups and aggregates. Good sculptors can produce, purely by surface inflections and handling in a single material, the feel of different sculptural colors on different parts of a work.

Physiology

Particular colors do carry with them emotive connotations, about which there has been much speculation and research, especially for the purposes of advertising. Combinations of colors have also been studied for their physiological and psychological effects on different groups of human subjects, and many tabulations of chroma, hue, and intensity have been published for architects and designers to use schematically without needing to commit themselves to personal aesthetic judgments. Color is not an actual "property" of specific objects, but a phenomenon that results when the three sets of retinal cones in the human eye, which respond to red, green, and blue light, read patterns of relative intensities of these basic colors across a visual field. Our brains conflate these patterns into what we see as colors, along with our human experience of contexts, both actual and cultural, in which we have responded to them. Here I propose to discuss only the contextual side of color experience, which is most likely to contribute to the overall sculptural image.

Elemental Colors

Color sets have been schematized in different ways, including color circles and diagrams. One specific set of color distinctions is deeply rooted in our languages and culture, and gives extent and coherence to colors' aesthetic values. For our purpose this oldest and most widely understood scheme offers the easiest approach: the set of colors attributed to the traditional Elements earth, air, fire, and water. It ranges up from black, through brown, either to green, blue to white; or through red, orange, and bright yellow to gold. We can look at each color not as a flat tint but as a cluster of possible modulations.

Black reflects no light, so it stands for the total absence of light, as in deep night or the bowels of the earth, or for the negative and as yet unformed Hyle, densest matter of the Neoplatonists. The black sculptures that embody all these meanings best are the famous Black Virgins of Gothic Europe, which have been variously explained, but most persuasively as Christian re-presentations of the pre-Christian image of the Celtic Earth Mother. In India the goddess Kālī, who represents the destroying power of time, is always shown as black. Among woods, the hardest, the heartwood of lignum vitae, is black. Some bronzes naturally turn blackish from a slight silver or lead content, and they have invited philosophical interpretation as the metallic reflection of light giving form to matter. Gray, which is the natural color of the heavy lead sometimes used entirely for mold casting, carries the connotation of slightly luminous base matter.

Browns are the colors of the upper earth, the ground over which we walk and which we cultivate. They range from the darkest, most fertile, to lighter, drier, and autumnal ocherous browns. Cut woods are brownish, often flecked with hints of other colors. The region of earthly life is often felt as yellow with an earthy, ocherous tinge. Most sandstones and many limestones are brownish or ocher, usually because they contain oxides of iron; they may show their layering when carved, which emphasizes how they were formed by long underwater deposition of surface layers.

Greens are the colors outstandingly of vegetation, the lighter shades being the more springlike. Vegetation also implies water, and as an element, water is green, shading up into greenish blue. We speak mythically of the "water of life." The level between earth and water, mud, is a combination of dark green and brown, and most people find it drab. There are many varieties of green stone, including jadeites, malachites, and agates, which have often been carved and polished, especially in the Far East. The Chinese loved the color of pale green jade (they admired other jade colors too) because it recalls the color of distant mountains—highly emotive to them for a range of cultural reasons. Other colors have similar cultural resonances for other peoples.

Blue, the next elemental color, symbolizes air, as the color of the pure cloudless sky. In many varieties of art blue resonates with overtones of atmospheric light. Since the Middle Ages, it has been the chief color in which the robe worn by the Virgin Mary has been painted in Christian sculpture. In some cultures blue refers to the ultimate mind, the whole or void from which all phenomena originate; this notion lends depth to our previous interpretations. Dark in tone, blue conveys a sense of shaded luminosity, and the Impressionist painters, obsessed with light, used it for shadow tones. As a ceramic color it normally has a darkish value. Many painters have treated a paler blue as a kind of envelope of luminosity for their shapes. And sculptors have "transcendentalized" pieces by painting them entirely blue. Given a slight tinge of red toward magenta or lavender, pale blue can become very "sweet," an effect many contemporary artists detest, though it has been popular in the past and still is with some people. Inflected toward green, as turquoise or cerulean, blue can convey a sense of supernatural vitality.

Color Sequence

The painter and writer André Suarès has illustrated how the two "upward" sequences of color, the "cool" and the "warm," culminate in two different maximum lights. The cool, which I have been tracing, culminates in white, the total absence of apparent modulated color produced when our human eye cone-receptors register maximum intensity. White therefore conveys a sense of utmost luminous blankness, a radiant emptiness.

The second upward sequence, the warm, begins with deep purplish red, the color of blood and dark wine, both symbolic to most people of ripeness and of human and supernal life-energy. Lighter in tone, it is often felt to have genuine erotic, as distinct from lustful, overtones. Strong red has the powerful overtones and elemental significance of fire, heat, and the most vivid human experiences of energy at work. Many people love red, but others find its intensity intolerable. Traditionally, as the substance color of a sculptured robe, for example, red is meant to convey the wearer's passionate devotion. The reddish tints of iron oxides—rust—are modulated down toward the brown of earth, to which they do, in fact, give its prime color.

Above red is orange, a yet more intense version of red. Many people find it even more intolerable than red, others more exciting. Sculpturally, it is rarely used save in its reduced rust versions. The next color, brightest yellow, represents the maximum degree of radiant energy at which the human eye can look, as when the sun just begins to set. Old elemental systems treated this energy as the subtlest substance of all, originally called "aether," but perhaps better indicated now by the term *frequency.* Physiologically it is the combination of red and green at their maximum intensities, and it may veer slightly toward one or the other of its two component colors, with correspondingly altered values.

Gold

Gold is more than a simple color, being named after the metal that virtually every major culture has interpreted as the congealed light of the sun itself, and as such has taken as the touchstone of ultimate value. Gold has been used to convey the idea of divine radiance, for example as halos around the heads of saints, for crowns, and as the hair of goddesses and mythical queens. Many sculptures of divine figures in various cultures— a root meaning of the word *divine* is "shining (light)"—have been cast in gold, coated with gold leaf, or cast in brass, which can look like gold. Some modern works, such as Richard Lippold's *Sunbursts,* may be cast in carbo-bronze, which resembles gold but is physically more rigid.

4
Scale, Environment, and Space

Scale

All sculptures adopt a scale for overall image and lesser components, both in relation to the normal human size and in relation to the distance from which the visitor is expected to see them. A sculpture can be far taller than a human, yet seem small-scale and mean if its lesser components are too small; conversely it can have broad and massive forms that seem empty because they have little modulation to lend them interest from the expected viewing distance, or because their *true* shapes cannot be seen at the available viewing distance. A small sculpture obviously needs to be appreciated from fairly close in, and the artist will need to adapt its lesser components to the scale of the overall image. This question of relativity can have important implications for sculptors who work in an Expressionist mode, signifying emotive utterance through finger or tool marks that need to be seen clearly along with the whole. Our responses to a piece depend far more on this relativity than some sculptors realize.

Sculptures can occupy a nearly infinite range of scale. The scale of an individual piece depends very much on the sculptor's intentions with regard to its setting and its expression in that setting. The sculptor usually works close up to a piece and tends to keep assessing its shape from that distance, but it is important that he or she back off frequently to check the work at its intended scale and distance. The match between scale of work and viewing distance can even influence a visitor's assessment of whether particular surface features are meant as texture or specific shaping.

Sheer size dominates and overwhelms the visitor, and may be meant to, but what matters most is how the subsidiary shapes and features relate to the human scale. A sculpture consisting of vast but relatively blank surfaces may overpower one as a blank wall does, with little further communication, and drive one to a distance. A genuinely colossal piece, such as some of the gigantic Classical Roman marble statues in the Naples museum or Michelangelo's *David*, may offer surface developments that, though large, both eye and hand can accept from a position close enough to experience the figure as gigantic. Surface developments also offer the possibility of reading the topic working for its expression of admiration and praise, in contrast to its dominating rhetoric.

Pieces with clear figurative implications that stand about life-size address the visitor immediately at the human level and encourage investigation of their shapes, as if one were meeting and responding to a person. Sculptures just under life-size can seem awkwardly diminished and can be difficult to exhibit. But pieces smaller still can be successfully placed on plinths so that the visitor accepts that they inhabit an imagined space generated and scaled according to the implications of their shapes.

Space: Actual and Imagined

Imagined space is an important ingredient in any sculpture well under life-size. Whereas a piece life-size or larger challenges our ordinary feelings about our lived-in space, a considerably smaller one establishes a space within which it creates its own consistent world, or "second nature." Our imagination scales down the measurement context within which we read the formal relationships among its shapes. The context shrinks progressively and consistently down through the scale levels from table piece to miniature down to super-miniature, as in some Japanese netsuke. At the most miniature level we can easily accept dreamlike conflicts of scale, appreciating, for example, the image of a mussel shell opening to disclose a collection of little figures or a boat.

One can hardly exaggerate the importance of the fact that, whatever the scale of a sculpture, solid body and space are dialectical correlatives, defining each other: without one we cannot understand or even perceive the other. Empty space is meaningless without bodily points of reference to make us aware of it. Only by setting up solid shapes and positioning them in relation to each other can we give value and presence to sculptural spaces. The specific qualities and indications of energy we give to the spaces energize and illuminate their correlative solids.

Gravity and Weight

It is easy to lose sight of the fact that all sculptures are heavy, and that the force of gravity plays some part in the imagery of every sculpture. Whether we feel that a piece squats on the ground, surges up, or even takes off, we are relating its expression in some way to its apparent weight in relation to its foundation on earth, floor, wall, table, or plinth. The place where a work and its foundation meet is important and should be considered carefully. Good sculptors—Brancusi is a prime example—give particular thought to their plinths. Even hanging pieces like Alexander Calder's mobiles gain much of their expression from the way they seem to deny the gravity that bears on humans. Many traditional sculptors include into their images representations of the earth on which their figures seem to stand or from which they emerge. This approach enables the artist to make a clear statement about the relationship and its meaning at the imaginative level, and thereby reduces the problem of creating a plinth.

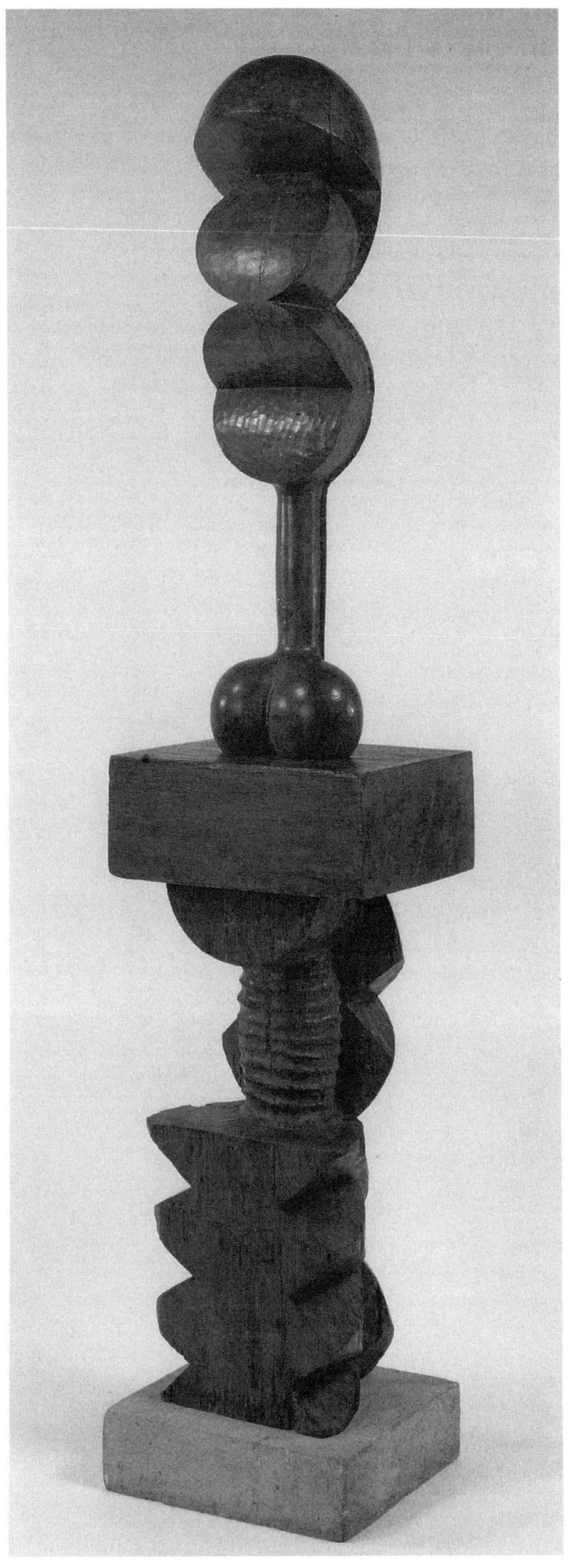

15. Constantin Brancusi, *Adam and Eve*, wood on limestone base, 1916–24. (Solomon R. Guggenheim Museum, Collection Mary Reynolds, gift of her brother; photograph by David Heald, copyright © the Solomon R. Guggenheim Foundation, New York. Copyright © 1995 Artists Rights Society, New York/ADAGP, Paris.)

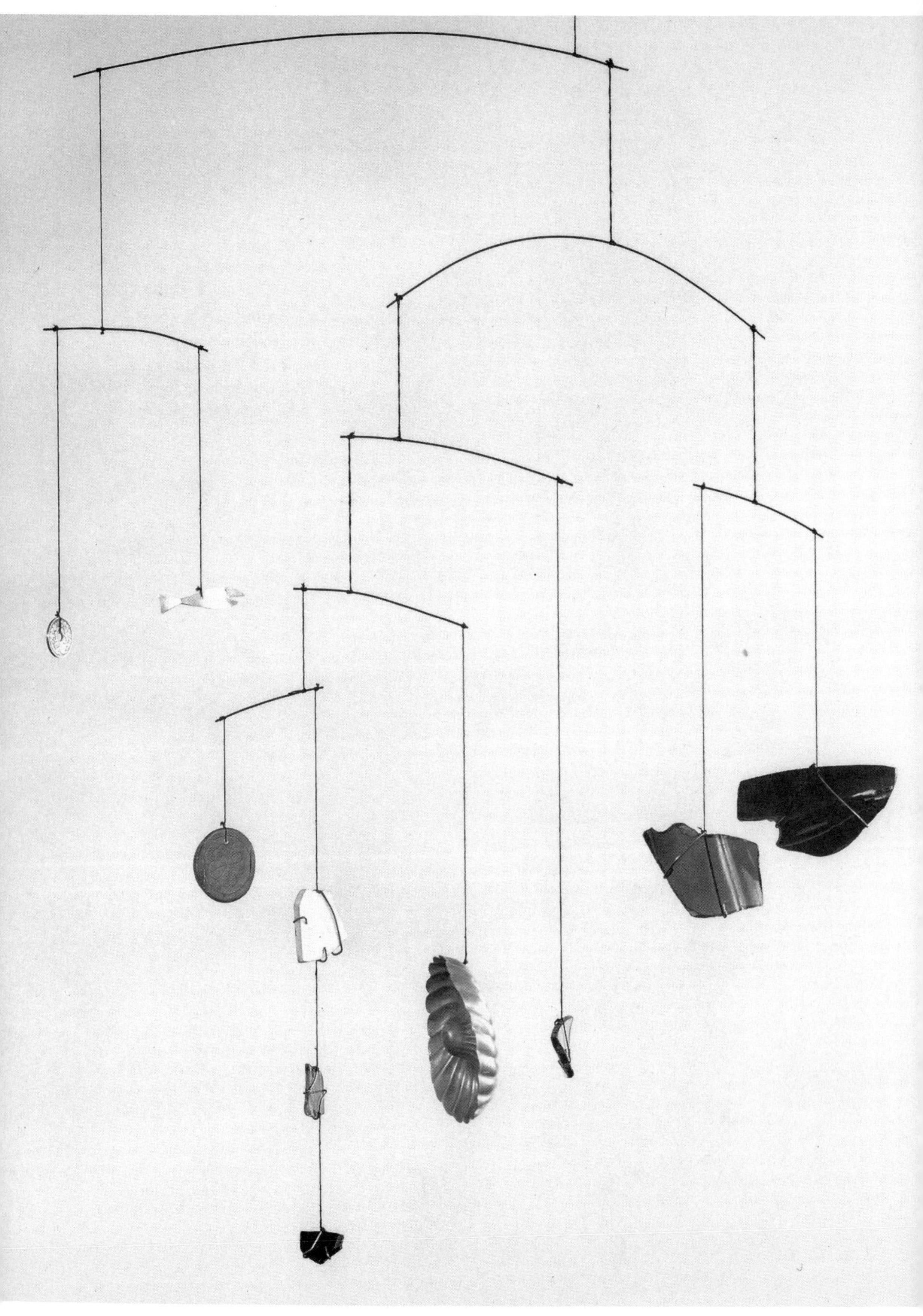

16. Alexander Calder, *Mobile,* mixed materials, 1935. The various shapes of different materials dangle and move like celestial archetypes in open space. (Solomon R. Guggenheim Museum, Collection Mary Reynolds, gift of her brother; photograph by Robert E. Mates, copyright © the Solomon R. Guggenheim Foundation, New York. Copyright © 1995 Artists Rights Society, New York/ADAGP, Paris.)

Mass, Bulk, and Volume

Three more factors operate in the making and reading of sculpture: mass, bulk, and volume. Each depends on our grasping it as fully three-dimensional. Mass implies relatively unformed sheer weight, and we read it intuitively, partly through our understanding of materials. Bulk appears as the whole quantity of space a body encloses, without reference to its actual weight, so it needs to show its three-dimensionality clearly. The sculptor does this not only by exhibiting a bulk's frontal spread, but by making sure the visitor can see the entire depth and extent of its side surfaces, and perhaps its top, without serious breaks or interruptions.

Volume is more specific yet less concrete than bulk or mass. A volume is a content of space given specific shape by its enclosing surfaces, which at the same time define the space around it and how it relates to that space. But we cannot actually see a volume, only infer it and its character from the visible surfaces that bound it. Conceiving and articulating interesting volumes are the most vital sculptural skills. During the early decades of the twentieth century, Cubist sculptors developed a method of implying volumes by omitting their enclosing surfaces and presenting them instead as sets of planar cross-sections, whose edges define the extent of the volumes. By relocating, intercutting, and angling these planar sections, Cubists produced a special sense of interpenetrating volumes.

The effects of mass, bulk, and volume contribute to the meaning of an image through the way the artist relates them to each other and to the environment. They can convey feelings of balance and tension by appealing to our inner senses of stable or unstable poise, forces, and mimicry of implicit motion. They can relate in specific ways to the scales and qualities of the environment and its size-compatible components, whether they involve gigantic spreads of raw concrete, massed greenery, calm white open space, or hurrying crowds. These factors suggest particular viewing distances from which the principal shapes look as they are meant to, neither blank and vapid nor jumbled and confused. In environments that visitors can traverse, pieces may be required to be effective from both near and far.

Place

In the West we have grown accustomed to thinking of all sculptures as self-contained objects that we can shift freely from place to place, even continent to continent. Some sculptures were made to be shifted around like that. But many of the world's major sculptures that we have carried off to isolate in museums, expecting them to offer us purely aesthetic experiences, were made for a specific, much more profound purpose connecting them expressly with the place where they were originally installed. Major sculptures were often meant not only to represent but literally to embody and make present live spirits, often identified by name, at specific locations in countryside or city. Their humanoid or animal tenors symbolized their indwelling life, and their topic working expressed their meaning for their people. The main icon of a shrine or temple was often identified literally with the sacred being to whom the place belonged, and the sculptor's ceremonial skill played a major part in bringing the spirit alive in the icon. Even lesser sculptures, of a kind we usually consider merely decorative, were meant to induce and contain live spiritual energies in the fabric of the sacred site they were made to adorn. We do need to try and recapture some sense of their original spiritual content if we are to grasp the "real" meaning of many works we meet only in museums. This places a responsibility on art historians and curators to perceive and respond to that need in their interpretation and display.

Modern societies have ceased to recognize and acknowledge live spirits that can be identified and incorporated as sculptural subject tenors in specific places. During the nineteenth century the Western conception of the recognizable tenor mostly degenerated to the level of the portrait image of the worthy citizen or kitschy church furnishing. Most art critics have grown accustomed to thinking of all works of art, including sculptures, as nothing more than personal "statements" by the artist that can be exhibited anywhere convenient and suitable. Many creative sculptors, however, still do feel responsible for capturing and condensing some general spirit of place. Patrons continue to commission large-scale works for parks, city squares, plazas, and building frontages because, at bottom, they feel the work adds something uniquely valuable and significant to its site. Whereas we may purchase or commission other kinds of art for a variety of status and investment reasons, public sculptures still have a special cachet which we need to nourish.

Environment

The general physical environment in which all of these considerations operate is significant. Sculptures may be expected to assimilate to a whole range of environments, including wide open spaces of landscape, park, and garden where one or more large pieces may be meant to focus the attention of visitors on a hillock, a body of water, the culmination of a vista, or a planting scheme. Another set of possibilities, however, is dominated by normally rectangular walled spaces of differing sizes. Street, concrete and glass plaza, mall, bare gallery, or living room, for example, can all establish either a frame or a prison. Even when, as with many exhibition galleries, the enclosing walls are neutralized as far as possible by white paint or dull fabric, they are nevertheless present, defining the space in relation to which a sculpture has to work. Because this type of space can be difficult to command—in the studio as well as the display area—it is easily ignored. This difficulty presents an advantage to working at a less than life-size scale, in accord with which a sculpture can generate its own space relations, such as a table piece, a miniature, or a handheld work, which appeals to the forms of touch even more than to vision.

Implications of the body image are important in this context, especially the sense of movement a piece conveys. The many sculptors who work with relatively static or self-contained images may be content that even their large work is conditioned by the three-dimensional frame of an interior space. In contrast, sculptors working with an imagery projecting energies bounding or floating into distance may find closed spaces inhibiting and require less restrictive space. Sculptors working with massive, highly stabilized imagery, like Calder in his big stabiles, may need considerable clear space in which to establish their stilled focus. The story of Rodin's violent disputes with purchasers of casts of his *Burghers of Calais* is relevant. He objected to their raising and isolating the work on high plinths, because he had designed it to stand at ground level, with the idea that the public should be able to enter among the group of figures, participate in their implied movement across open ground from the city gate, and so assimilate their implied feelings. Relief artists create such self-consistent imagined spaces that environmental problems for them consist mainly of whether and at what height the visitor can see their sculpture. Works meant to be handheld, like some early Inuit tusk carvings and small Native American pieces, we may need to imagine holding close in our hands, even inside our clothing.

Modes of Space

Artists imagine space in two radically distinct modes, though individual artists may not always work at the extreme of either. The modes were first defined and named by the French art historian Henri Focillon when he was developing concepts to describe the stylistic change from Romanesque to Gothic art. They are essential to our following discussions. The first mode is space as "limit," the second space as "environment." Space as limit means that the work defines its spaces inclusively, working inward from an established overall limiting frame through progressively smaller framed cells down to minimum closed shapes. Every shape is thus conceived as in some sense a subdivision of an overall cube of space. Normally the overall space and its cells are conceived in rectangular terms; Louise Nevelson's boxed reliefs are a paradigmatic example. Space as environment, in contrast, means that the artist conceives his or her imagery as springing outward from one or more centers as far as its energies carry it into an indefinite and unlimited environment of possibly infinite space. Early Chinese bronzes offer an ideal example of this mode.

We can speculate about the personal and cultural implications of each

17. (below) Woman polo player, tomb figure, modeled and part-cast low-fired ceramic, China, T'ang dynasty. A fully three-dimensional image of vivid life and energy meant to accompany the dead into the Western Paradise. (Courtesy Oriental Museum, University of Durham, England.)

18. (right) Scenes of heavenly love, Mahadeva Temple, Khajuraho, Rajasthan, India, sandstone, ca. 1000 A.D. Their deeply rounded and creatively active figures seem to bud from the temple exterior, filled with its supernatural juice. (Private photograph.)

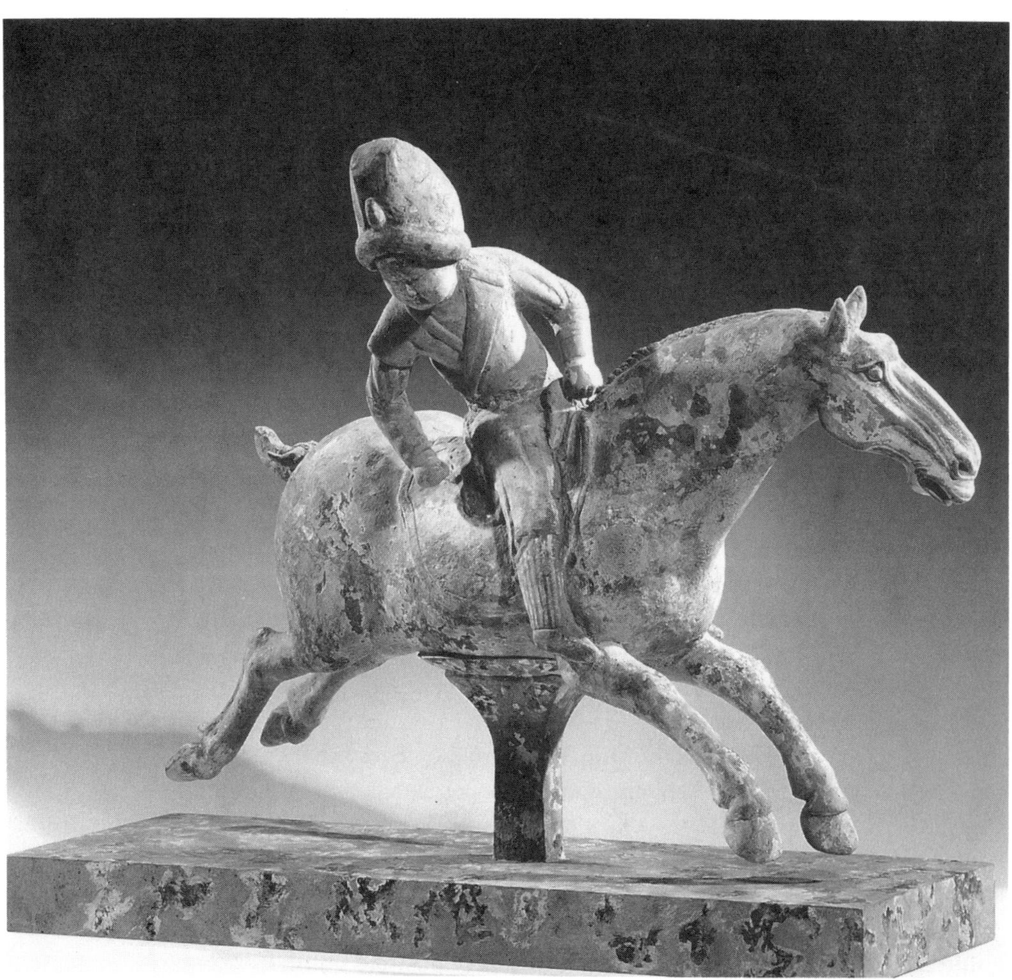

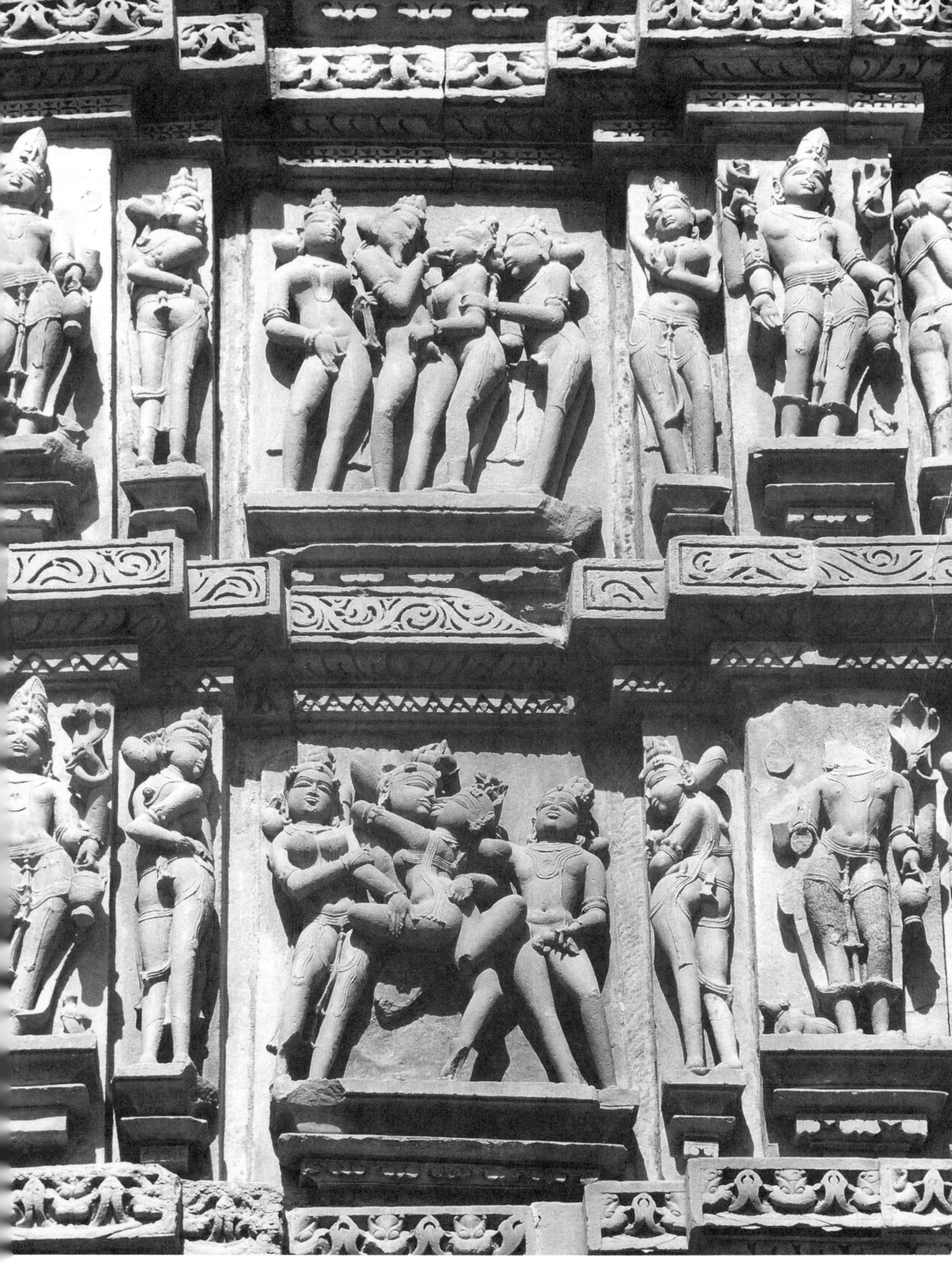

of these modes of spatial imagination and connect them with prevailing philosophies. Broadly speaking, space as limit implies an attitude that holds to clear conceptual classifications as absolute, social forms and personal disciplines as beyond question, and action according to procedures established in advance by custom, convention, or rule. It may also imply the will to set up such a state of affairs imaginatively in compensation for a fluid and ambiguous actual situation in which the artist feels lost, without steady ground underfoot. Space as environment implies an attitude that there is no real possibility of either understanding or ultimately controlling the vast processes of future time and of coiling, endlessly varying change which weave the phenomenal universe; it accepts that time is the ultimate imponderable and that in whichever direction one looks one sees not boundaries but infinite extension. Sculptors tend to favor one or the other mode; though some attempt a combination, this may be more or less uncomfortable and restricted in its expressive possibilities. Artists working in the second mode of environment, such as Chillida, are most likely to feel constrained within the rectangular gallery space.

Common Space

One further way of conceiving space ignores the possibility of creating an imaginative, second-nature space. This approach leaves the commonplace lived-in environment unquestioned and unmodified and treats sculptures as ordinary objects. It represents the most crass materialist attitude in the sense that it assumes that all the things simulated can only ever belong to the most inert and lifeless orders of external banal fact, and it implies that any figurative images portrayed belong to that same motionless order. In fact, few works of sculpture do discount the possibilities of movement and change which distinguish the living from the dead. But in the late 1960s certain American artists molded hyperreal, true-scale stand-ins for actual people and objects, meant as conceits to shock the visitor's recognition faculties, as wax fruit and waxwork figures do. The act of stilling into total inertia a life-size copy of, say, a naked or clothed person, or a group of people at a moment in some violent action as if in a three-dimensional high-speed photograph or freeze-frame, enables the visitor to survey and verify small frozen details impossible to recognize in the actuality. This sort of work may have the effect of lengthening the visitor's usually diffracted attention span and so provide an exceptionally vivid experience of external, purely visual perception. It also matches the scientific convention of verifiability. However, merely to shape an image "accurately" to fit actual space is not an effective sculptural procedure.

Common space is invoked by artists such as Claes Oldenburg who manufacture replicas of familiar objects on a vastly enlarged scale, translated into distinctive and unnatural materials. One of the most famous examples is Oldenburg's huge hamburger of stitched and painted canvas. Apart from other implicit readings, its effect depends on its most emphatically *not* setting up an imagined space for its presence, but requiring the common space setting to point up its grotesquerie.

Earth art, at the opposite extreme, also depends on the visitor accepting the space and scale of the actual for its effect. Vast furrows ploughed in the desert, strange platforms and walls of immense size, or Christo's stretches of coastline wrapped in plastic sheeting amaze and promote inner queries about relations between forms and shapes, and about imposed integrations, precisely because such artifacts are made on that scale in common space. What matters is that they are done rather than how they are specifically shaped.

Magical Space

One final way of treating actual common space has been followed by installation sculptors, who have set out to convert an assigned real space into a magical hyperspace by placing around its interior floor, walls, and ceiling a variety of differently shaped and grouped objects, maybe on different scales, meant to be encountered in a particular sequence. Lighting can play an important role both in illuminating specific areas and objects and in drenching, for example, a passageway in single or shifting colored lights. Video and sound can also be included. This art is probably descended from a combination of tribal ceremonial setting, interior architectural decoration, theater, and Surrealist assemblage with fairground "ghost train" and "tunnel of love" constructions; its aesthetic possibilities are by no means exhausted. It is, of course, itself a variety of assemblage.

Viewing Aspect

Although full-round sculptures are essentially three-dimensional creations, they do stand up erect in front of the visitor. Their shapes thus have a two-dimensional composition from whatever direction they are seen. It has become a cliché among some modern artists and critics that sculptures ought always to be so fully three-dimensional that they can be appreciated only by walking all around them. This cliché has been taken so far by some museum curators that they have displayed solid stone works from traditional cultures mounted on permanently revolving turntables—even with little radial fences to stop the visitor following them around to catch their principal aspects.

Taking this proposition as the sole yardstick for all sculpture making can have disastrous consequences for the vigor and coherence of a piece. Carried to the extreme, it would mean that a sculpture could only make sense as a pattern of memories of each aspect in the walking visitor's mind. Whereas it is obvious when one confronts a good sculpture that it has a strongly constructed frontal presence, and that even though it shows clearly how its major continuities of three-dimensional form are

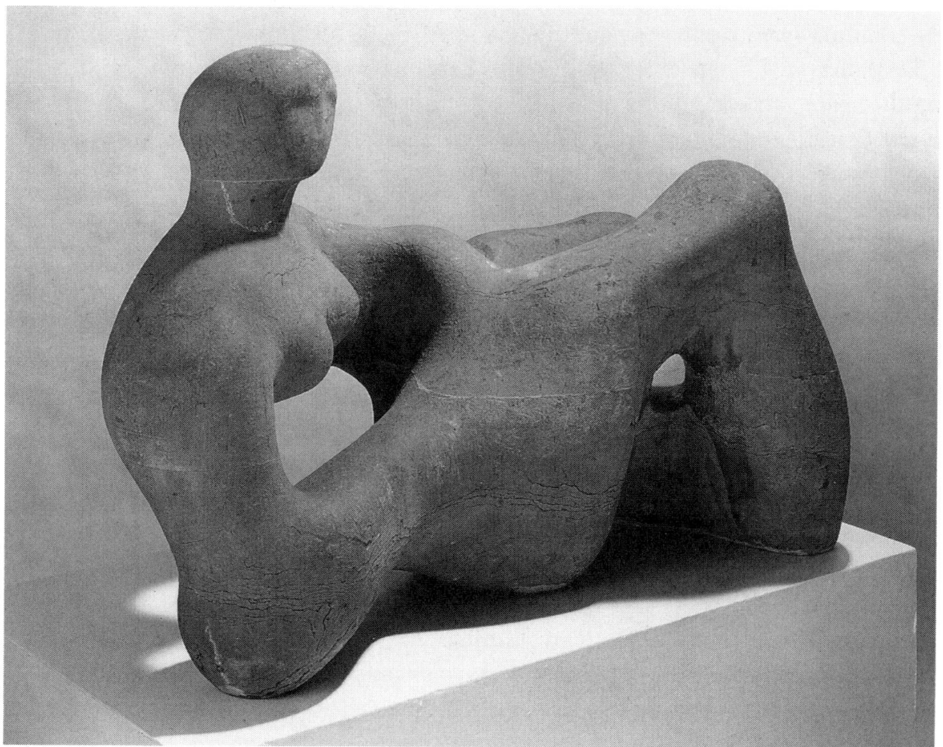

19. Henry Moore, *Reclining Woman*, lying figure, stone, ca. 1937. Freestanding, to be walked around, this work combines into a single complex of symbolisms the meanings of stone, female, and hollow in the earth. (Copyright © the Henry Moore Foundation.)

likely to run on when they pass round out of sight, it also offers fresh and interesting two-dimensional compositions from successive aspects. Compositions, of course, need to be intentional and carefully developed. It may be important for the visitor to study the three-dimensional continuity of a whole piece by shifting viewpoints. But there are serious risks that a piece's two-dimensional compositions can be spoiled or weakened if the sculptor ignores or sacrifices them for the sake of walkaround appreciation. A simple example makes the point: a vivid coiling curve which is the primary idea of a piece may be properly effective only from a main viewpoint, and attempts to modify it into a total three-dimensional shape may destroy its initial energy. The solution to this difficulty lies in composing the whole piece as a single three-dimensional entity, as for example African sculpture does outstandingly, from basic shapes and structures that are individually conceived and visible as fully three-dimensional.

Taking Possession of Space

The importance of the all-round totality of a fully three-dimensional piece is that it should "take possession" of its space by one means or

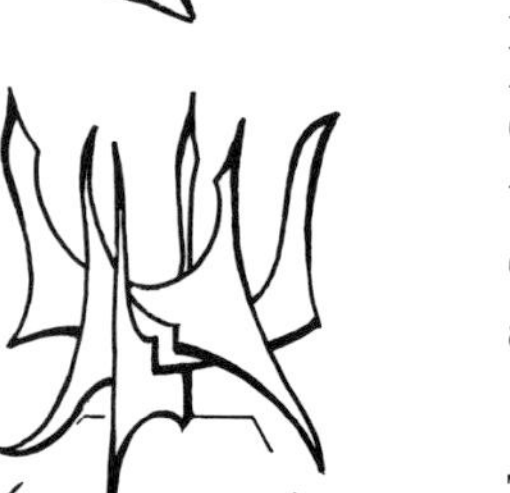

Figure 4. Taking possession of space.

another. This does not mean simply occupying space; all objects do that. It means developing its shapes and their implications so as to build in readable connections between the piece and the spatial environment. Several specific ways of achieving this result depend on the type of sculptural work involved, of which there are three main ones: full-round; what is called in French *ronde bosse* (deep forward projection); and relief of various grades. Each calls for a different approach.

Spatial Skeleton

Full-round sculpture demands that both artist and visitor identify their inner fully three-dimensional mimetic experience in the layout of the piece, the sculptor projecting, the visitor responding. Distinguished modern sculptors, including Henry Moore, have pointed out that the prime characteristic of the human body on which we base our sculptural imagery is its skeleton of long bones, spine, and upper and lower arms and legs, which extend it through space, and that sculptors use a parallel system of extenders to take possession of space. Another term for extenders is *axes*, though that word has implications, unwanted here, of the right-angled axes used in plotting positions mathematically. Extenders are axes in the sense that they constitute central directions for connected aggregates of volume which may be built around them like kabobs impaled on their skewers. Normally the axes are straight, as are the bone extenders of the human body, though they can be curved. Straight extenders multiply and deliberately vary the angular directions of the main axes of the piece in and through space.* Anthony Caro, who in his early years worked with Moore, used principally axial girders. Around curved extenders, the artist may construct sequences of connected shape that snake and coil through space.

A second important spatial method reflects even more strongly the basic human skeletal structure and is especially valuable for directly figurative work. It includes, along with the principal long-bone axes already mentioned, a set of notional straight horizontal axes that define the body's postures and gestures. These axes are, reading from the ground upward: that connecting the feet; that joining the knees; that running through from one hipbone to the other; that running between the outer top rims of the pelvic basin; that running from one shoulder tip to the other; that running from ear to ear; that extending as the forward direction of the face; and that extending as the implied direction in which the eyes are looking. The central column of the spine may flex from side to side and to and fro as the axes tilt and twist in space; and the head may tilt and twist on the neck. The central column of the spine may thus support a complex set of spatial directions based on these axes, plus extra directions extending through and beyond the directions of the hand gestures. To multiply and vary the angles and stretches of all such axes is a primary method for

* The floor rectangles I have drawn in the diagrams are only a device to compensate partly for the missing actual third dimension.

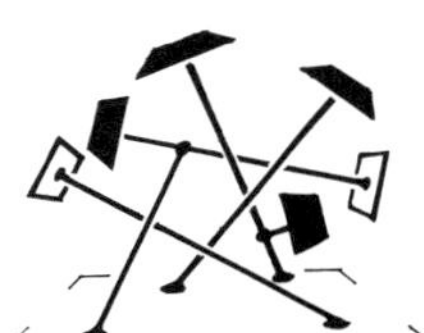

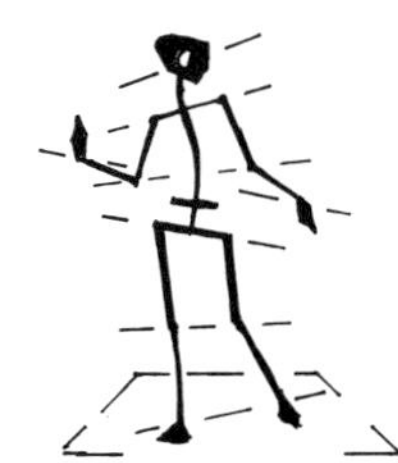

Figure 5. Axes occupying space (above) and human body axes (below).

giving to any figure or figures a sense of life and interaction. It was used especially by Roman sculptors, by Donatello in his big monuments, and by Baroque sculptors. It can be used implicitly in reliefs to enhance their sense of space. Even ancient Egyptian flat reliefs gain some depth by implying the presence of the hip axis running into the depth of the figure.

Assemblage sculptors who work with open structures use both multiple straight axes and sinuous axes, sometimes in combination and visible right through the piece rather than clothed in shaped volumes. The relationship of the axes with the floor on which they stand can be highly significant, as with the bridging spans of some of Calder's stabiles. Or, inverted, they may cage space like tree branches either poised upright or streaming off in a common direction, or they may move within a region of space into which they are suspended, as Calder's mobiles do.

20. Alexander Calder, *Standing Mobile*, painted metal and wire, late 1930s–early 1940s. The imagery of the dangling shapes is complemented by the spiderlike reach through space of the support. (Solomon R. Guggenheim Museum, Hilla Rebay Collection; photograph by Carmelo Guadagno and David Heald, copyright © the Solomon R. Guggenheim Foundation, New York. Copyright © 1995 Artists Rights Society, New York/ADAGP, Paris.)

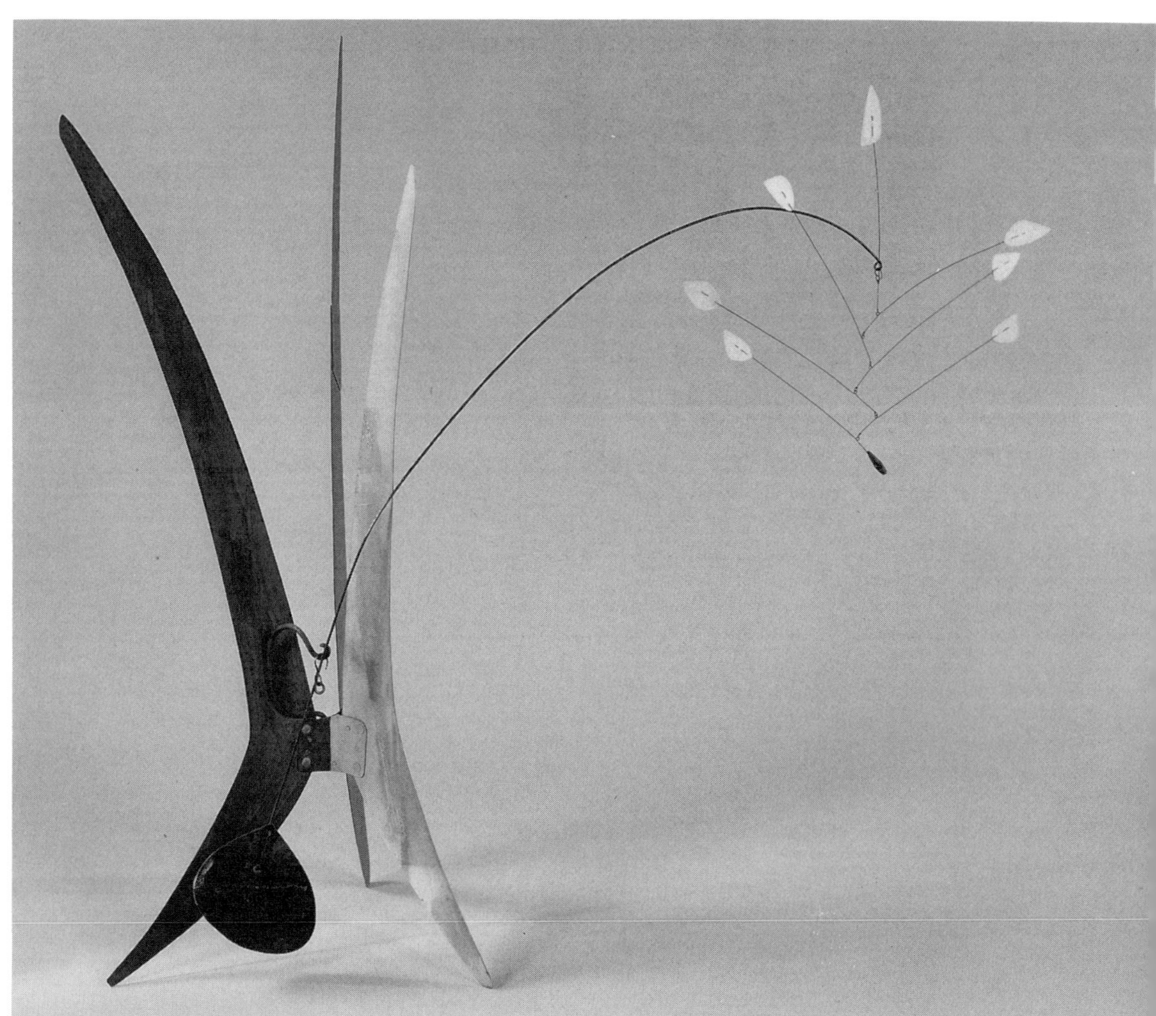

Space Cages

In the 1950s and 1960s many radical shaping sculptors followed an example set by Picasso, derived from tribal precedents, in fabricating fully three-dimensional sculptures composed as wide-spaced open cages made of wire or thin modeled lengths of bronze. These enabled the entire inner space content of the cage to be grasped, along with the standing places of its feet, its character implicit but invisible. Some of Picasso's related paintings are based on linked up, rodlike streaks and show how the three-dimensional constructs were also meant to read as two-dimensional images from particular viewpoints.

Hyper-Depth

Among the most important of the ways of treating space, and rarely used because it is the most difficult to achieve, is to expand or extend the spatial depth contained within a piece far beyond what is natural to the tenor. This has the strange effect of somehow "transcendentalizing" the image by lifting its content of space to a higher value. The method is the exact

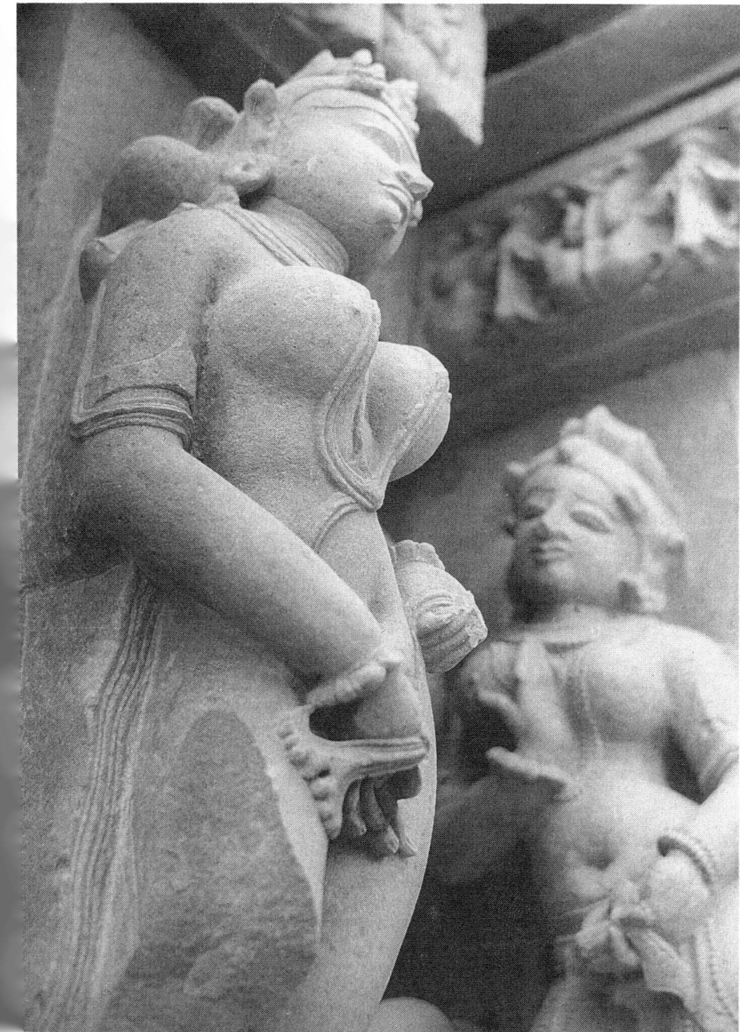

21. Celestial girl, Mahadeva Temple, Khajuraho, Rajasthan, India, sandstone, ca. 1000 A.D. This figure illustrates the long side-recessions which give the volumes their amplitude from viewing angle and distance. (Private photograph.)

opposite of normal relief: instead of compressing the distance between the frontal and the rearmost features, it is stretched. The frontal features reach far forward into space toward the visitor, and the rearmost recede far away. This technique may work most effectively for a principal viewpoint, but it can work well for multiple viewpoints. The force of this description of depth may be nearly impossible to realize from photographs—which itself suggests that it may represent the acme of three-dimensional expression. Prime examples are some of the woven masks from New Ireland in Oceania, many of Africa's great masks such as the Baga's immense Nimba heads or the Songe masks from Zaire with their fantastically prominent eyes, nose, and mouth, or some of the prophets carved on the main portal of Strasbourg's Gothic cathedral whose deeply cut features loop far out through environing space.

Solid volumes can also be made to contain a preternaturally deep content of internal space and produce a particular powerful effect. The vivid French term for this technique is *ronde bosse*, which means "projecting roundly far forward" and implies that the piece stands separate with a pronounced frontal aspect, its receding side surfaces being exaggerated in length to lift the frontal presentation face far forward. This formation gives the whole image its extraordinary depth, bulk, and volume. For full effect the side surfaces need to be visible from the main viewpoint for the whole of their length, from the edges of the presentation face to the contours.

Such a piece can also convey a powerful effect from other viewpoints by clear statement of its shaped volumes, but it will always seem to be directed toward its front. In practice *ronde bosse* belongs to the radical shaping mode, though it could be adapted to assemblage. It resembles exceptionally deep relief projecting against an actual or, if it is freestanding, an invisible background, its back also being worked. The method is used especially for major icons. Some of the greatest are Indian and Khmer Buddhas and Hindu divinities in both cut stone and bronze. Michelangelo's immense *David* is a fine example, the back being markedly broader than the frontal presentation face to allow for the reach of the side recessions.

Frontal Surface Mobility

This notion of *ronde bosse* raises a point of the utmost importance for the whole of sculpture, especially radical shaping, which is related to the true psychology of perception. Most experimental work on this psychology seems so far to have been done on the recognition of flat silhouette shapes. These are certainly important in sculpture, but when we are in the close physical presence of a person, roughly within the thirteen-foot range of binocular parallax, we do not run our eyes around his or her edge contours to grasp that presence. We look instead at the nearest frontal surfaces to assimilate their humps and hollows, the undulations

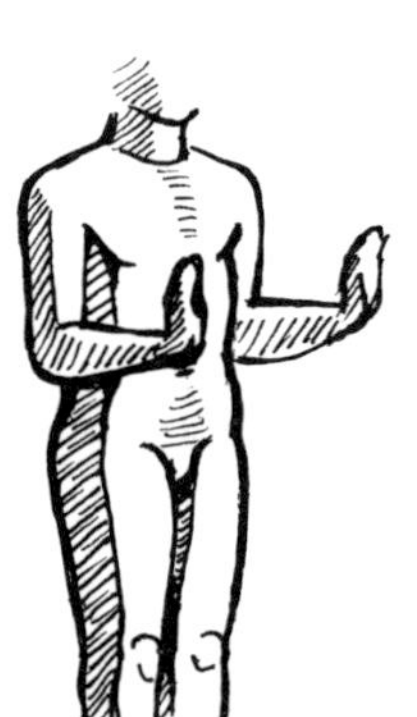

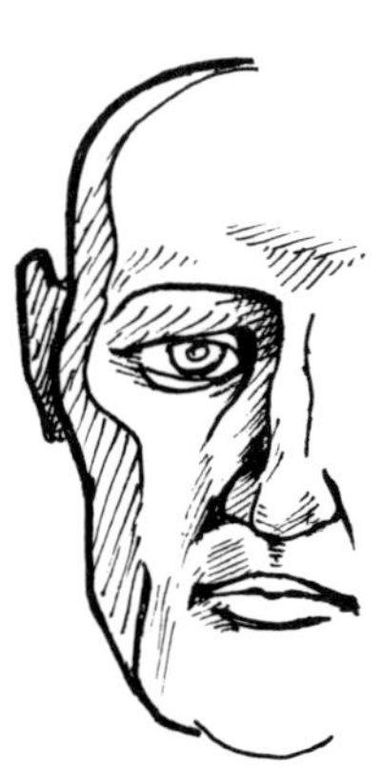

Figure 6. *Ronde bosse* (above) and shed-lines (below).

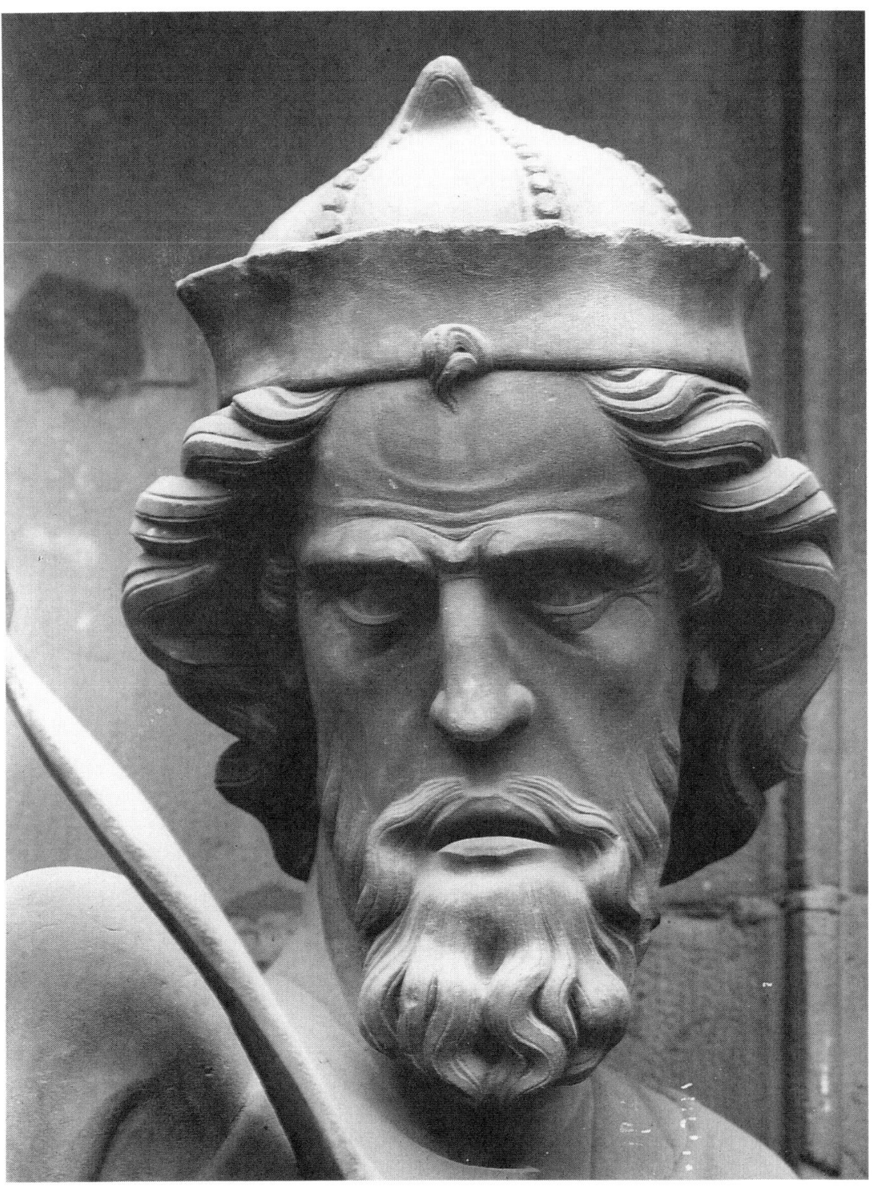

22. Head of a prophet, front of Strasbourg Cathedral, sandstone, ca. 1225. No flat photo can do justice to the way the sharply formulated features of the head loop out magnificently through space. (Courtesy Bildarchive Foto Marburg.)

and stretches of material that emerge toward us and recede from us defining volumes in the sculptural space. We are secondarily aware of the edge limits to which the side recessions of the whole body turn away from us. Sculpture works most effectively when it offers the visitor this order of bodily presence and face-to-face relationship, within the thirteen-foot range of binocular parallax, each eye then being able to bear on a substantial stretch of its own side of the sculptural bulk.

Depth and Shed-Lines

In creating a sculpture with genuine and powerful presence, the artist must define as strongly as possible both frontal and receding side surfaces. This can be achieved by drawing in space clearly readable demarcations between the two kinds of surface that position the transverse extent of the frontal surfaces, and the extent from frontal face to back contour of the receding side surfaces. These are most readily composed and given coherence as three-dimensionally mobile "shed-lines," analogous to a geographical watershed, from which run away the frontal and side surfaces.

If the piece is to be seen from much farther away, even a sculpture with well-defined, coherent, and mobile front faces may need particularly long and clearly inflected side recessions, to avoid seeming bodiless. However carefully developed and interesting its frontal silhouette may be, from a distance it may look nearly two-dimensional. To develop a true sense of bodily volume, the sculptor may need to work progressively around the piece to give its sequence of changing mobile silhouettes both variation and continuity. The silhouette of the frontal surface may be the most important, but viewing it from the side can reveal the importance of shaping and inflecting, even substantially broadening and deepening, the continuity of the receding side surfaces.

Humps and Hollows

Studying the silhouettes from various viewpoints helps to establish the relationship and placement within the sculptural depth (whether expanded or compressed, as in relief) of the humps of maximum volumetric prominence and hollows of maximum indentation. These components are important in defining the main proportional or modular scheme of the whole image, as is especially clear in African carvings. The force of a volumetric sculpture can depend on how robustly it clarifies and enhances the three-dimensional scope and mobility of all its enclosing and defining surfaces. These depth and surface relationships defining the inner full and the outer adjacent void volumes of a piece lie at the root of sculptural thinking. To reduce shapes to flat objects identified only by one set of edges as seen from a single viewpoint, as in plan drafting, may perhaps be allowed to stand as "abstraction."

Relief and Site

A very large proportion of the world's sculpture is relief, standing vertically face to face with the viewer. The various kinds of relief sculpture are attached to or set against a background support, and so amount to decoration as defined here, since they are meant to present in sculptural terms the meaning and value of the place or structure to which they are attached. Modern sculptors do make reliefs that are portable like paintings and have no specific relationship to the places where they happen to hang. Nevertheless, in that they are attached to a ground from which they project into a limited depth of space, they maintain a connection with the architecture, however tenuous. Reliefs normally ask to be seen directly from the front; but some assemblage reliefs, particularly those that form parts of installations, may propose themselves as sections of three-dimensional objects which seem to emerge through the surfaces of wall, floor, or ceiling.

Types of Assemblage Relief

There are at least five broad varieties of assemblage relief. First is the type that is suspended against the interior or exterior surface of a site, projecting substantially from it and addressing visitors either rhetorically, if it is placed high and open, or intimately, if it is low at the person-to-person level. Its distinctive address to the visitor is an element in all relief art; all relief pieces, especially figurative ones, need to be placed so that they can be read clearly. The second type of assemblage relief consists of an arrangement of elements that project minimally from wall or hung backboard and are meant to be read frontally as transverse designs: for example, Charles Biederman's rhythmic rectangular arrangements of small colored plastic slats stuck vertically onto a colored backboard. Third is the boxed relief, a flat arrangement of open-faced boxes containing sets of varied enigmatic shapes or objects, as in Nevelson's major pieces. Fourth is a type of which Arp made many examples. Differently or particolored flat panels of substantial thicknesses, usually of wood, are cut into outlined shapes and superimposed on each other directly or spaced slightly apart. Picasso made similar pieces from cut out sheet metal. Fifth is the glazed wall display case filled with various objects and shapes.

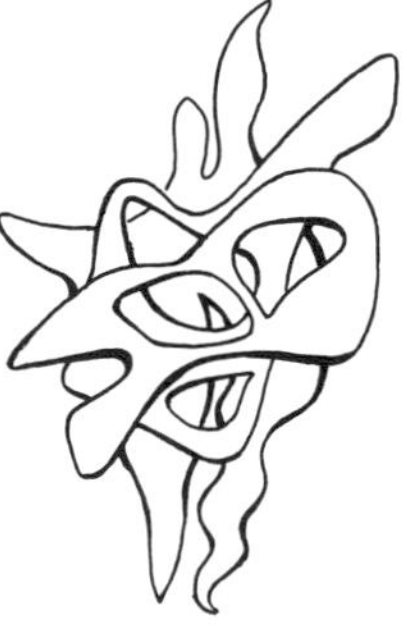

Figure 7. Layered relief.

Radical Shaping Relief

Whereas assemblage relief depends on the nature and relative placing of the objects assembled, radical shaping relief is far more demanding technically and has a much wider range of possible expression, including the imaginative presentation of deep space. Because none of the seven broad types of radical shaping relief uses components that have a preexisting identity as solid objects, the artist has to shape and construct images of solid bodies generating notional space. In figurative relief of this kind, the

Figure 8. Sections of relief types, top to bottom: low relief, raised relief, attached relief, undercut relief.

long-bone-like extenders are nearly all shown laid out in two dimensions across the ground; foreshortening is used not at all or sparingly. The basis of the whole method lies in skillful outlines subtending beveled edges of varied widths and slopes running from front faces to background.

Types of Relief

The true low relief is normally carved within a small thickness of a flat surface, which is cut back closely round the image to a ground level that represents the furthest limits of depth. The broad areas of visible solid body are thus defined by the same front level as the original surface. Ancient Egyptian art is full of such reliefs, and in the twentieth century Ivan Meštrović adopted the method. It implies that the image represented is generated within the fabric of the surface; this approach is especially significant when the relief is part of a sacred building, such as a temple or memorial. Usually the figures are presented in orthographic projection, as if the observer's eye is located at right angles to every part from top to bottom.

The raised relief resembles shallow relief, in that its bodies are compressed between the levels of the background and a frontal face. The bodies thus stand out flat but are raised well above the level of the general background into the visitor's own space. They may then be incised with shallow channels and beveled modeling across the bodies, which define subsidiary shapes but do not cut in as deep as the background. Sumerian and Assyrian reliefs use this method with wonderful effect.

The attached relief is also worked into a relatively shallow depth of surface and keeps to a maximum forward projection, but outlines solid bodies overlapping each other. The fifth-century-B.C. interior frieze reliefs from the Parthenon at Athens refined this technique to an extraordinary degree, and since then it has been a staple method. In fact, the practice of overlapping the edges that define solid bodies is fundamental to all arts that set out to create an image of deep space, including graphics, painting, and architecture, as well as sculpture.

The undercut relief involves cutting material away behind the contours of each body so that from the front it looks as if it is freestanding, though it remains attached to the ground. The principal bodies may overlap others executed behind them in attached relief. Many Roman sarcophagus reliefs follow this method, as do Renaissance reliefs imitating antiquity. These figures are never simply the front halves of complete rounded figures that are then slightly flattened; rather they are composed to present those mo-

23. *Dormition of the Virgin* (detail), south portal of Strasbourg Cathedral, sandstone, ca. 1223. Here the deep relief has been cut from a thick slab, its emphatic heads aligned in actual space are spaced notionally and linked by a network of melodic folds. (Courtesy Bildarchiv Foto Marburg.)

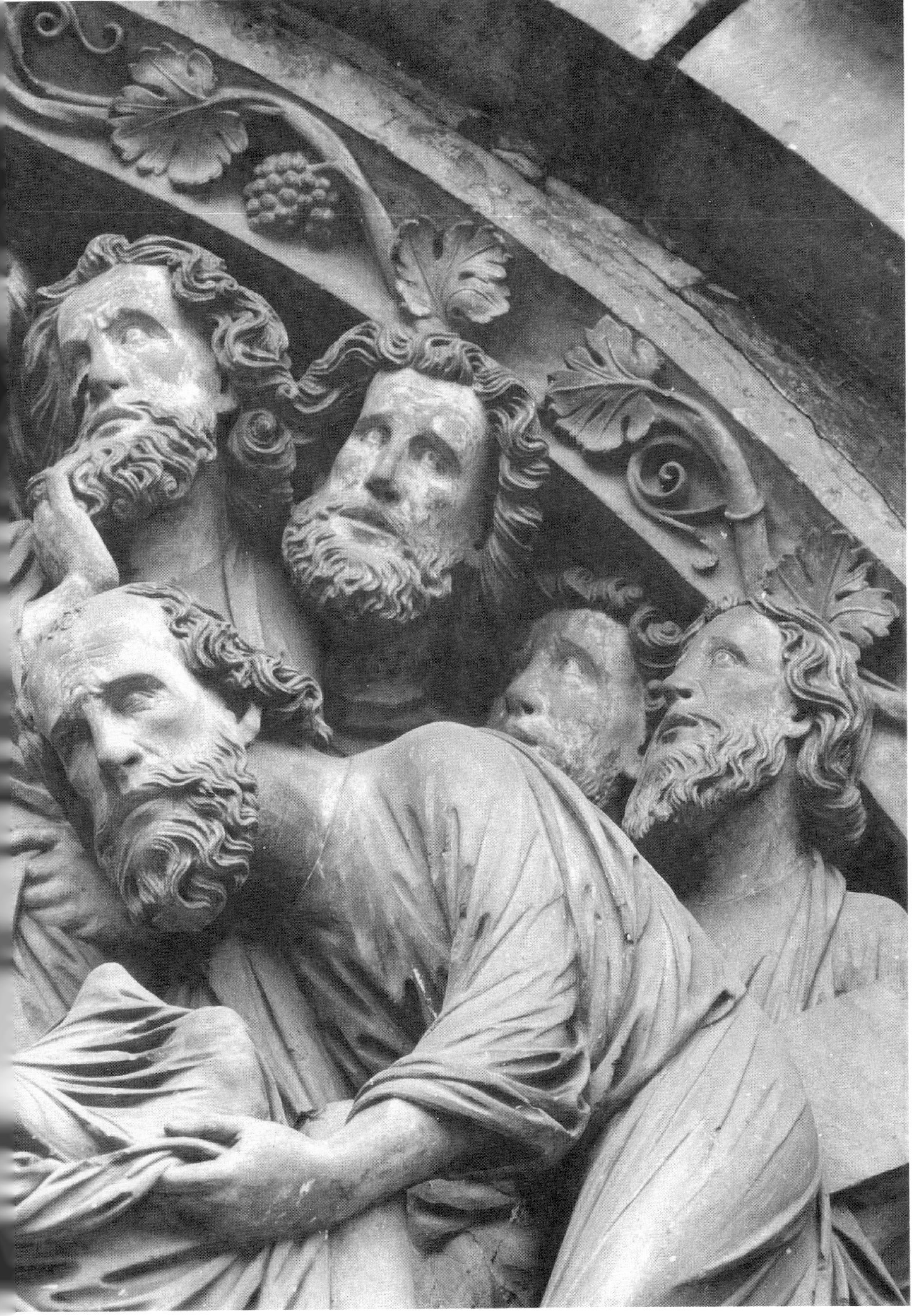

bile front faces mentioned earlier, with overlaps and side faces receding to limiting contours, which are themselves variously positioned in space.

The next type of relief is *rilievo stiacciato*, or suppressed relief. This is a kind of graphic sculpture using channels, minimal bevels, and surfaces only slightly raised, lowered, and inflected to render a wide range of things and settings, including deep-space perspectives over water, trees, and shores, as if the sculpture, which in fact protrudes from its background toward the eye, were a window opening on reaches of depth beyond its surface. In the previous types of relief, what is read as levels of close-up relative depth, here becomes reaches of implied deep space, extending toward the infinity of the sky. Two great Italian artists of the mid-fifteenth century used this relief especially effectively: Agostino di Duccio (at Rimini), who worked primarily with fluent linear channels cut in stone surfaces to generate his overlaps, and Donatello, who developed, in addition to beveled channels, extraordinary abrupt and harshly fluttering, reflective bronze surfaces, modeled originally in wax.

Another type of relief combines undercut, almost freestanding foreground figures, freely projecting and not contained by a consistent frontal surface, with more distant *stiacchiato* features. In addition, rising from the lower, near edge of the relief, modeled floors of landscape or pavement link these to produce an effect of deep space. Lorenzo Ghiberti, in his bronze doors for Florence Cathedral in the early fifteenth century, and Rodin in the late nineteenth, developed versions of this method.

The last type of relief was followed particularly in sixteenth-century Germany and eighteenth-century China. It consists of open working of two or more distinct layers of shallow attached relief, superimposed with narrow gaps between them—the nearer layers more openly spaced, their elements framing and overlapping the more distant layers.

Any relief in almost every material (though often a precious one, such

24. Donatello, *Christ Handing the Keys to St. Peter*, meant as a predella, marble, ca. 1435. The shallowest possible relief ("rilievo stiacciato"), subtly drawn into the surface as sets of overlaps and hinting at volumes by delicate modulations between them. (By courtesy of the Board of Trustees of the Victoria and Albert Museum.)

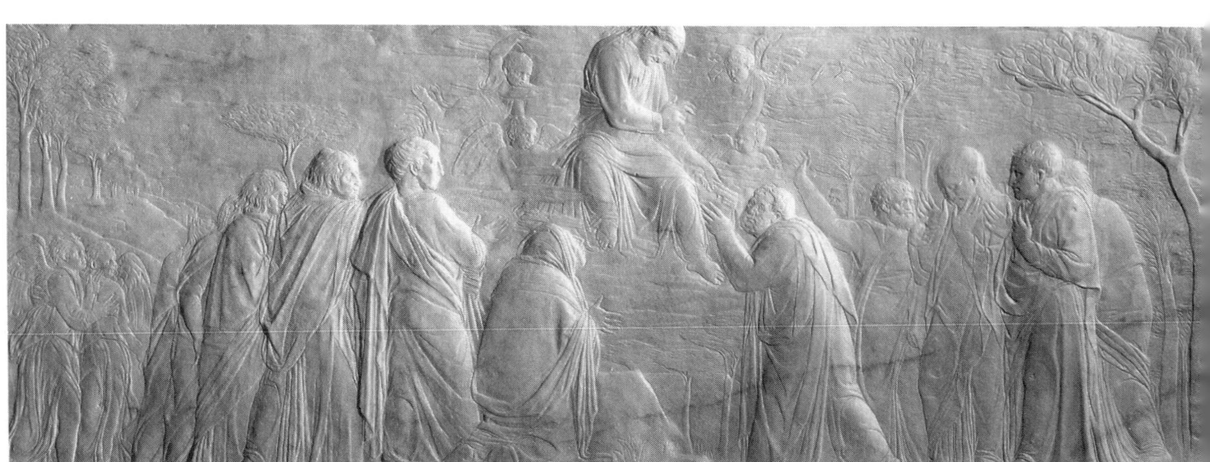

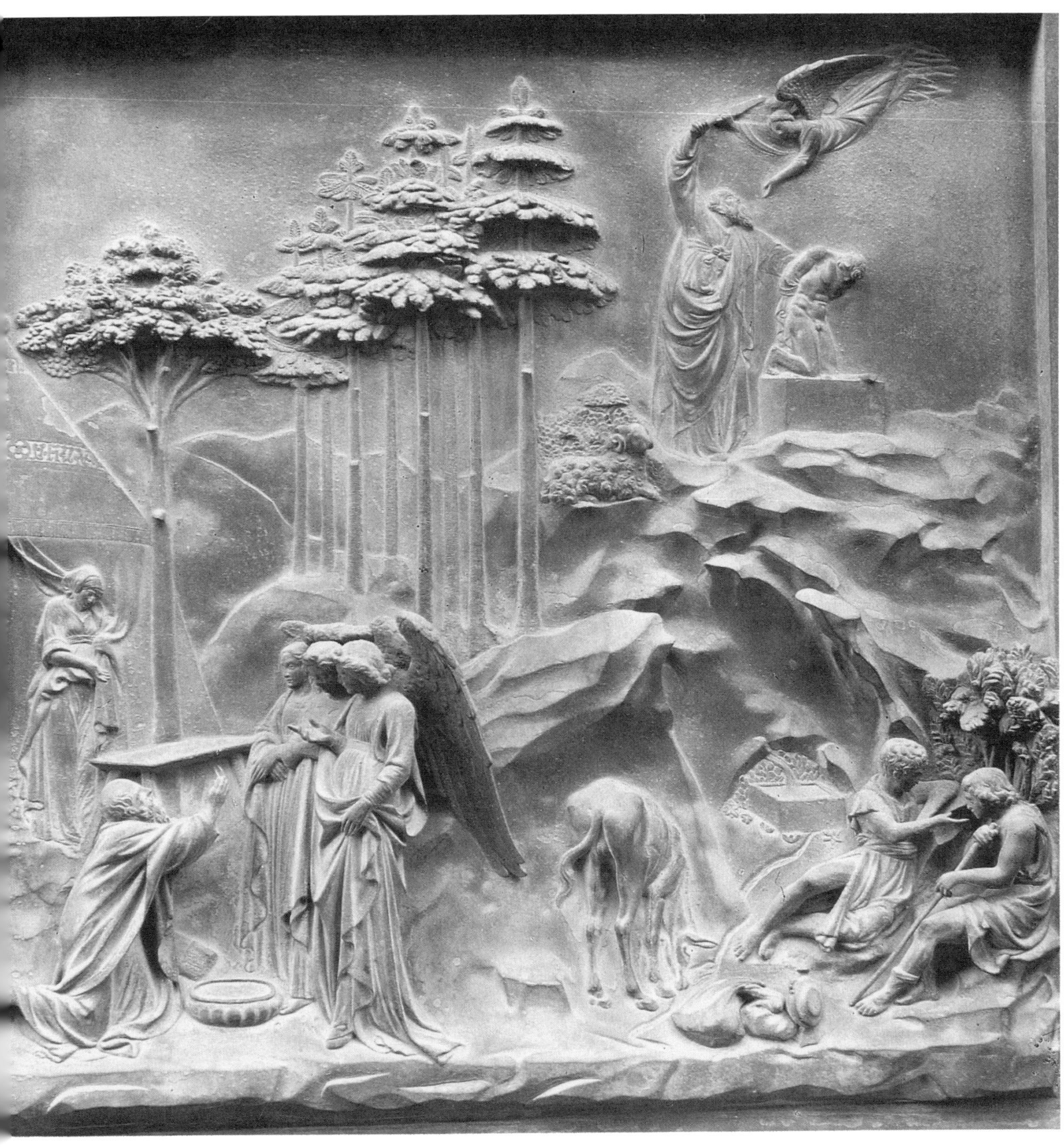

25. Lorenzo Ghiberti, *The Story of Abraham*, bronze, 1436–52. This work conveys
a sense of deep notional space by graded depths of relief in actual space, the nearest
figures standing virtually free. (Courtesy Opera Santa Maria del Fiore.)

as ivory) can be pierced through around the contours of the principal tenor-objects, either singly or in clusters, and then attached to some other background or supporting frame.

Overlaps

Carefully devised sets of overlaps are a basic element in all sculpture, especially reliefs. They are not as simple and commonplace as they may seem at first sight. To invent sets of defined overlaps of many kinds among both notional bodies and the edges of their parts introduces a sense of notional depth, even deep space. To our human perception of the space we live in, the edges of nearer things overlap and their surfaces so defined occlude more distant things. We estimate the depth of space between each overlap according to our estimate of relative scales of size. The front surface of a close thing, such as a human body, cuts off successively broader stretches of objects behind it, eventually perhaps a mile or two of notional distant landscape. By contrast, an apparently human body poised behind a horizon line may appear a colossus.

Overlaps are the true basis of visual perspective, rather than schematic arrangements of man-made straight lines "converging" optically on vanishing points. Optical schemes do give a sense of the length of a straight city street, but to produce a sense of environmental space the sculptor needs to develop sets of overlapping edges belonging to notionally solid bodies that interrupt our view of others that lie "behind," farther away. Before and behind, near and far, become dialectic features of visual structure. A sculptor can produce a powerful sense of spatial depth, even within a minimal actual depth, by devising and arranging series of overlaps within the tenor, as part of the topic development, rather like the wings of a stage set but more complex, moving step by step into notional distance. When rendering a tenor all of whose components are "close" in space, an artist may not need to differentiate much between relative expected sizes. Picasso, for example, late in his career made some close figure reliefs in shapes cut from sheet metal spaced a little bit apart. To produce images of deep pictorial space, however, the sculptor may need to differentiate relative sizes quite sharply.

Overlaps imply specific viewpoints, though the artist can build the overlaps into successive views of a fully three-dimensional piece around which visitors are expected to circulate. Henry Moore took this approach sometimes with his largest pieces. A special version of this method has been used by stone carvers who would otherwise be faced with impossibly heavy work in cutting away masses of stone from large voids, for instance in some Maya Chac-Mool lying figures. Provided the implications are clear, the sculptor can outline a "frontal" part with a shallow recession set off against a long facet that recedes behind the contour of the front part.

Many twentieth-century assemblage relief sculptors have deliberately avoided using overlaps, probably because they have rejected for them-

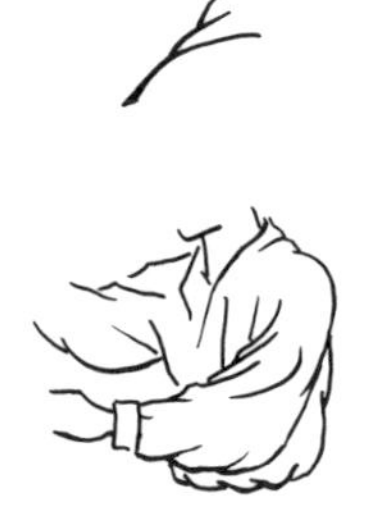
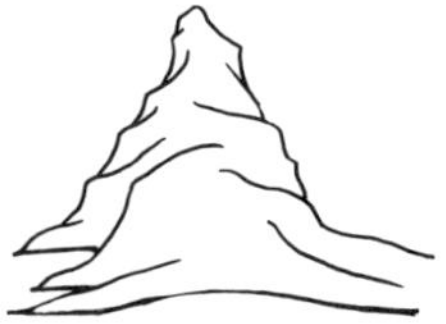

Figure 9. Overlaps generating depth and space.

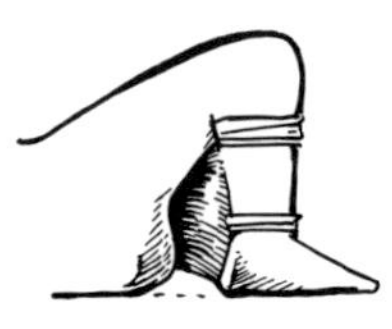

Figure 10. Chac-Mool undercut.

selves any suggestion of imaginary, as opposed to actual, space, insisting instead on laying out objective elements across a background that remains factual. This presentation accords with a theory of the art work as a pure if special object in common space among other objects; Biederman's pieces are good examples.

5
Form and Realization: General

Meaning and Being

The American poet Archibald MacLeish wrote two lines that are quoted frequently in literary criticism: "A poem should not mean / but be." This statement was meant to authenticate a kind of post-Symbolist poetry that seemed not to have any easily identifiable convergent meaning; nevertheless, both *meaning* and *being* are highly relevant to artistic realization. So, too, is a term already used here, *expression*. These three principles all exist in close relationship to form.

Meaning is normally taken as pointing to something obvious and already known. This interpretation is probably what MacLeish had in mind when he dismissed the idea that a poem might be expected to mean something. In this book, however, I take *meaning* to have a more fundamental and interesting significance. The twentieth-century scientific philosopher Michael Polanyi, in his books on human knowledge and meaning, showed how meaning is never so direct. He follows through the basic facts of the simple process of exploring the shape of the interior of a cavity into which one cannot see, using a stick as a probe. All one has to go on are sets of varying pressures on the skin of one's hands and small muscular movements in various directions. One progresses to a mental image of the moving tip of the probe. From these bits of information one builds a final mental image of the shape of the cavity. I would add that one also connects the sensory data with elements in one's mental stock of differentiated forms to produce the full image, which then produces the meaning of the investigation, although it is based only on those fragmentary sensations and one's intuitive reach for an image beyond all of them. Polanyi suggests that all meaning follows this pattern: meaning is a focal synthesis we intuit by interpreting progressive grades of contributory structures. So we discover and realize the meaning of any whole, in either the making or the reading, as a composite, prompted only by what we physically perceive and filled out by subsidiary intuited meanings. Since our minds seem to continue to combine those meanings unconsciously, even while we sleep, we may find ourselves thinking thoughts we never knew we had the capacity to think. The Austrian writer on aesthetics Karl Kraus called language "the mother of thought." Through languages we strive to convey meanings, though, as we saw, there are meanings that lie beyond the immediate scope of language—beyond the text. I take nonverbal sculptural language to be the mother of three-dimensional thought. As such it has evolved its own vocabulary of three-dimensional distinctions and categories, and its own structural grammar, in terms of which it reaches toward its own kinds of meanings. This may be what lies behind the often-quoted artists' phrase that "art is about itself," though good aesthetic propositions always point beyond themselves.

Being

We usually take Being for granted, without questioning it. The unre-flecting commonplace attitude views "things out there" as being nothing other than what they seem, omitting the vital phrase "to us." We ignore the fact that world and human person, subject and object, are functions of each other, that the terms in which things exist are human terms, articulated through human languages. Almost every statement that we make (including those in this book) amounts to an assertion that "such and such *is* the case for me." In our everyday transactions we draw con-tinually on Being to validate the meaning of our assertions and the truth of the judgments they express, as if Being were a mysterious, continually open bank account into which we never need to pay any deposits. But one of the functions of the arts, as MacLeish's statement implies, is pre-cisely to search out the source of such deposits, and from it replenish the account. Reflecting on Being is not the same as "thinking about things" in a calculating way. We can best think of meaning as the encounter that progressively unveils Being.

What seems the sheer concrete spatial reality of all sculptures may seem a sufficient guarantee of their being the images they present. Most assemblage work accepts the concrete reality of its object-material at face value, questioning only the conventional use-identities of the specific ob-jects—drinking glasses, wire netting, bits of surfboard—to generate re-mote images. Radical shaping sculpture, however, takes as part of its brief the forging of a language that transcends the commonplace attitude of ac-cepting thoughts as internal and separate from the "external" world. Such language expressly reveals in its shape-propositions what it means for its images to *be*. This it does by exhibiting its forms and formal structures at work, coordinating analogical references and evocative correspondences.

Despite the great importance of the hand with its sense of touch-shaping, we rely mostly on light for making and reading sculpture. Light casts brightness and shadows through which we interpret the shape-modeling of a sculpture. There is no escaping the fact that through hand and eye we assimilate the most concrete shapes as images of focal mean-ings only on the basis of original sets of minimal sense perceptions inter-preted through mental forms and structures, which give not only coher-ence to what is perceived but also conviction of the outstanding quality we recognize in a good sculpture: we can call it "presence." This quality implies far more than that the piece is simply there when we happen to come across it; rather it asserts a work's being as part of its meaning, through which it sets up a relationship between itself as "the other" and both artist and visitor. Such "presence" has a factual basis that can best be explained by contrasting it with what we normally, if loosely, understand as "abstraction," which we take in art as meaning to treat shapes only by their linear outlines, as if they were plane-geometrical diagrams drawn in two dimensions with a point.

Abstraction and Presentation

This symbolically "abstract" procedure takes no account of the vital "presentation faces" which a sculpture offers to the visitor, and which the sculptor works and develops. These faces serve as dialectic structural correlatives to the shaped two-dimensional contours that establish the linear limits to their spatial extension. We have seen one aspect of the significance of the presentation face in connection with spatial *ronde bosse*. If in everyday life we look at a man standing near us—within about thirteen feet—and experience his immediate presence, we find that we do not grasp that presence by looking aside to his outlines and running our eyes along them; instead we focus on the middle surfaces of the bulks nearest to us and read the way their humps and hollows approach or retreat from us. The nearer they are the more strongly do we focus on the middles. Thus we readily accept the sculptural value of those small, flatly worked terra-cottas from Neolithic societies like the Middle Eastern and Mesoamerican whose outlines, though important as correlative spatial boundaries, are not intensely worked—and the famous Cycladic stone figurines have clear-cut contours and mathematical proportions delimiting their pronounced presentation faces.

Presence

To give a piece real sculptural presence the sculptor must focus on the middles of its presentation faces, however much attention is also paid to their outlines. Side recessions and consequent three-dimensional volumes can then be developed as derivatives from the spatial movements of the presentation faces. (The same kind of central focus is characteristic of the best Western painting, though it is often disguised in the scheme of illumination.) The form sets are built, either consciously or unconsciously, as functions of the expanses of mobile frontal surface. The sculpture thus confronts and stands as a kind of mirror, reflecting its imagery into the viewer's mind and sensuous memory fund, illuminating, awakening, and linking up contents through the different levels of form it evokes. A sculpture can only awaken what is there to be awoken; but a viewer may not know what lies dormant until the awakening happens, which can be a highly numinous experience. If the sculpture is meant, as sculptures often are, to reveal the sanctity of a special location, then the aesthetic experience can amount to an immediate sensation of the numinous embodied

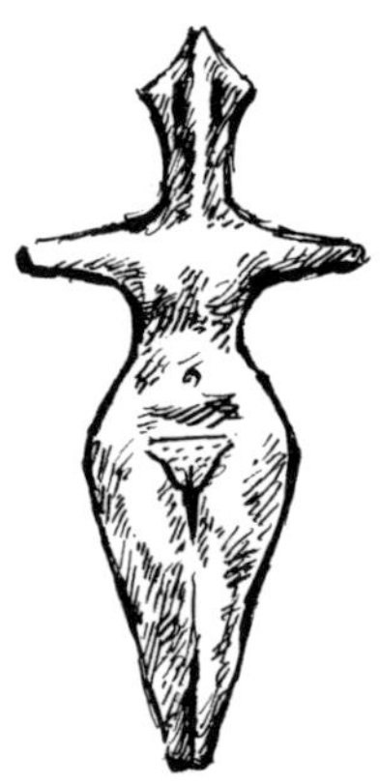

Figure 11. Front face, ancient terra-cotta method.

in three-dimensional form. We can then say that the sculpture offers us its own definition of sanctity: a combination of meaning and Being.

For sculptors who compose assemblages of already existing things, however, forms exist as the shapes those objects already possess. Being is assumed, not symbolized. In this case it can be particularly difficult to bypass the visitor's natural tendency to be content simply with identifying the objects, and instead reach further into the viewer's inner matrix of analogy and response. Consequently, subtle assemblage artists may choose to baffle the public initially with their pieces.

Expression

Expression means pressing out something internal, shaping it on the way. For sculpture it must mean transforming an internal image into an outer physical three-dimensional medium. All projection or progressive formal building and shaping of originally inner content amounts to expression. But critics and art historians have adopted the term *Expressionist* to imply that the artist so called works under the immediate impulse of feelings and unconscious promptings that burst through all prior conceptions of form, which the artist sees as restrictions on artistic freedom. In fact, Expressionists develop their own routines and formal conceptions, which we can easily recognize when we have seen them often enough. The importance of Expressionist manifestation is that it calls for technique that looks to the future rather than the past, waiting for formal discoveries to appear unanticipated from behind layers of routine. The usual Expressionist methods rely on the speed of the moving hand to outpace habit, setting off open-ended processes of creation that have only the most general intended results. This technique involves trying for formal promptings from the human unconscious fund.

Most sculptors develop ways of stimulating and enlisting such promptings into their shaping. Some methods of bypassing formal procedures that seem to have grown stale rely on pure chance or on mixing parameters. These methods accept the Surrealist notion of "the certainty of chance" (André Breton's phrase) to reach beyond both old method and already consciously accepted elements of the human matrix.

Some assemblage sculptors have devised techniques for deciding on their next creative step by following the fall of dice or using other oracular devices. Most of the sculptures based on mixed parameters so far constructed have been kinetic; that is to say, they are designed to move either in whole or in part by electric or mechanical engines. The parameters can be set up as programs (for example, on tape or in computers) and either repeat themselves or combine in overlapping numerical sequences that are random or remote (for example, thirteen and fifty-eight). The moving elements may range from small projections that are parts of the structure, to small tracked mechanisms, or lights and transparencies switched in single sequences or as groups. The results of purely random procedures may be unforeseen within limits, but results arising from structured programs may seem random to the visitor who witnesses only parts of the programs that the artist has previously formulated. Generally speaking, the creative input of form from the artist to these procedures is meant to be as impersonal as possible, though the artist's initial choice of formal elements to combine is necessarily personal.

Form and Scale

Forms, being mental, have no given size or position. Realized as shapes, they take on scale and place in relation to the human maker and visitor, amplified by other properties of the material in which the shapes are worked. The same form may lie behind a four-inch brush scrawl and a ploughed land-art ditch half a mile long. This kind of formal congruence enables us to make maps of landscapes or small models of larger works. Through its forms, we give to the physical phenomenon we produce as a sculpture its human meaning, presence, and expression, thereby lifting it to a level transcending that of common object.

"As If"

Previously we discussed the factors of mass, bulk, and volume. They refer to our common experience of the everyday world and play an important part in our reading and making of all shapes and realized formal structures. A few examples show how both forms and their corresponding shapes can constitute diagrams of energies at work through the implications of all three factors.

Imagine a bulky rectangular beam lying propped up at an angle on a shortish thin rod. To read the forces involved we need information, especially about the materials and their natural weights and strengths. If, on the one hand, we know the beam is solid concrete, we also know the rod can not be fragile wood, but has to be some material such as steel. If, on the other hand, we recognize that the beam is a fragile box of card, we realize that the rod could be a mere stick. If, as is often done in stage sets, the beam is painted to look like concrete, the rod like steel, the viewer can be deceived into reading the shapes "as if." Stage design relies on producing "as if" illusions to simulate impossibly heavy parts of realistic sets. Conversely, a sculptor such as Anthony Caro has induced more complex readings by painting manifestly heavy and bulky steel girders in delicate colors normally used for interior decoration.

The "as if" factor plays an important part in all sculpture for producing formal effects of different substance properties within the same integral material. For example, the stone pillars of a temple may be given capitals with an outward-bowed contour that implies they are bulging under pressure of the roof they support—which, of course, they are not—while elsewhere the same stone may be carved to represent flesh, floating fabric, even water. A massive bulk may seem to be pierced by and rest on three slender legs, though it may or may not be actually heavy or pierced.

In contrast, materials shaped with precisely machined surfaces, such as flat card, hardboard, molded fiberglass, or spun metal, may look as if they have neither weight nor, by extension, materiality, seeming as if they are meant to be read as "abstract." In a similar way one common formal construct in traditional sculpture—the long, thin, horizontally undulating shape with significant upward convexities—may seem to be resisting the force of gravity, invisibly borne up on currents of air.

Symmetry, Asymmetry, and Balance

Related general features of form and shape are symmetry and asymmetry. The effects of both derive largely from our inner human sense of balance in stance and posture and our reading of it into experienced outer phenomena. Similarly, we respond to top and bottom as "natural" features of sculptural objects; artists such as Georg Baselitz have featured deliberately discomfitting upside-down images.

In the context of sculpture, symmetry is the visual equality of size and shape on either side of a vertical central axis, on which also the center of gravity lies, either high or low. The standing or sitting human body is itself broadly symmetrical when seen from front or back, but it is not symmetrical from front to back. A profile view of an otherwise balanced anatomy always suggests a readiness to move or address in a "forward" direction. Artifacts are rarely symmetrical all around: only ceramic vessels may make a feature of such symmetry as part of their expression. Many sculptural styles use specific side-to-side symmetry, or near symmetry. Peoples of ancient Egypt, Archaic Greece, Buddhist countries, and many tribes in Africa have insisted on side-to-side symmetry of the human body, with a minimum of the asymmetry that suggests agitation, to portray a highly valued inner condition of spiritual balance, equanimity, or "coolness." Traditions valuing bodily exertion, such as the Classic Greek, may emphasize a high center of bodily gravity, equally balanced even if on a narrow footing. In contrast, Buddhist traditions in particular have aimed to suggest a low center of bodily gravity located in the relaxed stomach, representing a broadly based state of inner calm and powerful stability that permits the immediate, unruffled response also characteristic of Zen and its military arts. The symmetry of African sculptured figures we may feel to be poised on their characteristically springing bent knees.

Asymmetry or nonsymmetry implies instability, either falling or moving in the direction of greater weight or tilt. Whereas we may express energy by highly asymmetrical or twisted postures or gestures, so long as the center of gravity is well inside the straddle of the legs or lateral extent of its support, we do not feel a body to be unstable. Sculptors can convey a wide variety of sensations of types of balance by means of the relative positioning of center of gravity and footings, of weights and leverage lengths across central axes. The artist can introduce such readings of symmetry and balance into all kinds of sculpture, including that which is not obviously representational.

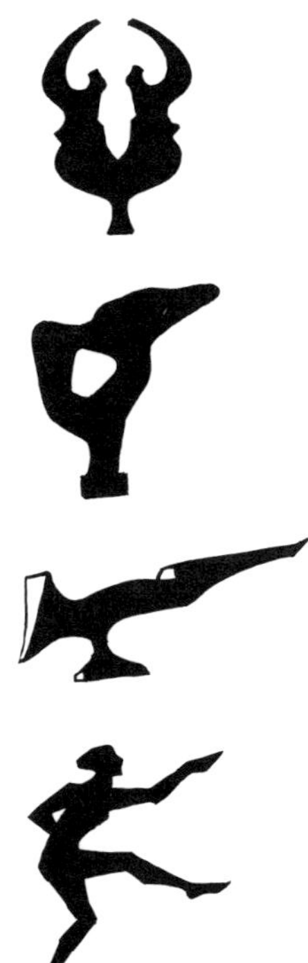

Figure 12. Symmetry and asymmetry (upper two); balance and body image (lower two).

Symmetry, asymmetry, and balance also condition the expression of component shapes, especially volumes. Whereas volumes that are symmetrical can generate a sense of poise and calm, slight asymmetries can generate a sense of subtle motion within an aggregate or overall image, stronger asymmetries a sense of more powerful energies at work, even multiple asymmetries acting in several directions at once.

Initial Approaches

A sculptor can approach the execution of a piece from one of two principal directions: either by imagining first the overall image as an idea for an objective "other" standing in opposition to him or herself, which will then be divided up inventively into well-differentiated formal groups and invested with lively shapes projected into the material; or by beginning to play with the material in a state of mind that sets aside conscious preconceptions as to what may emerge—that is, looking to the future. This second approach, however, may prove difficult to sustain over a long period of physical production of sculpture; each work also, as it arrives and reaches complete expression of its image, becomes the past for the artist, and helps to ossify his or her artistic personality and intentions before his or her own eyes. At some stage, therefore, the elements of artistic language may lose distinctness and degrade, becoming themselves consciously intended. The artist may then need to adopt a version of the first approach, maybe allowing for continuous and drastic revision as the work proceeds. This means that the sculptor becomes a craftsperson in the full sense (described in Chapter 1), creating through inventing and developing form rather than repeating formulas customary to the material.

Assemblage Base

Assemblage art, so fashionable and widespread in the late twentieth century, omits most of the problems faced by the radical shaping sculptor. Some people may wonder why, therefore, radical shaping needs to be considered at all. The answer must be that its language exists, ready and inviting to be explored at any time, for the sake of the particular deep insights it can offer into meaning and Being which assemblage never ventures on. The assemblage sculptor takes as basic shapes objects readymade, or fabricates them, then arranges them in actual space, either two- or three-dimensionally, leaving the visitor to reach into his or her knowledge of what they are, past experience of where and how such things have been encountered, and then to correlate what deep-seated common factors or relationships they might have. Correlations may often be remote, as with Mike Kelley's *Brown Star* (1991–92), which consists of bundles of stuffed toy animals suspended from a steel frame. Picasso's bull head, composed of the handlebars and saddle of a bicycle, is one of the most famous assemblages ever made, based purely on putting together objects that become formally related through a visual analogy. But in another famous piece, designed by Marcel Duchamp, a bicycle wheel in its fork is mounted upside-down on the seat of a stool; here there is no obviously intended visual analogy, but many possible interpretations—one being a cosmic symbolism, another being a jokey common factor (of which we know from sources Duchamp was well aware) that both objects support human posteriors. The aggregation in each of these examples is minimal, the image immediately visible, however remote in significance.

Where assemblage does not question the mind and its knowledge of visual and tactile reality as such, taking these as given, radical shaping sculpture, in contrast, aims to invent the very terms in which it conceives and states the reality of its imagery, as Cézanne did in his paintings. Most of the vigor and interest of radical shaping work is contained in this kind of invention.

Contrast and Articulation

One of the principal sources of energy in any three-dimensional design lies in the creation of those initial sharp contrasts and imbalances between the forms of all levels of component shapes. The work of articulation then consists in reconciling these contrasts by inventing linkages, combined shapes, and sequences that expand on and lead from one contrasted shape to the others. The process is clearly displayed in certain African masks. The commonest characteristic formal contrast is the offsetting of sharply angular and rounded shapes, expressed through boundary lines, surfaces, or volumes.

Certain tribal sculptures show clearly this process; their formal openness was one of the reasons Western artists were so attracted to tribal arts in the early decades of the twentieth century. It contrasted sharply with the smeary and indefinite shaping to which Western sculpture had become habituated during the course of the nineteenth century. This practice may have resulted partly from the gradual fading of clarity and definition of the characteristic and long-established Western technique for combining angular and rounded shapes within single volumes, a distinctive way of working that Archaic Greek, Southeast Asian, and Renaissance sculptors had developed with particular clarity.

6
Form and Realization: Specific

Interpreting Shapes

In ordinary life we may interpret forms we read from cracks in walls or groups of shadows in a hedge as faces, because of the way their arrangement provides context. In the great Paleolithic and Magdalenian caves of Europe, early peoples seem to have interpreted marks or humps on the rock face as parts of beasts, then added to them drawn signs for the "missing" parts to complete the images. In the Font de Gaume cave in the Dordogne, one artist interpreted a long vertical crack as a "river" by incising images of animals seeming to "drink" at its edges. All such meanings depend on our readiness to read contexts and arrangements, thus illustrating Polanyi's suggested process for arriving at meaning.

Tangrams

A further schematic illustration of how we can apply this interpretive process in the field of art is the Chinese game of tangrams, which became popular in the West in the 1960s. To play the game, first set up a matrix of shapes and rules by cutting up a square of card into a set of small basic shapes according to a simple system that makes them distinctively different, yet interrelated as part of the whole. Arrange these smaller pieces of card into clusters or aggregates within the format of a larger sheet of paper or card to construct pictorial images of familiar kinds. Depending on how the pieces are arranged as clusters within the format, the same basic shapes will be read as different parts of some overall image of reality, according to the various contexts of other shapes and placings in which they appear. One rule is that bits of shapes may not overlap or obscure bits of others. The original shapes of the pieces may not be altered in the process of developing an image, and normally the pieces are treated as components of solid objects, not of spaces between objects. The underlying system of distinctions between the shapes results from the way the pieces are initially cut, which then gives to each different composition an inner coherence.

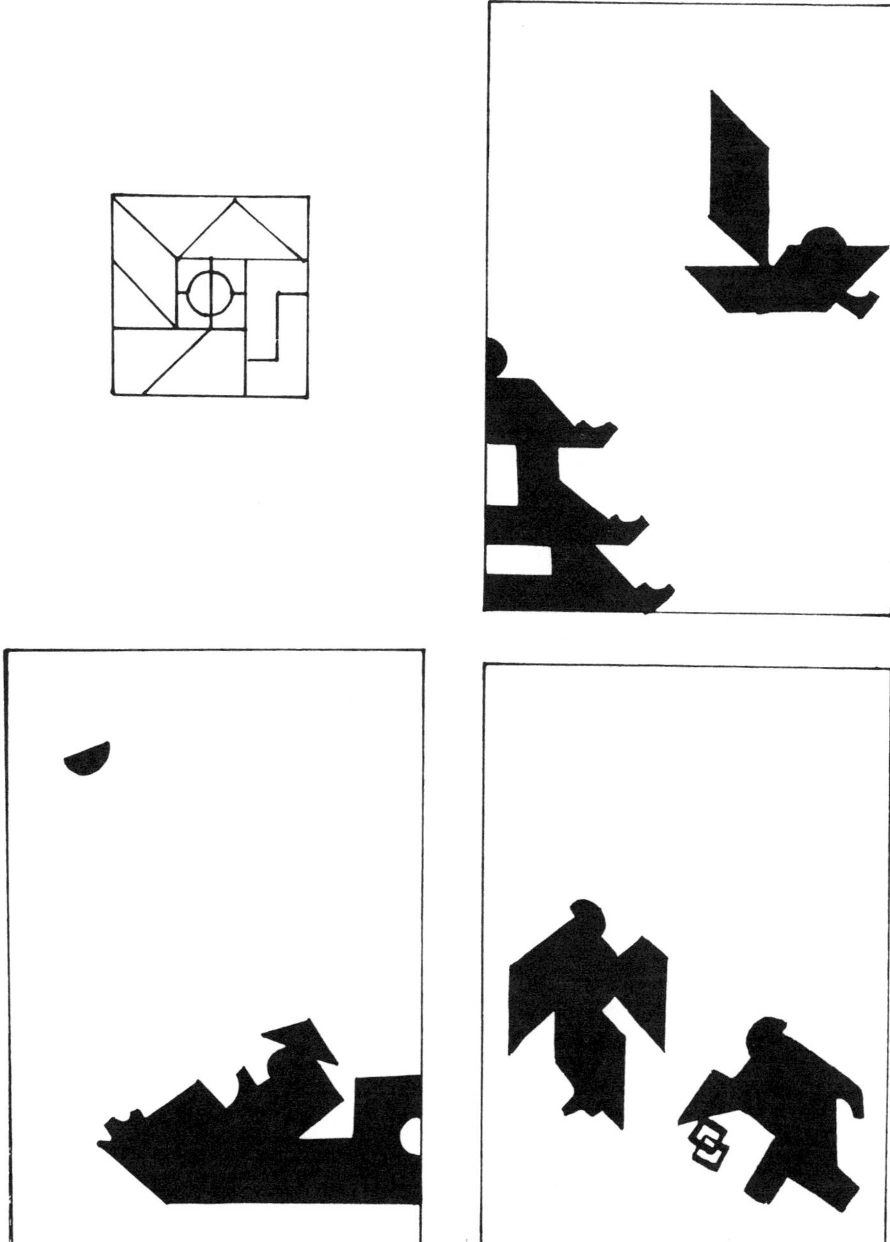

26. The Chinese game of tangrams, from an eighteenth-century book. Each image is constructed from the same set of shapes cut from a square of card, illustrating how relative positioning and context can radically affect overall meaning.

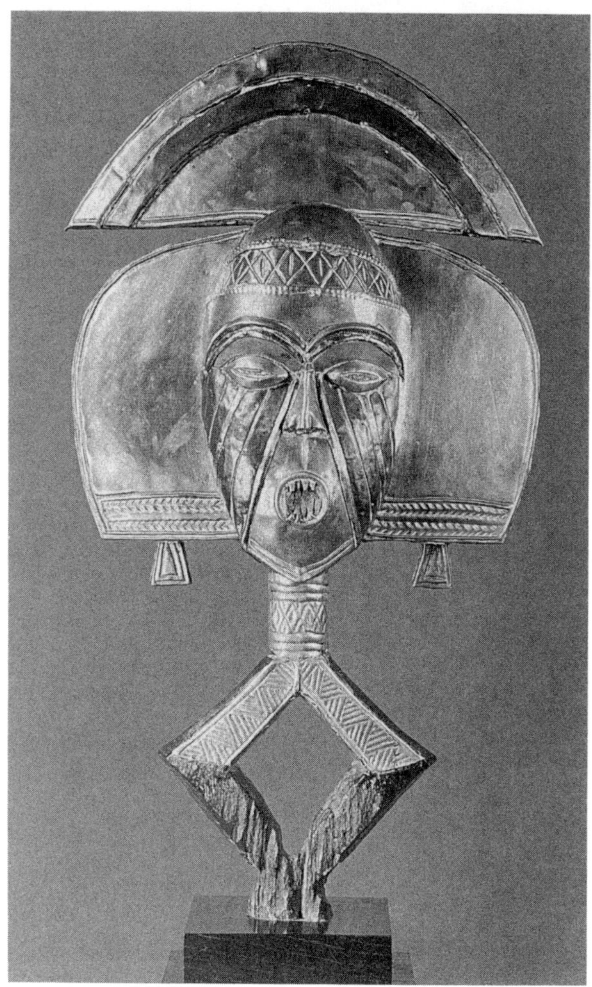

27. Spirit head, Bakota, Congo, brass, nineteenth century. Provides a physical presence for the evoked spirit of a dead person, its clear-cut shapes able to present spiritual rather than more objective reality.

The game parallels to some extent the process of realizing meaning in sculptural language. Every sculptor builds up, sometimes deliberately, a vocabulary of distinctive basic forms by means of which he or she differentiates the *basic shapes* from which a final image is composed. We can think of these forms as analogous to the words that poets combine and recombine for each new poem. Like words, they too may each have a wide range of possible references—by three-dimensional analogy—which are interwoven and made more precise and colorful when the artist contextualizes and connects them through a kind of grammar and syntax into *aggregates*. One important quality of genuine three-dimensional sculptural shapes, unlike tangram pieces, is that the artist is free to modify them according to their places and roles in aggregates and the final *over-*

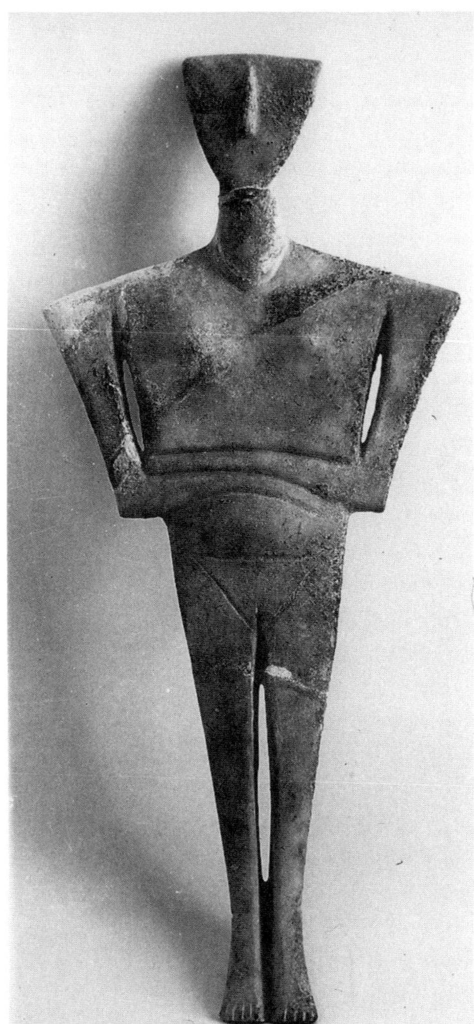

28. Image of a goddess, perhaps of the dead, Cyclades, marble, early Bronze Age, third millennium B.C. Such flat figurines, with their sharply formed, barely modulated shapes, much admired by early twentieth-century artists, were abraded from fragments of flat strata (and widely faked). (Courtesy National Archaeological Museum of Greece.)

all image, including void spaces, so long as their formal characters remain distinct. And this image is *not* an abstraction, but a matching synthesis from a repertoire of shapes.

Structural Categories Defined

I use the terms *basic shape, aggregate,* and *overall image* to denote the roughly equivalent levels of sculptural composition, while fully recognizing how approximate these words are. The order in which I discuss them is intended to parallel the level of their structural role rather than the temporal order in which the artist conceives them.

In practice, the forms of basic shapes represent the first, "primitive" level of formal differentiation which makes the structural dialectic of sculptural language possible. Real invention — the discovery and articulation of those mysterious, "previously unknown" forms that good artists "find" and project as three-dimensional images — takes place at the levels of aggregate and overall image. Paul Klee's drawings reveal this primitive level most clearly, as he himself recognized. Their basic shapes are measured lines, curves of different kinds, angles, and enclosures, which he intuitively varied and aggregated into original and continuously inventive sequences. It is worth mentioning that not all basic sculptural shapes are solids. There are others, which may appear as forms of relationship, such as linear arrangements or sets of rhythmic indentations.

It is not always easy to recognize the basic shapes of a sculptural repertoire, in either one's own work or that of others. One must focus on a more fundamental level of perception than usual, just as one does to recognize individually the syllables and words of normal speech. The forms of basic three-dimensional shapes can also be very difficult to describe in words; one might say, for example, "that partly conical open-ended bulb which appears in the shape of the bowl of a wineglass," or "the crisscross crested concavities that appear where waves in water cut across each other." Someone experienced in three-dimensional thought easily recognizes the single forms referred to from the instances quoted. Some sculptural traditions, such as the African and "primitivist" twentieth-century, make a point of keeping the basic shapes distinct, connecting them only in clear-cut ways. Other traditions, notably Western post-Renaissance, set out expressly to overlap and interweave basic shapes and aggregates so that none stands out separately. Henry Moore, for example, started his career making clear "primitivist" distinctions between basic shapes, but in later work he superimposed and interwove subtle linear surfaces over hidden axial volumes.

Individual sculptors have developed general theories about shape repertoire usually on the basis of their own practice, but these theories are not necessarily valid for the practices of other people. Brancusi, for example, affirmed a crucial distinction between bulk, rod, strip, and wall, categories that may be apt but do not cover all aspects of sculpture. Here I discuss each kind of basic shape in terms of mental form, then consider some of the physical shapes in which it may be realized. There are four principal kinds of basic shape: lines, surfaces, volumes, and rhythms. Each of the basic shapes may also function at the levels of aggregate and overall image to coordinate and connect other basic shapes.

29. Henri Laurens, *Head of a Young Girl*, terra-cotta, 1920. An early twentieth-century attempt at spiritualizing the subject by abstraction and sculptural faceting. (Solomon R. Guggenheim Museum, Collection of Peggy Guggenheim; photograph by Carmelo Guadagno and David Heald, copyright © the Solomon R. Guggenheim Foundation, New York. Copyright © 1995, Artists Rights Society, New York/ADAGP, Paris.)

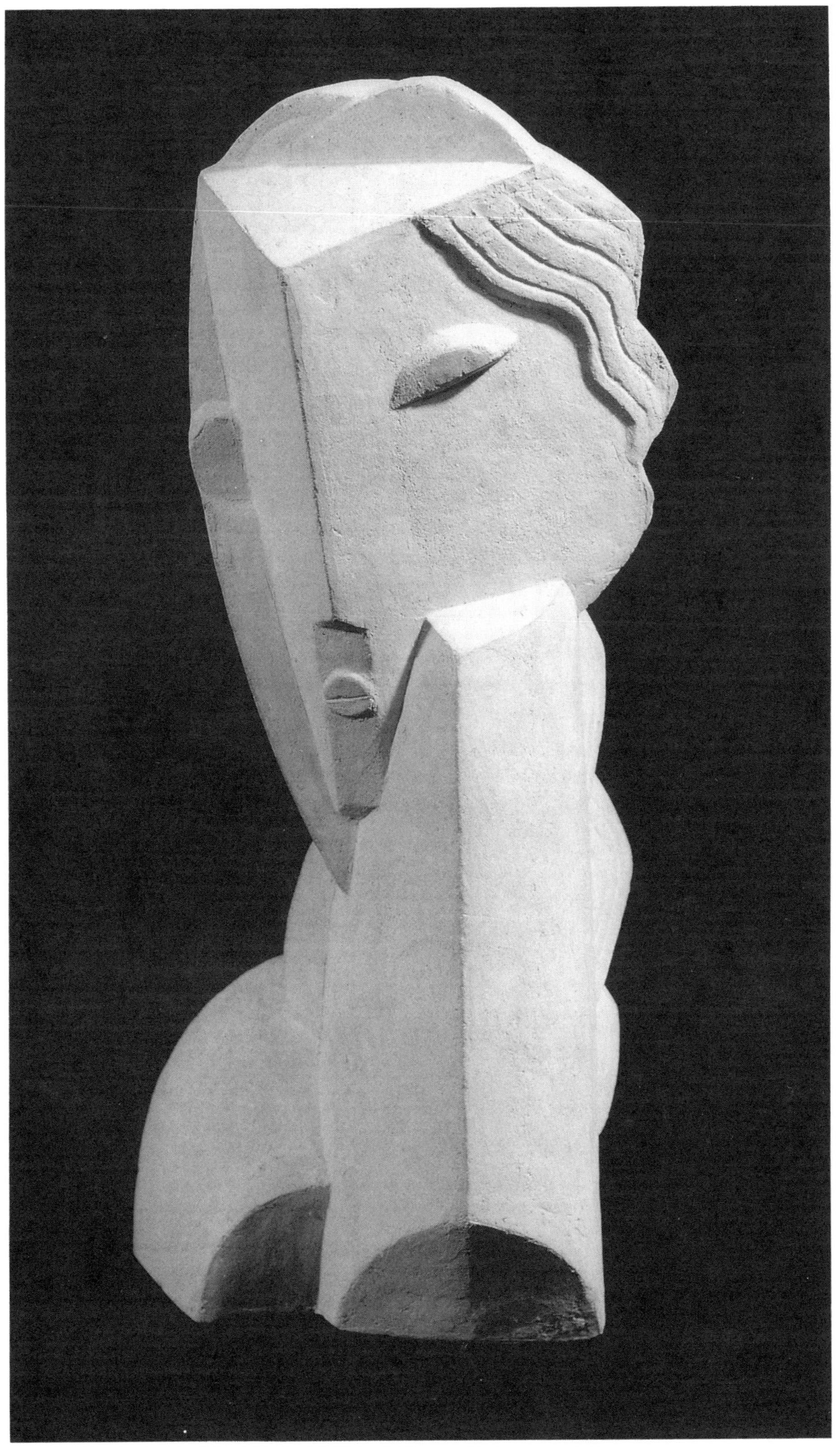

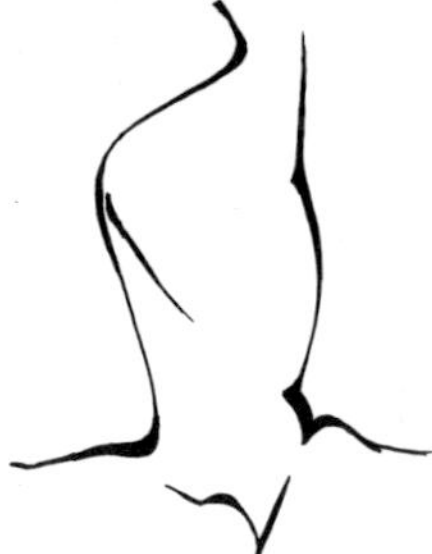

Figure 13. Interacting lines.

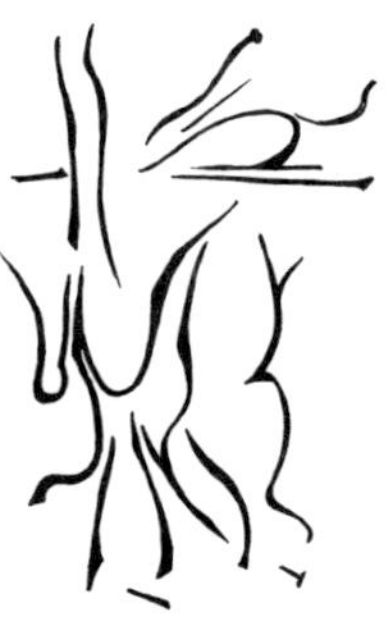

Figure 14. Varieties of linear interaction.

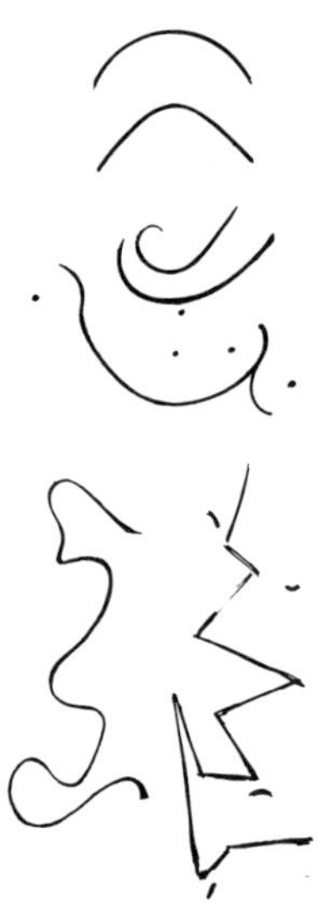

Figure 15. Basic categories of linear sections (top); spirals based on segments of centered circles (center); characteristic linear movements compounded of basic categories of linear sections (below).

Lines

Lines come first because they are what other shapes, especially surfaces, are compounded from. In formal terms, we can think of any line as the mathematical function of a moving point. That is to say, it has specific kinetic value, and we both make and read it as the track of a sustained act of unbroken attention. A drawn line is made by a physically moving point, and we may be able to tell from its physical features in which direction the point moved, hence in which direction to read the line. Lines in sculpture may not have this quality, and their direction of implied movement may be ambiguous. But the essence of a line is that it has directional kinetic value along its length, according to its particular qualities of successive curves and/or angular breaks. Sculptors build these qualities into each line, along with expressive properties of pace, of changing direction, and of rhythmic feel; unless viewers scan the length of any line to read and experience these in succession by their own faculty of inner mimetic response, they will miss the sculptor's primary meaning. Lines thus naturally have directional run-on effects, resulting from their kinetic energy, which can carry them invisibly across gaps between one shape and another. I call these "vectors," and they are important in knitting compositions together.

Lines also serve as separators, cutting apart the spaces on either side of themselves and, if they are developed into enclosures, giving these enclosures specific shapes. Lines therefore invite us to take account of what is happening on either side, and we also scan them transversely across their main kinetic direction to discern their relationship to other lines on either side. Lines may interact in various ways for which we have no exact standard words, save a few metaphorical verbs such as imitate each other, enclose, fan apart, step across, jump to and fro, take up direction from each other, quiver together, approach, and part. These effects are based on transverse relations of angle between successive segments of the lines, all the way from parallel to right angle and reverse. Since lines in sculpture may be realized in three dimensions, so too may their transverse interactive interrelationships, which is one reason for recognizing the immense potential richness of sculptural composition, as well as the special insights and skills it can develop.

The successive segments of lines referred to above follow a limited number of possible shapes, like the finite number of phonemes from which the words in our basic vocabulary are compounded. What matters for expression is how the line-segments are inflected and connected. The basic line-segment shapes are the pair of straight and curved. Curved are the arc, angular curve, and exponential curve, often called "the curve of life," since growing plants, shells, and animal horns follow its inflection. The artist's main skill is in both stringing these together in varied melodic sequences and combining deep curves with sharp stereometric angles. An artist working in two dimensions or a relief sculptor normally works within a rectangular format with top, bottom, and two sides, and can make lines that rise, fall, sag, leap, and so on, in relation to the format. An artist working in three dimensions usually has top and bottom, in and out, as well as side to side to explore as "limit" or "environment" within the kind of overall space he or she uses.

Straight lines alone can have an expression derived from our normal human stances, according to how they are set up and combined. A horizontal line lies passive; a vertical stands steady linking above and below, poised, yet able to "go"; a slanting line is dynamic according to its slope, falling or reaching in one direction.

Western curves tend to be flattish and single phased, reluctant to undulate or stream onward into fresh shapes. This may reflect the Western adherence to transverse sets, right-angle relationships, and geometric enclosures. Eastern curves, in contrast, are often developed into long lines incorporating different degrees and directions of curvature, re-entrant, or multiple and varied S-curves. From the 1880s to Henri Matisse, Western art adopted these as "arabesques." The strength of lines usually derives from the depth of their curvatures and the clear shaping of their ends.

One function of lines is to create enclosures. Such enclosures draw their expression primarily from the complete outlines or partial contours that define them. Enclosures may be organic or stereometric: the former have curved and perhaps undulating contours; the latter have contours composed of stretches of more or less straight sections of line. Organic contours particularly may include inlets of surrounding space as well as distinct promontories, which we readily interpret as the results of spatial pressure from either outside or inside the enclosure. The liveliness of enclosures depends on the variety and rhythmic consistency of their kinetic outlines. Stereometric contours may enclose areas of many different shapes according to the lengths of the straight lines and their angular relations. When organic enclosures are connected, they easily lose their identity in one overall shape, whereas chains of stereometric enclosures may be linked without the individual components losing their identities. The outlines of stereometric enclosures, however, do not naturally have the kinetic continuity of the curved contours of organic enclosures, and their sense is directed primarily inward on their content of space.

Some stereometric (straight line) forms have a feel about them derived from the basic lines they assemble, which has led to their being interpreted as having specific areas of meaning within symbolic languages. I mentioned earlier how certain linear signs have been used by artists at widely different times to convey similar meanings. A cross refers to the four directions and links them; with another axis added it refers to the six directions of space, and we use it for most three-dimensional planning. The square has a static, fixed enclosing feel; small squares easily connect into large squares; and on a large scale a square can seem both emphatic and threatening. The long isosceles triangle, pointing upward, can give the sense of rising, when it is pointing downward, of descent or creation. Equilateral triangles may express passivity, while extremely irregular triangles can convey a sense of imbalance and extravagant direction. The

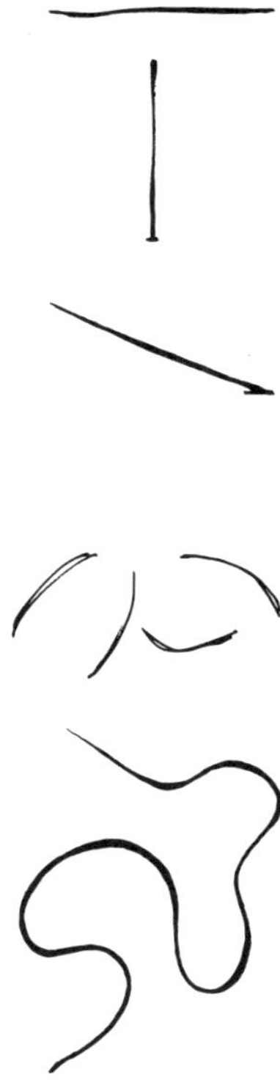

Figure 16. Top to bottom: horizontal, vertical, unstable diagonal, Western curve segments, "Oriental" linear arabesque.

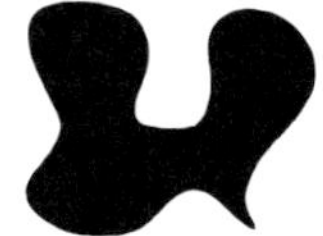

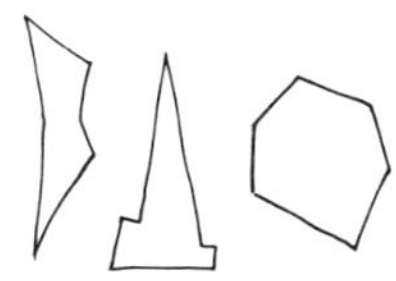

Figure 17. Enclosures: organic (above) and stereometric (below).

circle, which has no top or bottom but focuses on its center, is universally seen as signifying the all-embracing or containing. The oval contains an implied axis, which suggests it can link up at its ends and possibly rotate.

In accordance with the distinction made earlier between rounded and angular conformations, suggesting that they can be combined, the variety and interest of both ordinary open lines and enclosures can be increased by joining the two conformations into a continuous line. Another distinction is that between "crystal" and "fruit," crystals being stereometrically faceted and fruits organically rounded. Of the two principal ways to combine these, the first is to treat each curve of an organic line as, in a dialectical sense, composed of sections of straight lines of rhythmically varied lengths—quanta of direction—set at developing angles. The second is to lead a long curve, perhaps a closed organic outline, according to an un-

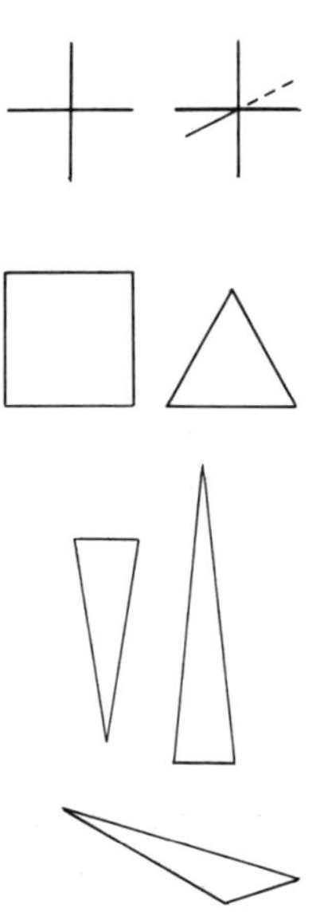

Figure 18. Top to bottom: cross spatial axes, square, equilateral triangle, isosceles triangle, dynamic triangle.

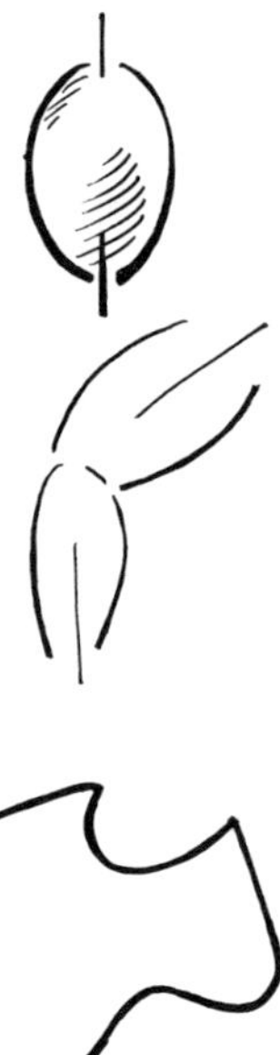

Figure 19. Above, ovals; below, enclosure combining curves and straights.

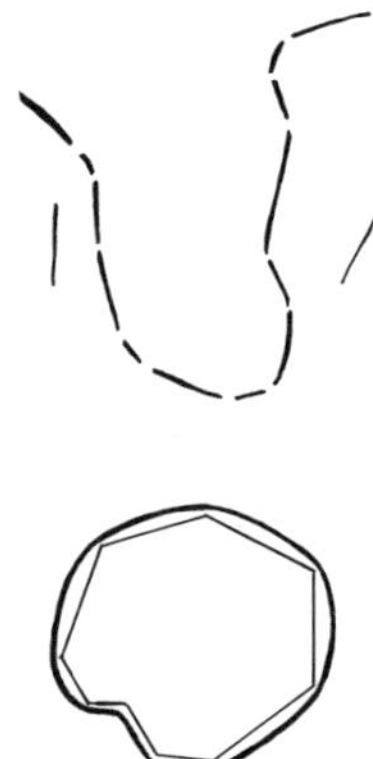

Figure 20. Directional elements within a curve rhythmically organized (above); stereometric enclosure within an organic outline (below).

stated but implicit, angular, stereometric shape lying beneath it. This can be particularly relevant to developing curved volumetric surfaces over shed-lines.

Since the diagrams in this book are of necessity two-dimensional, we can best consider the realization of linear forms into material shapes by beginning with relief sculpture, then moving on to the full three dimensions. In any case, as we have seen, the two-dimensional aspect is important to even the most fully three-dimensional piece. Its most basic form is the linear channel cut into the face of relief material, either as a complete outline (for example, in ancient Egyptian low relief or flat decorative carving), where it may show only implicit in-and-out movement, or as the partial contour of a body defined against the flat surface of its background and emphatically raised above it, as in Assyrian relief. Assemblage reliefs may depend on the flat outlining of components against a backboard or each other.

The primary role of lines in most relief is to define the edges of solids, awarding them some degree of kinetic energy, and to define stacks of overlaps, where one solid passes in front of another to indicate depth. In other styles of relief, lines with minimal in-and-out movement define surface features as well as bodily contours. They may also link different solids at various depths into their own continuity by subtending at different parts of their length, on either side, differently beveled segments of surface. The relative degree of emphasis on the linear continuity of the channels and their side bevels is one of the features that distinguishes relief styles. Far Eastern artists emphasized long calligraphic continuity of channel, whereas Donatello in his *stiacciato* disintegrated his channels into sets of bevels.

Organic or stereometric linear enclosures can be realized as two-dimensional shapes in flat cut-out sheets of materials such as wood, metal, or plastic. The thickness of the edges of such sheets may have some sculptural value, but their expressive qualities derive from their linear contours, of whatever kind and in whatever way they are combined into aggregates.

The simplest purely three-dimensional realization of a line is string or wire. So-called Constructivist sculptors such as Naum Gabo have used them strung taut in series of straights between main members. Wire, however, can be bent into complex, totally three-dimensional shapes. Rods, poles, and tubes also can be used to realize complex three-dimensional shapes that rely almost entirely on their linear forms. Pure lines and enclosures, singly or in groups, can be incised or even drawn onto mobile three-dimensional surfaces, so that they too have three-dimensional value. Gestures, either impressed into malleable materials or gouged with tools into carving materials, can likewise embody three-dimensional linear forms. Raised lines can be added to a surface either by incising them into the face of a negative mold before casting the positive or by affixing them.

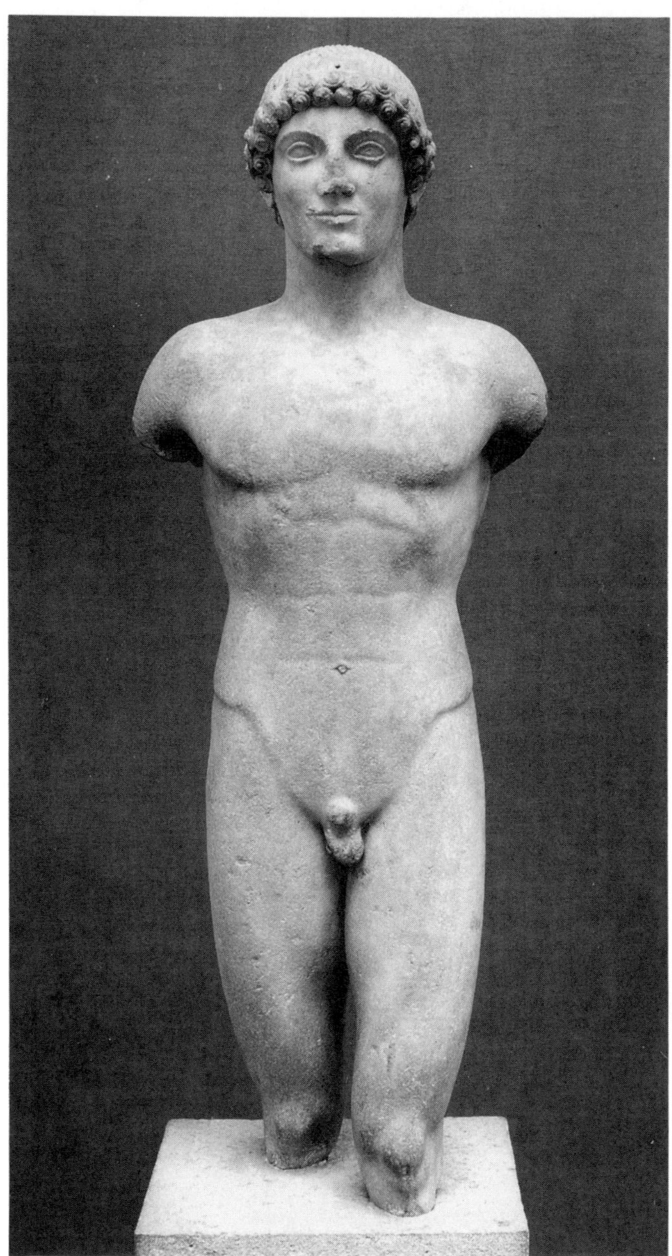

30. Strangford Apollo, Archaic Greek, marble, ca. 500 B.C. This sculpture was carved by first hammering, then abrasion; the maximum linear continuity of surface is punctuated by defining channels like those drawn on contemporary vases, but running through actual space. (Courtesy the British Museum.)

The second category of basic shape is the surface, which is a direct function of the line. It is the fundamental resource of most sculpture and establishes the primary relationship between inner and outer, or between one body and another. All sculptures set up surfaces, however narrow, as the impediment to human sight and touch that separates an object or bulk from its enveloping space. We can define surface as the trace or locus of a line moving through space across its linear direction. Like the line, the surface exists only by virtue of its continuity. If the line does not change shape as it moves, the surface will be simple, the flat plane being the simplest of all. If the line does change, the resulting surface will be complex. Surfaces do not have to be totally smooth: they can be implied by arrangements of solid crests or textural prominences.

Early twentieth-century Cubist sculptors favored surfaces given by straight lines "moving" across flat or rotating tracks. Gothic carvers created stone surfaces based primarily on long lines developed transversely according to profile sections resembling those on pillars, with convex and concave curves and steps, but changing along the main length. Other traditional sculptors, including late Gothic carvers and Michelangelo, worked deep convex and concave undulations into their surfaces, conceived as the functional tracks of continuous and highly varied expressive lines, running in several directions across the surface together. Such tracks are revealed in crossing patterns of claw-chisel traces on the marble of many of Michelangelo's unfinished pieces. Sculptors used to refer to this linear complexity of surface as sculptural "color," affecting the feelings in a way similar to, but not the same as, actual color.

The true sculptural surface is thus a fully three-dimensional continuum. Some sculptors do make a point of fragmenting their surfaces by irregular handling, for their own expressive purposes. Linear continuity is valuable because it provides the kind of scanning tracks for the visitor's attention to follow that can awaken genuine focused formal and feeling echoes, which a disjointed surface quality does not. The latter becomes texture rather than form. This is an important distinction. We can define texture as surface quality imparted to the material which only matters when taken broadly en masse over a surface already defined. It may range from smooth polish, say on metal, which reflects the light brilliantly, as on Richard Lippold's *Sunbursts*, to a heavily eroded surface of natural stone or wood, to carefully contrived rhythmical roughness in clay or dribbled plaster, perhaps meant to be cast in bronze. All such textures have their own symbolic values, general rather than formal: polish for its implications of light, natural erosion for its overtones of time and change, and roughness for its record of the artist's nervous vitality, as in Alberto Giacometti's later work.

The simplest realization of a surface is a flat plane. Its contour determines its complete shape and appears as the linear enclosure edge. It can also be thought of as the result of the length of the straight line of which

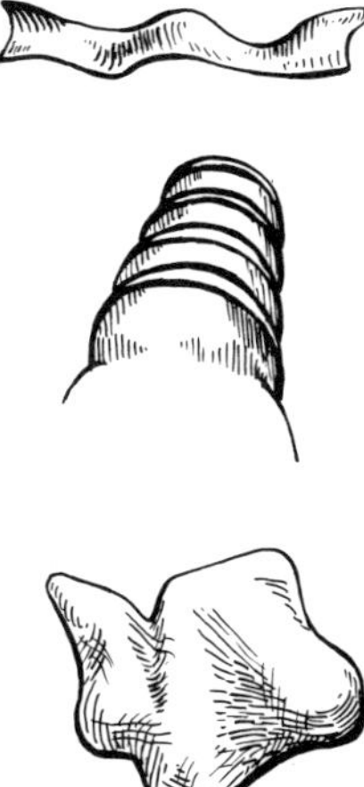

Figure 21. Top to bottom: linear plane, crests, sculptural "color."

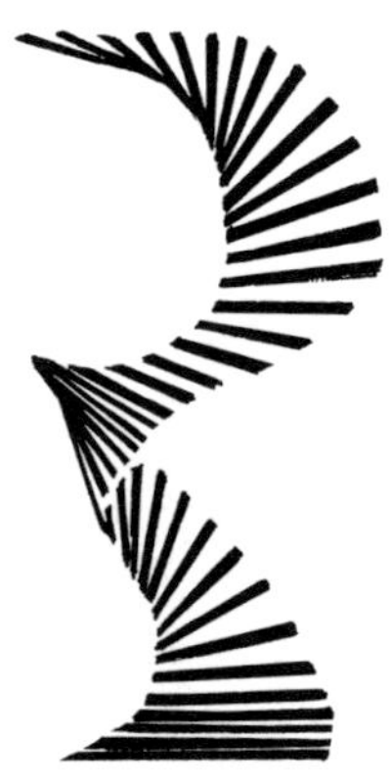

Figure 22. Locus of a straight line "moving" through space.

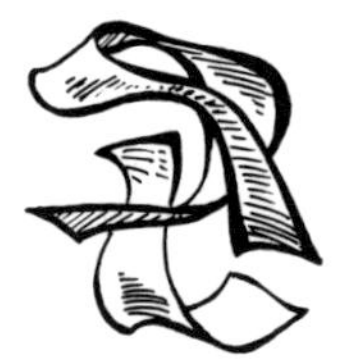

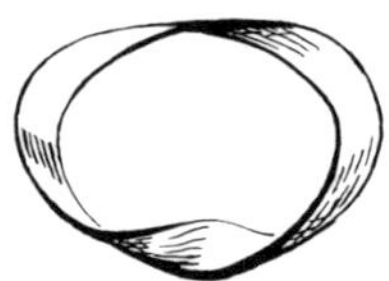

Figure 23. Spatial complex of linear surfaces (above) and Möbius strip (below).

it is a function expanding and/or shortening as it "moves" across a level space. Realized in transparent plastic, for example, a flat plane can seem virtually bodiless, though it is the bodily properties of the material that help to produce such an effect. A similar "abstract" effect can be generated by developing a straight line through space following a geometrical curve, with maybe a twist as well. The surface will then move in all three directions of space.

More complex and interesting still are those surfaces that carvers and modelers can develop which do not simply move through a featureless space but, by the ways they modulate from convex to concave, imply shapes of inner and outer space impinging on them—as with the organic linear enclosures mentioned earlier. Sculptors such as Arp and Brancusi have developed continuous surfaces that enclose and define entire three-dimensional enclosures, and whose linear conformations can be read for their continuous and differing variations in any direction across the surface.

Surfaces can be developed in any material as long linear ribbons which turn and twist in space, their small transverse developments remaining constant, flat, or with a single curve, or varying along the ribbon's length. Such ribbon surfaces can seem to defy gravity if their bodily bulk is minimal, appearing to float on air, or coiling and twisting through a region of space. They can also represent topological images such as the Möbius strip, which Max Bill executed in bronze.

Volumes

No one can see a volume. All that anyone sees in a sculpture are surfaces, and from them one infers the forms of volumes that they might contain and shape, lying invisible behind or beyond them. And yet volumes are essential to the three-dimensionality of all bodies, especially to sculptures, which have to convince the visitor of their presence. It is significant that certain sculptors, such as Calder in his mobiles or Biederman in his reliefs, create their airy and luminous effects by deliberately suppressing the volumes of the thin, flat components they use. Just as we specify and characterize the realized shapes of plane geometry by the arrangement of their contours, so do we specify and characterize the shapes of volumes by the arrangement of their surfaces and angles.

The two principal and contrasting orders of volume are the "crystal" and the "fruit." The crystal is composed of flat plane surfaces that are

31. Naum Gabo, *Linear Construction No. 1*, plastic and plastic threads, 1943. A static object figuring a succession of locations and dimensions defining an active energy. (Copyright © Nina Williams.)

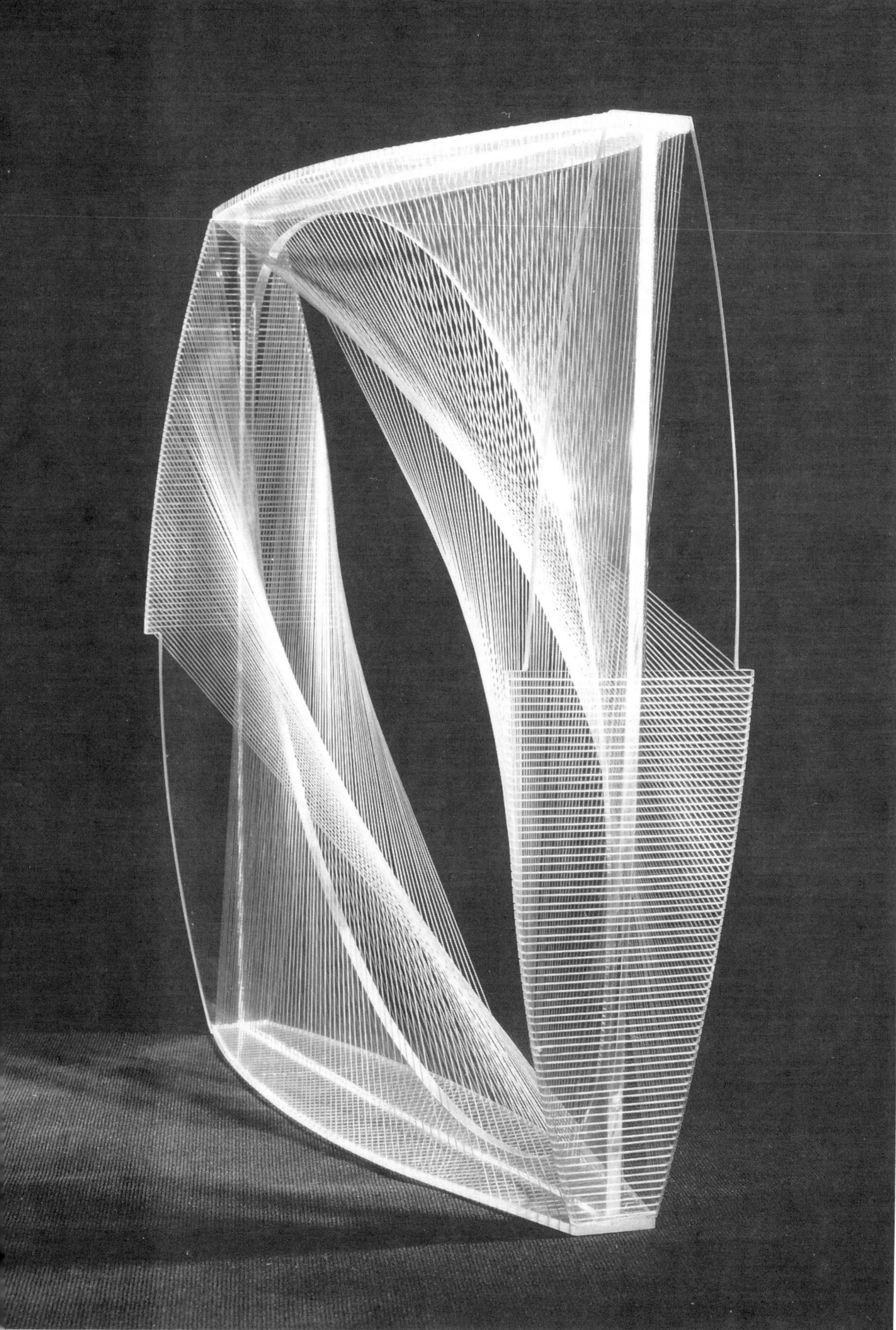

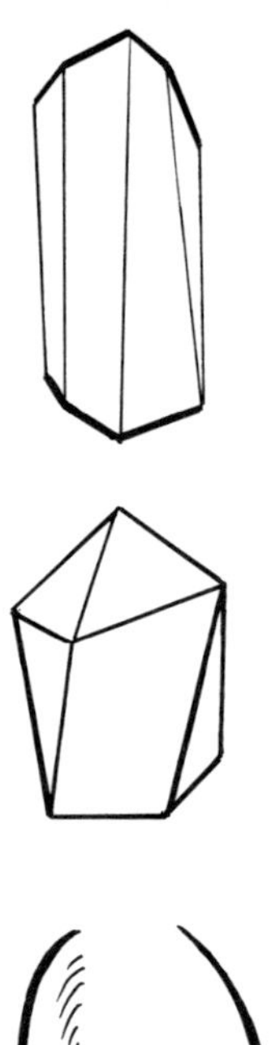

Figure 24. Volumes: crystals (top and middle) and fruit (below).

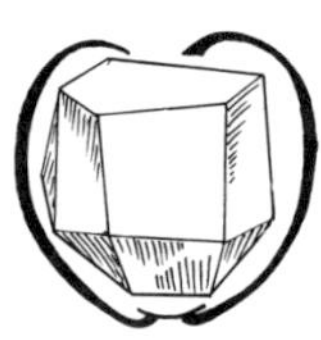

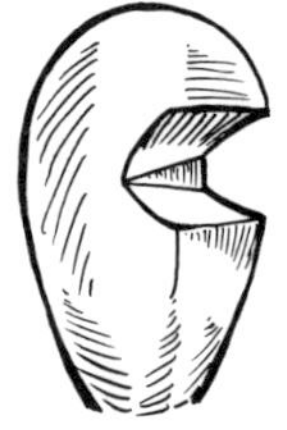

Figure 25. Crystal underlying fruit (above) and crystalline void cut into solid fruit (below).

assembled edge to edge so that they meet at angular crests. A cube's surfaces are square and meet all at right angles. Other geometrical volumes composed of rectangular, triangular, and other geometric planes are likewise regular. In addition, innumerable irregular crystalline faceted volumes can be created from a variety of planes of different shapes, from which the artist can generate a wide variety of linear crests at different angles. The sculptural importance of crystals is what they signify in the particular contexts of other forms in which they are realized.

The second of the two orders of volume, fruit, is implied by continuously convex, forward-projecting curved surfaces which appear to be closing around a unit of spatial content, by reason of the longitudinal and transverse inflections of their curvatures. The surface of a thrown ceramic vessel is a function of the revolution of an unchanging line, which does close fully around its contained volumes. Curved fruit surfaces do not need to close, however, only to imply that they do when seen frontally from the intended viewpoint, so long as the whole implied volume that backs them is sufficiently deep to "complete" the volume they seem to enclose. Fruit volumes always imply by their total convexity a live pressure expanding or bulging out of their surfaces. They also suggest that they fit comfortably within a two-handed clasp, and a series of them may imply a running and changing series of clasps. Fruit volumes, complete or partial, do not have to be symmetrical, though they may have an implicit axis, which can be important for linking them into aggregates and for taking possession of three-dimensional space. Indeed, asymmetry is essential to the creative processes of variation.

Both orders of volume may appear as either solid or void, positive or negative. Of course, they can only be seen as void if they are open to view or touch, and so incompletely closed. We have seen how they may be produced naturally as part of the carving process. Both Medardo Rosso and Umberto Boccioni, however, deliberately modeled large, fruit-curved concavities to suggest the pressure of external space on their central images. African wood carvings have used both curved and faceted hollows in abundance to articulate their positive volumes. Many Classical and post-Classical Western sculptures use hollows of clearly defined curvature as articulating elements in their continuous undulating surfaces.

There are several ways to combine crystal and fruit into a single volume. To do so can impart a definite but inexplicable sense of energy and strong analogical overtones to the form. Tribal wood carvings show many versions of this combination particularly clearly, and it is a main source of their expressive power. As in their approach to linear enclosures, Western traditions usually shaped the curved surface inflections of fruit volumes according to underlying crystal facets.

One of the most demanding imaginative and technical processes in sculpture is to realize and articulate clearly varied volume conformations in materials. The surfaces of both convex and concave fruit volumes need to be modeled or carved—virtually stroked into shape—so that their curvatures in all directions are continuous and varied, without flat spots, accidental gullies, or humps to destroy their linear integrity. The sculptor needs to take particular care over the way the curve-ends turn inward and make sure the volumes do not flatten off in the working. The pre-Socratic philosopher-sculptor Polykleitos of Argos was referring to this problem when he made the recorded utterance (which has baffled so many philosophical commentators) that "the most difficult stage of the work is when the artist's clay is within a nail's breadth." One can most easily check all this by rotating the work and watching the continuity of its contour for blemishes—easier with a solid than a void. The surface of a positive or negative crystal is more readily distinguished and controlled because of the run of its crests and channel lines.

Provided that the underlying volumes remain clearly intelligible, the sculptor can handle their surfaces with all sorts of irregular and evocative humps and hollows, cuts and openings, violent roughnesses and textures. Joan Miró often used this technique successfully. A nearly endless variety of qualities and evocative inflections can be given to any clear volume by modulating its surfaces and their arrangements.

Rhythms

Rhythms are a formal feature of all vital art works, both as basic shapes and for the articulation of aggregates and overall images. Rhythms are externally measurable and internally powerful. Both our bodies and our world are imbued with various overlapping regular beats: those of the heart, breath, gait, peristaltic contractions, day and night, lunar phases, planetary circuits, and so on—to say nothing of the less easily identifiable frequencies in which we live immersed. We might even define life as being the participation in the regular shifts and changes that rhythmic activity involves. To participate in the rhythms of music and dance can enormously enhance our inner sense of vitality. Good sculptors incorporate lively and effective rhythms among all the elements of their pieces, and since few sculptures do move in time, visitors need to discover where to find and how to respond to the particular kinds of rhythm its sculptor has realized in any specific piece. The word *time* is the clue to both making and responding to rhythms, for their essence is that they give shapes to time by means of their spatial layout.

The idea of rhythm in visual art has been slightly tarnished by two sets of overtones that have become attached to it and may cause difficulty in understanding it. The first arises from the way *rhythm* was used as an emotive catchword in post-Symbolist art discourse between about 1900 and 1940. Originally identified with the antirealistic swirls of art nouveau, it was inspired by a combination of the cult of the long Japanese line and the immensely influential dancing of Loie Fuller, who whirled loosely floating silk cloths in shifting colored stage lighting she had invented, and who became the subject of numerous sculptures as well as paintings. Sec-

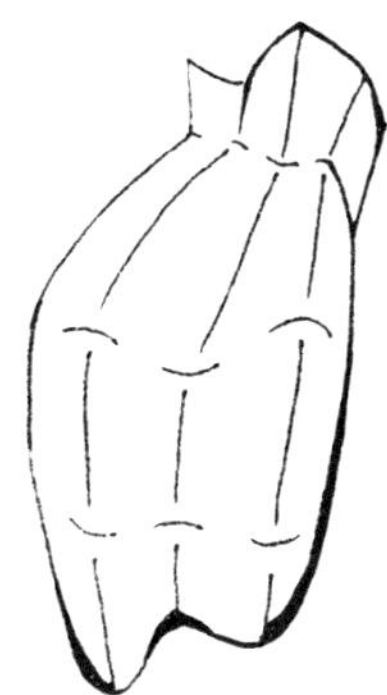

Figure 26. Crests controlling surfaces.

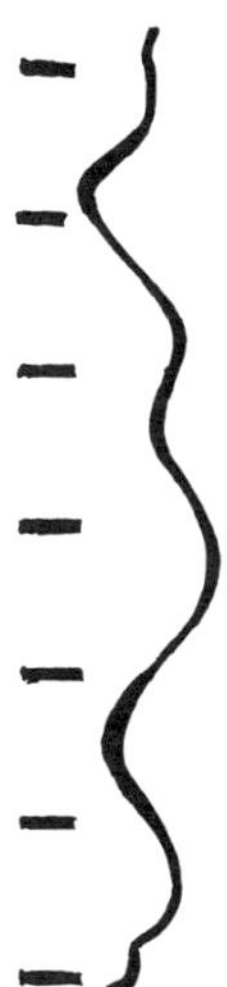

Figure 27. Free rhythmic line over modular spacing.

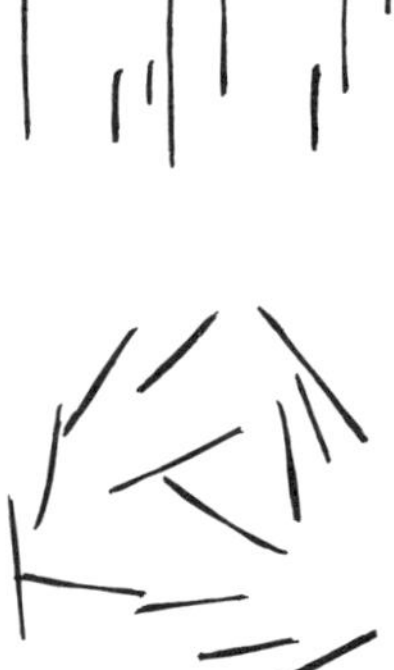

Figure 28. Transverse rhythms.

ond is the way the idea of rhythm is discussed in the sciences to refer to unvarying frequencies or cycles.

Although artistic rhythm is certainly based on equal beats or intervals which we scan in time, and does engage our bodily and mental responses to produce a sense of urge and uplift, the regular and mechanical repetition of identical intervals is aesthetically deadening rather than vitalizing. Artistic rhythm does depend on identifiable patterns of more or less equally spaced points of reference or stress, shaping either the lengths and changes of curvature along lines or surfaces or the transverse intervals between them. But artistic phrasing does not adhere rigidly to equal intervals; rather it refers analogically and mimetically to human experiences of clusters of feeling-filled events imbued with similar rhythms. Therefore its expression depends, as musical performance does, on subtle variation of module, meter, and phrasing, the organic stretching and shortening of intervals, rather than on measured exactness. Every beat or interval marker need not be stated or emphasized, only felt. It may also be doubled or tripled and so on to produce wider intervals which remain nevertheless based on the same rhythmic spacing.

Again, as in music, the sculptor may incorporate and overlay rhythms of different pace and quality, of both longer and shorter span, among the basic shapes and spaces in a single composition, so as to avoid exact repetitions. These varied rhythms may be anchored together by their coinciding at focal points in the sculptural structure.

Rhythms, therefore, may function not only as basic shapes but also, and more importantly, as forms broadly integrating both aggregates and overall images. They articulate shapes *of* time, which the visitor needs to scan over *in* time to grasp. The rhythms that the sculptor builds into the physical features of any piece may appear as lengths and widths of surfaces and volumes, as spatial spans between sharp or curved crests and troughs of linear surface, as transverse intervals between volumes and channels, or hidden within longer stretches of surface or open space. Transverse intervals may lie more or less parallel or angled in loose, fanlike arrangements.

7
Aggregates

Aggregate Types

Creating lively and varied aggregates, without losing the clear distinctions between basic shapes, is the central activity, the syntax of sculpture, in which the artist's formally inventive reach is most clearly revealed. Aggregates link conceptually the basic shapes to the overall image, articulating the former into the latter. In much twentieth-century sculpture, however, the overall image may be contained in little more than a single aggregate, a complex reaction to foregoing artistic styles. Many twentieth-century sculptors and painters came to reject the nineteenth century's cult of sweet-flavored naturalism, which was based on a minute copying of the live human model and often extended to casting from life or using the pointing frame to replicate a posing model. These techniques were frequently employed by Victorian and Paris Salon sculptors to produce their finished works. Both methods demand that the model remain resolutely motionless for a long time, as in all traditional art-posing; this absence of motion in overall images infected much of the work of even the most revolutionary artists of the first three decades of the twentieth century, though with some outstanding exceptions. Most important for our discussion is that these nineteenth-century techniques virtually eliminated the basic shape/aggregate level of formal invention, which would have been incompatible with their methods, substituting sheer accurate measurement of surface-point positions along three-dimensional axes between which surfaces would be smoothed by abrasion. When twentieth-century revolutionary sculptors began to learn from the African mask, whose emphatic basic shapes usually constitute a single, no less emphatic aggregate, they reinstated the clear aggregate of strongly defined shapes as the prime factor in their own sculpture.

We can witness this change in the career of one of the most important early twentieth-century sculptors, the Romanian Constantin Brancusi. He began as a highly skilled fabricator of nineteenth-century simulacra of the model, modifying his ideas only after he had reached Paris and encountered tribal arts at first hand, and developing his own kind of aggregates of clear-cut shapes as integral sculptures. Simulacra may be interesting for their own sakes, as are sound recordings of live events such as an awakening farmyard, a railroad train, or people making love.

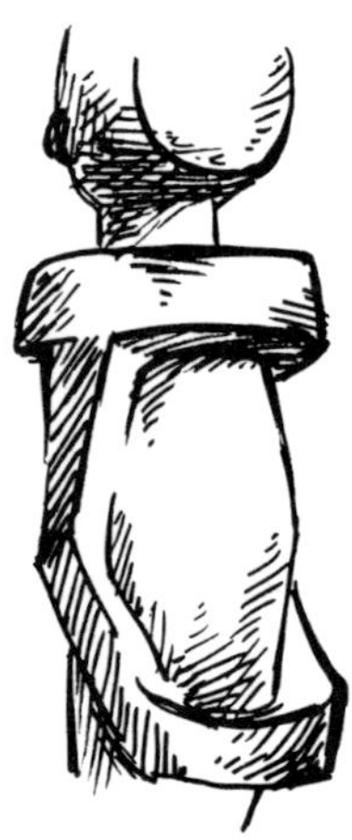

Figure 29. Three-dimensional signs.

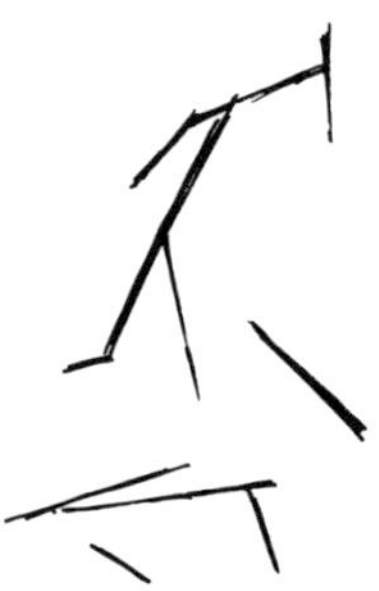

Figure 30. Open right-angled relationships.

But just as these recordings are not themselves shaped music, though they may provide fragments of raw material for concrete music, so three-dimensional simulacra are not sculpture, though they may supply raw material for assemblage.

One way of thinking of the nature and role of aggregates is to compare a sculpture to a flowering plant. The plant itself parallels the overall image, and in it we recognize functional distinction between parts—flower, leafage, branching stems, root—each sharing basic forms with others. These parts parallel the sculptural aggregates that constitute the overall image. Within each part of the plant are further differentiated functional and formal distinctions, such as sexual components in the flower, capillaries and hairs in leafage, and so on. Similarly, each of the aggregates constituting a sculpture may be made up of distinctive types of basic shape developed and arranged in ways unlike those employed in other aggregates. Highly developed examples include the Gudea sculptures of Lagash in the second millennium B.C., in which the head, right arm, and body are handled as distinctly differentiated aggregates, though all are finished with the same abrasion technique. In major Gothic sculpture of the thirteenth century, the face and neck, whose role is to convey human type and expression, may be developed as an aggregate in terms of one or two dominant basic shapes, the hair in terms of others, shoulders and arms in terms of yet others, while the lower body may stream off into rhythmically arranged folds and pleats of fabric. The works of the twentieth-century German sculptor Barlach take this functional differentiation to an extreme in the face, garments, hands, and feet.

Possible aggregates seem to be infinitely various in their composition, in the relative proportions between components, and in expression. Here we can examine only a few actually realized combinations and look into how the basic shapes are assembled to form what are effectively three-dimensional signs aggregating analogical reference content.

Linear Aggregates

Aggregates of basic lines can be composed in several specific ways. One we have mentioned already: sets of parallel or radiating fanlike sections. Curved lines, long or short, may spring off from each other like continuously branching plant stems. Deep and complex curves may for one stretch imitate each other, then run apart, sometimes setting off invisible vectors from particular directions of their movement to generate further curves. Collections of lines, straight or curved, may follow each other with a streaming motion. One final linear connective is the right angle, which Western artists have used constantly in interlocking versions for all sorts of features and in all directions within a composition, laid out close or widely spaced.

We have seen already some of the material shapes in which linear forms can be realized, including pure lines incised on surfaces. Some sculptures are incised only as scarcely modified lines on a plane surface, perhaps the

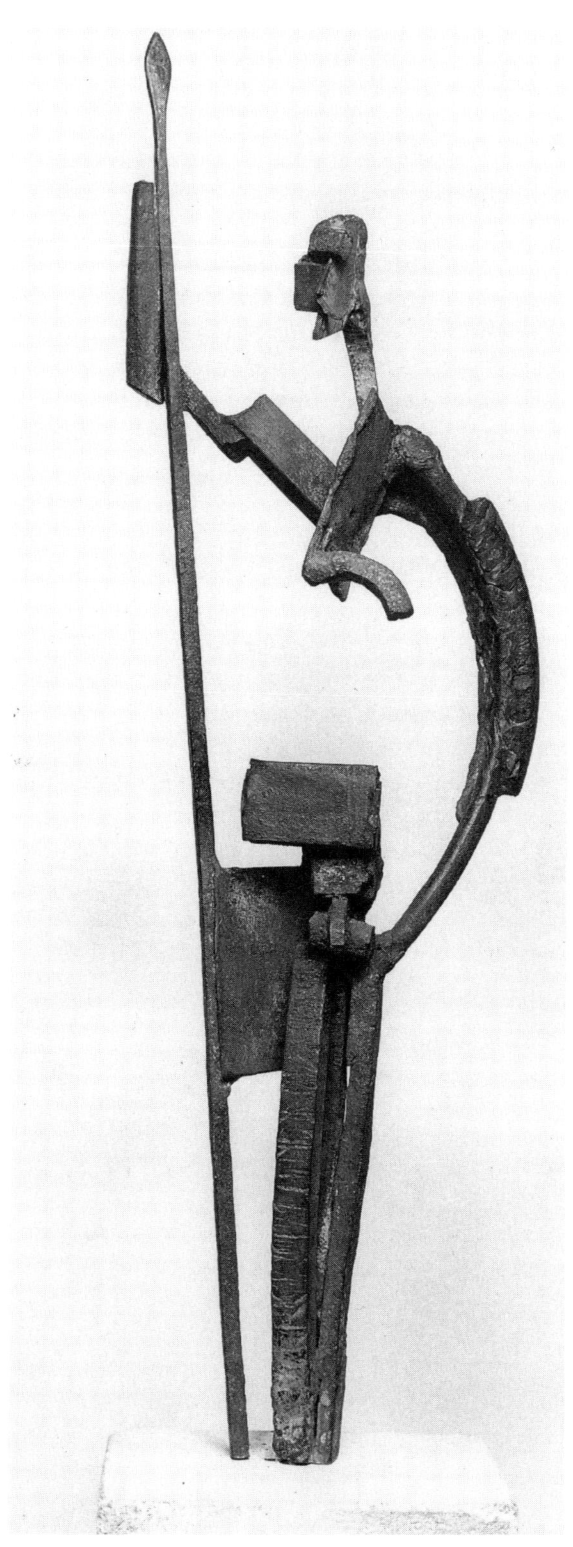

32. Julio Gonzales, *Don Quichotte* (Don Quixote), welded iron, 1929. A three-dimensional sign for the spirit of a famous literary character. (Courtesy Musée National d'Art Moderne, Centre Georges Pompidou, Paris. Copyright © 1995 Artists Rights Society, New York/ADAGP, Paris.)

best examples of which are on the tomb lintels, sarcophagi, and stelae of the sixth-century-A.D. Wei dynasty in China. Their beautiful, musical linear shapes and aggregate clusters are easily distinguished. These works are particularly important because in China they led directly to relief carving that consists of cutting back minimally the ground around the objects so outlined, and developing the standing areas as three-dimensional linear surfaces.

Such images do raise the issue of the symbolic nature of the material surface onto which the image is laid; usually that surface is carefully flattened. The linear image then interprets each of its surface areas as an imagined reality, borrowing, so to speak, the objectivity of the material surface and attributing it to each passage in tenor and topic of the image. Indeterminate smoothness of such a ground allows it to serve as an image of the universal ground of Being which modulates into appearances only superficially independent, according to fluid linear processes proposed by the drawing. In fact, all drawings borrow the objectivity of their ground support for their subject matter, including their open spaces. But sculptured drawings gain an extra dimension from the strong physical presence of their material. This reveals clearly one of the special characteristics of sculpture as a distinctive art form, and helps to explain why many sculptors have felt it essential to include the uniform identity of the material as an identifiable component of the overall image.

One relevant philosophical consideration operates in the flat linear

33. *Episode from Stories of Filial Piety*, from the lid of a sarcophagus, limestone, Northern Wei Dynasty, ca. 525 A.D. Shallow pure lines realize both a sense of passing time and the different feeling-qualities of trees and rocks. (Courtesy the Nelson-Atkins Museum of Art, Kansas City, Missouri [Purchase: Nelson Trust 33-1543/1 detail].)

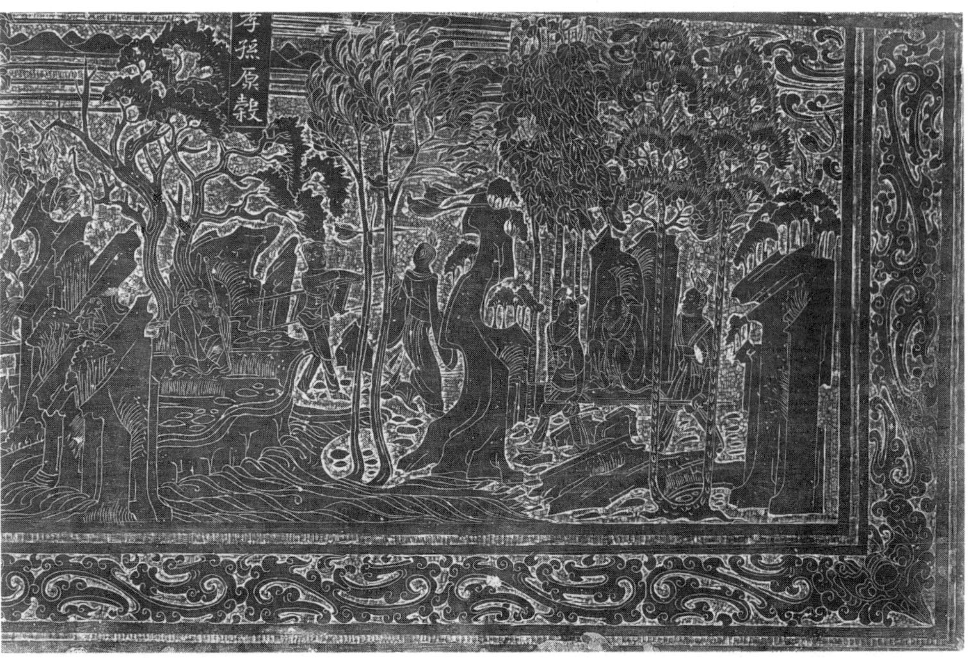

sculptural design of the Muslim world. For several religious reasons, such relief decoration as does appear in mosques and palaces remains shallow and firmly tied visually onto the ground that carries it. The stucco decoration on the walls, arcades, and ceilings of the Great Mosque of Córdoba, Spain, is an excellent example. Such art is meant to convey a specific religious lesson. All the fluid and intersecting appearances of standard shapes on the extended surface symbolize a higher archetypal layer of the many veils of apparent material reality which God interposes between himself and human perceptions. The linear aggregates combine together into extremely complex patterns—straight-sided geometric figures such as pentagons, hexagons, and octagons, combined at times with varieties of foliate arabesque based on S-curves and spirals. This example can give some insight into what has often been seen as the spiritual role and value of form as such.

Other art traditions use somewhat deeper lines cut into a flat surface, accompanied by some side-beveling. Particularly fine examples are found

34. The goddess Athena, Acropolis, Athens, marble relief, ca. 500 B.C. This piece illustrates the underlying linear structures out of which fully three-dimensional sculptural surfaces may develop. (Courtesy Acropolis Museum, Inv. No. 581.)

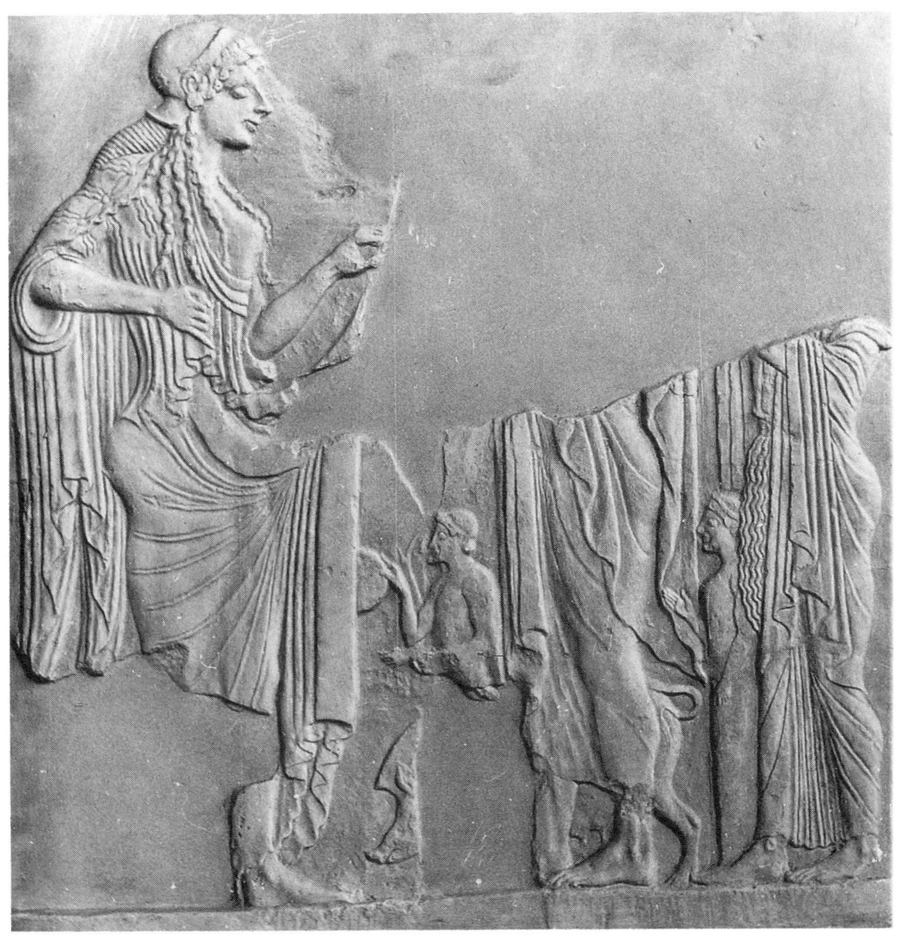

among the work of Agostino di Duccio at Rimini in the fifteenth century. His aggregates of smooth curves delineating drapery folds accompanying and overlapping each other differ markedly from the enclosed areas of modulated surface he uses to render human faces and bare limbs. In these works, which were attached to the stone surfaces of the Little Temple, the intention clearly was that the images should represent elements of the imaginative structure of the Classical Christian humanism that the whole building was designed to symbolize, manifesting from within the body of the material structure.

On many works of tribal art, especially from Oceania, linear shapes are incised or cut raised on the more or less planar surfaces of, for example, wooden dance shields, panels, and frontages of houses. The aggregates are usually long, undulating organic loops, sometimes concentric, or spirals. In ways specific to each culture, they incorporate signs of magical and social status indicated by both the forms of the design and the winding passage of the lines. In some areas of New Guinea the raised lines of wooden reliefs may be so deeply undercut that visitors to displays are meant to use their fingertips to follow through and appreciate their channels and undercuts behind raised shapes; where the groove access may be too narrow, visitors use the end of a little stick that has been chewed soft. These sculptured lines are therefore fully tactile, not only visual—a fact from which Western culture might learn.

There are sculptural traditions that superimpose purely linear shapes onto fully three-dimensional surfaces, including Celtic, certain Muslim, and Central Asian animal styles. Some scholars have proposed that nomadic Central Asia was the origin of the whole group of intensively curling linear art, which also extended into China during the second and first millennia B.C. The evolved linearism of later Chinese art may be a direct descendant, while features of late Gothic sculpture in northern Europe may also owe a debt to remote Central Asia. A similar linear inheritance in Islamic art seems to have been regulated by the geometric methods adopted from Greek Byzantium that survived in the Middle East. The flat but deeply twisting curves of the animal style were modulated toward three dimensions through serving as the enclosing contours of raised areas representing animal bodies. The linear aggregates in all these styles are based on interlaced, twisting, and twining curves, sometimes punctuated by sections of straight line and sharp angle. The original versions of the style were infused with a sense of vigorous movement derived from the winding kinetic quality of the lines. This linear movement was amplified in Chinese linear sculpture, especially relief, and appears as a lively element in European Gothic wood carving. In Islamic art, however, the movement, though still forceful, became repetitive rather than varied, thereby inducing a sense that the essence of all movements lay in archetypal patterns, however complex their appearances.

Enclosure Aggregates

Outlined enclosures are aggregated in two principal ways: by connecting them along their edges, or by intercutting, superimposing, and overlapping them, perhaps eliding sections of the overlaps. We have seen already that to join up two organic enclosures can simply make a single new one, but by superimposing two or more organic enclosures realized as cut-out sheet, the sculptor can create a valid aggregate, provided he or she considers all the factors of inner and outer pressure, correlates the shapes of inlet and promontory, and so on. Stereometric enclosures can be connected along their edges in almost endless variety, and it is not necessary that the edges connected remain visible: they can be omitted provided their angles are left clear to indicate their character and extent. What matters is that the aggregate the edges constitute has valid formal significance—meaning beyond the text.

All the linear aggregates so far mentioned can be realized as physical three-dimensional surfaces, being incised, inlaid, or raised. They then take on extra formal significance according to how they lie in the third dimension.

Theme and Variation

Thematic variation is one of the central techniques of sculpture. It is far easier to understand this technique by using line aggregates as illustration, though thematic variation operates in all categories of basic shape. The artist builds an image out of sections of basic shape—line in this case—derived from one or two main ideas that are modulated to fit the places in the image in which they appear. The main linear ideas are the source for the other varied shapes used in the composition. They are thus in a sense counterparts to the original tangram cut-out pattern, whose shapes are supposed to be immutable, whereas the point of thematic variations is

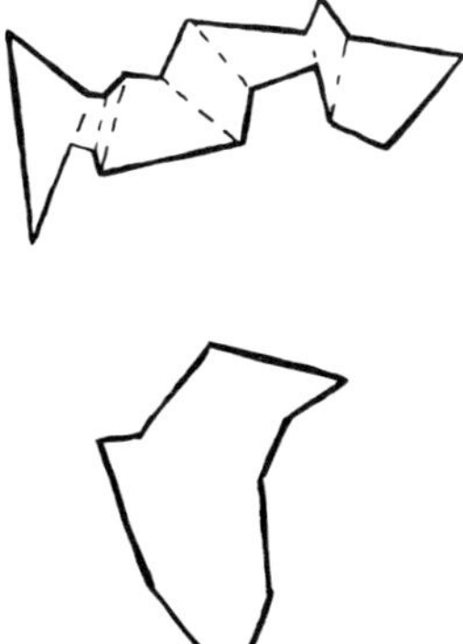

Figure 31. Compound stereometric enclosures.

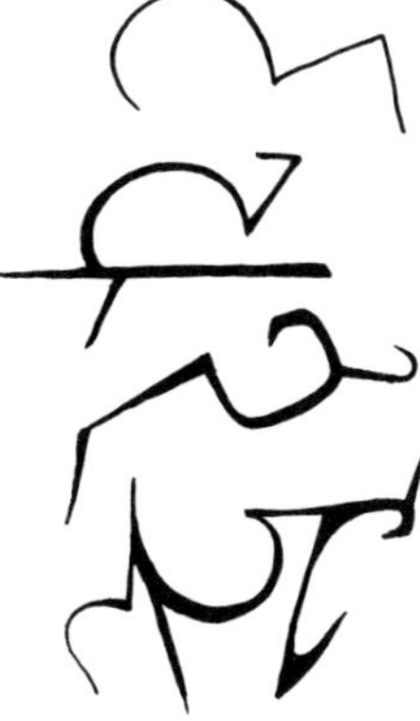

Figure 32. Linear theme with variations.

that they are all mutations. This comparison shows how an artist generates, develops, and modifies basic shapes, as distinct from shapes created through tangrams.

Surface Aggregates

We can view lines as being the primary images of extent in space and as carrying the kinetic implications of continuous time-sequence. We can perceive a complete line as a unit, but unless we do follow through its movement, going along with it imaginatively, we can never grasp its real expression and field of meaning, which are absent from the formally vague and indecisive surfaces used to copy literally realistic, standard tenors in three dimensions. Similarly, since true surfaces are continuous functions or locuses of complexes of lines "moving" to and fro in three dimensions, we need to follow through their implicit movements in all directions with sustained attention, if we are to discover their full content of meaning beyond the text. It is easy to miss the extraordinary wealth of surface meaning in, say, a piece of Gothic drapery unless we consciously determine to read its shapes thoroughly, in which case they can move us profoundly. We have grown used to taking little notice of shaped surfaces largely because most of the artifacts among which we now live, such as buildings and furniture, are manufactured with flat and three-dimensionally featureless surfaces assembled for manufacturing convenience at right angles. As a result, we bother only to grasp their outlined shapes with a single superficial glance. (This is probably a consequence of our prevalent purely two-dimensional drawing board design.)

In the 1960s several sculptors working primarily in rolled sheet metal fabricated pieces, often very large, from irregularly shaped stereometric flats welded together along their edges. Their expression conveyed overwhelming industrial power, and the absence of emotively subtle surface-leading was part of their specific point. Historically speaking, heavy and blunt-surfaced sculptures have usually been made expressly to overwhelm, frighten, and crush the spirits of hostile or subject people, as were, for example, the colossal ancient Middle Eastern dynastic stone sculptures.

The effective shape of a flat plane may reside only in its outlines. Modernist sculptors often reduced their surfaces to such outlined planes, but properly developed three-dimensional surfaces are inflected in space and achieve continuous and expressive movement toward and away from the visitor, readable by hand as well as eye across several directions into and

35. Helmet mask, Bakota, Gabun, wood (nineteenth century?). To be worn during ritual for possession by a spirit presence; the shapes are all variations on arch and triangle forms.

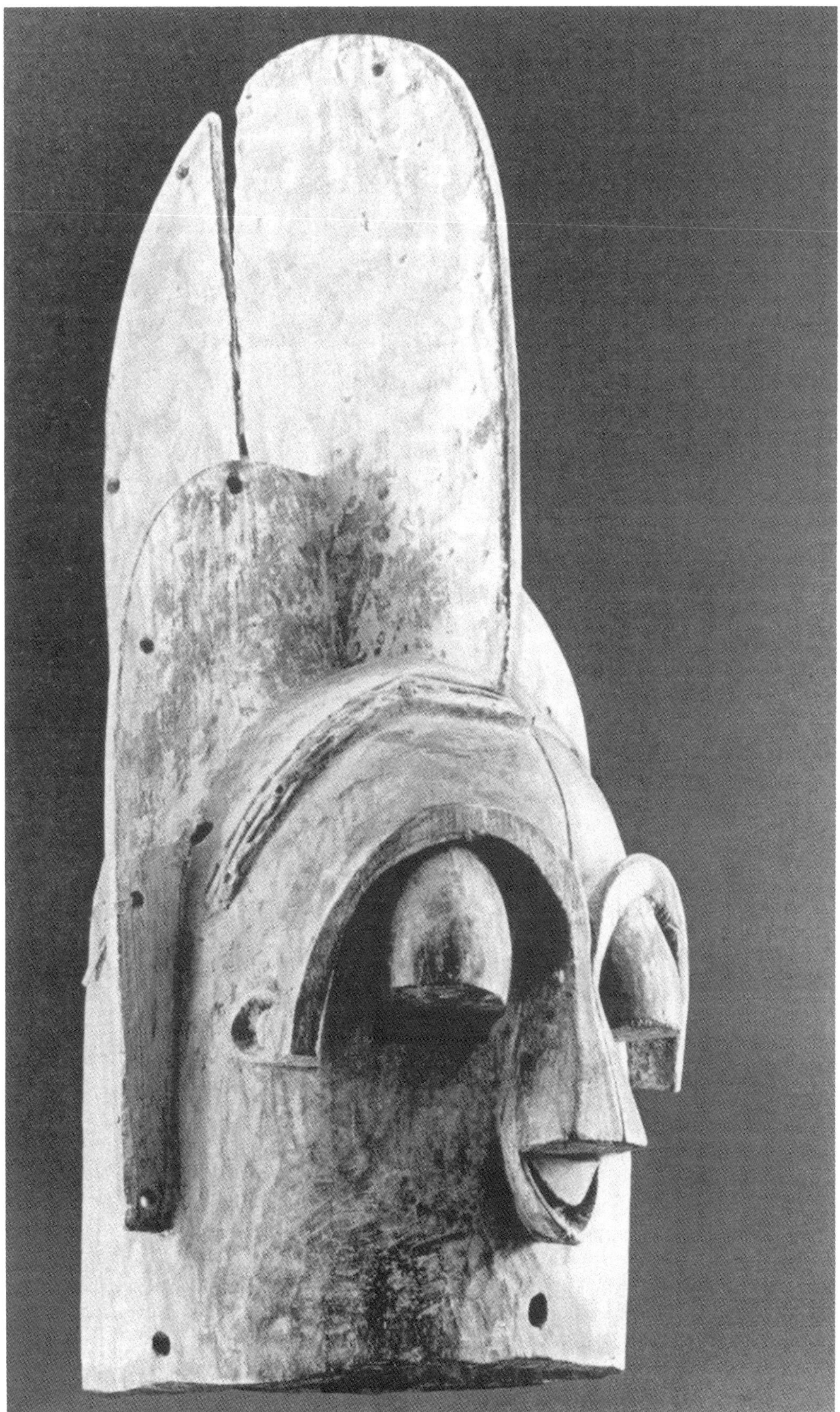

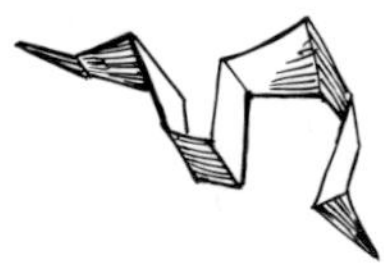

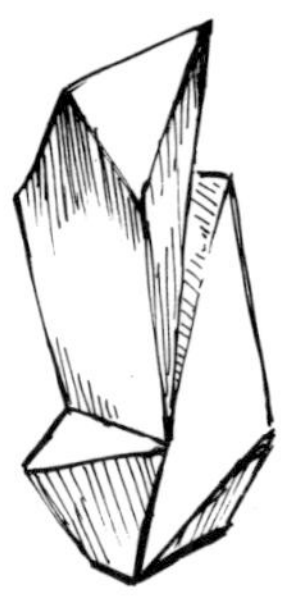

Figure 33. Three-dimensional volumetric developments of two-dimensional plane assemblies.

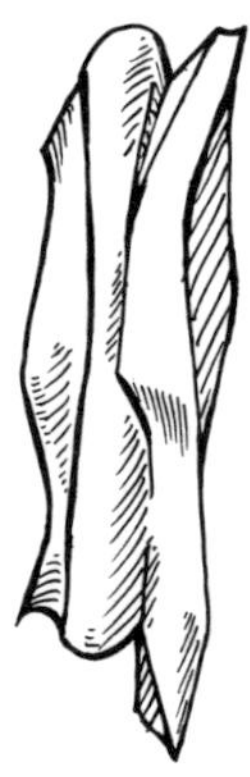

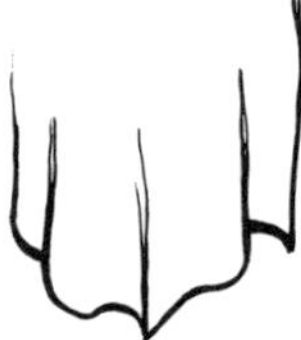

Figure 34. Aggregate of varied linear surfaces (above) and coordinating profile of surfaces (below).

out of depth. Such movement may depart radically from that of the contours seen from a principal viewpoint, and reading these surfaces may take some time. The sculptor working on them needs to ensure that their inflections do not lose but rather gain definition and variety as the work progresses, becoming "more so" rather than flattening out. To aggregate and articulate surfaces of this kind calls for a high order of formal imagination and shaping skill.

The simplest surface aggregates can be realized as sets of flat planes, each the function of an unchanging straight line, and each moving through space at a different angle, distinguished from each other by their outlines. They can be jointed along their edges to produce open, angular steps, or stacked at various angles to imply content of volume by their edges read as sections through, in Cubist fashion, or formulated to produce enclosed or open crystal volumes.

The next type of surface aggregate is the jointed collection of enclosed areas of convex or concave curvature. The convexes may imply volumes of solid lying behind them, but without defining them precisely. Both versions can give a sense of kinetic direction, and hence of pressure from internal or external space. Alternating them can produce an effect of controlled undulation either lengthwise or crosswise, or both together.

Another type of aggregate consists of clusters or bunches of linear surfaces, each having primary lengthwise movement, clearly shaped linear outlines, and a beginning and end. They may be joined long edge to long edge, or end to end, and flow into each other in a variety of ways. They may have varied convex and/or concave curvatures toward the eye, and their individual edges may connect as crests, steps, or convex-concave ripples. The predominant transverse linear sections are normally at approximate right angles to the main lengthwise movement.

A sculptor can extend linear surfaces twining and twisting lengthwise through three dimensions, so as to embrace a three-dimensional bulk. This was the technique of certain major Buddhist sculptures preserved in Japan, such as the great black bronze Yakushi Buddha in the Yakushiji, Nara. If we pick any one place on a fold and start to follow its surface lengthwise, it will lead us along an extended track through the three dimensions of space, during the course of the time taken to read it. Even though we cannot see exactly how the track carries on around the back of the figure, the artist convinces us that it does, and it reappears modified in other nearside surfaces. At the same time its convexities and concavities are fully continuous and consistent. The long aggregates are further aggregated into transverse continuities which articulate the lengthwise channels and steps as punctuations in the continuum. Some older Chinese pieces, such as the Han bronze lantern-holder, succeed in creating almost totally unified convex-concave linear surfaces over the entire composition.

Egyptian sculptures and Arp's major full-round pieces aimed for a similar integrated three-dimensional surface (though enclosing less com-

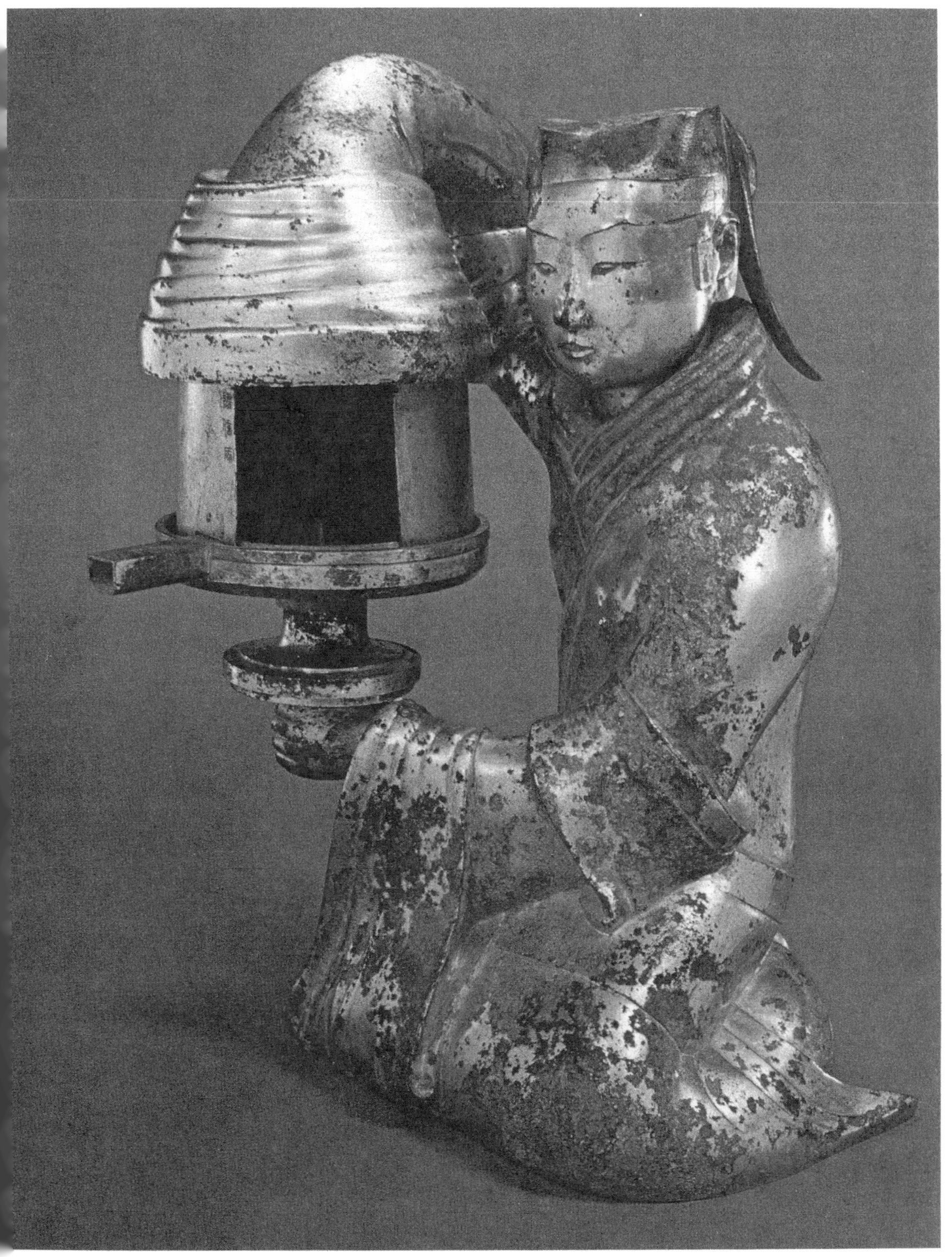

36. Chinese tomb lamp, gilt bronze, Han dynasty. The sculptured girl attendant was supposed to be a "reality" in the spirit world, aided by the almost totally continuous and fluid surface.

plex bodies than did the Chinese works). They follow the principle of the organic enclosure to the fully three-dimensional limit, so that nearly any flat section through the piece is distinctive and operates effectively in relation to contained and containing space. Egyptian sculptors used strongly faceted crystal underlay to define the frontal and receding faces of their volumes, which neither the Chinese nor Arp did.

One particular way of using linear surface is to lay it out so that it runs visibly away into the full depth of the whole piece or some part of it. By following this surface as it recedes, the viewer's eye is led to interpret the depth of run as actual, or, according to clues provided by the rest of the image, as an imaginary depth. In a full-round piece the sculptor can organize aggregates of a variety of such surfaces running into different depths, so that they enclose between them shaped bulks of space they position in three-dimensional relationship to each other. Moore did this on occasion, also supporting his bulks according to the implicit axes by which they take "possession" of space.

Another way an assemblage sculptor can aggregate surfaces is to join up manufactured sheet and strip (often welding steel), which are initially rolled or hammered out as surfaces. Ragged cutting, three-dimensional twisting and deforming of the sections, and inspirational jointing belong to the class of searching procedures that look to the future in pursuit of never-seen-before imagery. The result may be a variety of post-Surrealist imagery in fabricated materials which is open to many interpretations personal to each visitor. Several sculptors have turned to producing enigmatic three-dimensional shapes manufactured from sheet, often on a large scale, which they then suspend or lay out on a floor or the ground, inviting visitors to read into them unprescribed formal analogues and relationships.

Volume Aggregates

We have seen how surface shapes are generated from lines and shaped volumes inferred from surfaces. Aggregates of volumes are at a "higher" stage still. In thinking of volume aggregates we need to keep in mind two pairs of distinctions: first between the full, positive solid and the void, negative hollow, and second between the convex fruit and the angular crystal. Both of the second pair may appear as formal modulations of either of the first, and represent developed versions of the dialectic combination of straight and curved lines mentioned earlier.

The simplest aggregates of the first pair are the common negative volume cut into a clearly readable positive, and the opposite, a positive shape

37. Colossal head, possibly representing the divine nature of the Pharaoh Thutmose III, granite, eighteenth dynasty. Continuous abraded and polished surface, admired but unmatched by many twentieth-century artists. (Courtesy the British Museum.)

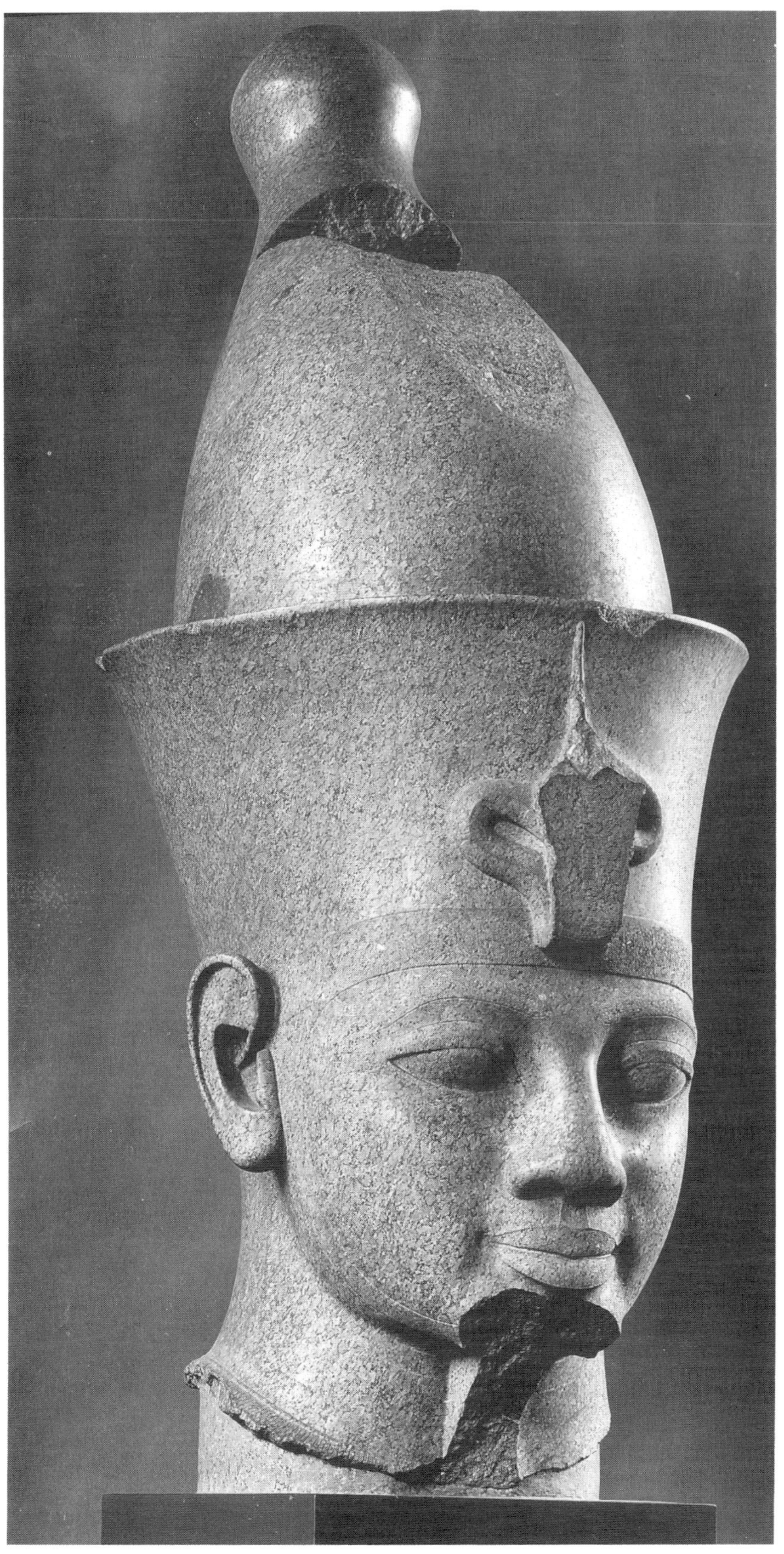

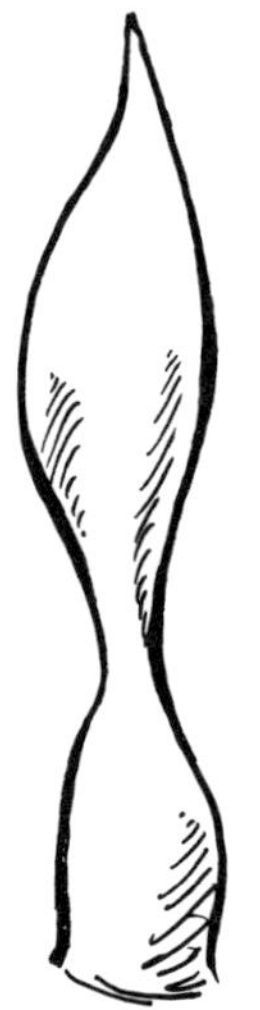

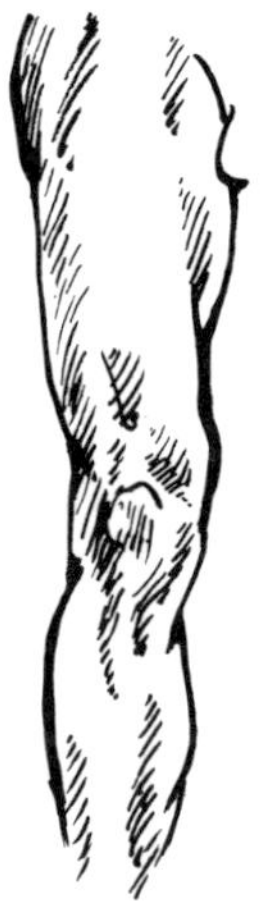

Figure 35.
Sequences of oval
volumes.

intruding into a negative. A less simple but common aggregate is the waisted spindle, either smoothly curved or faceted. A rounded fruit and a sharply angled crystal element may be combined into a single continuous volume. African sculpture uses all such aggregates freely, alternating thematic variants of each, either as individually symmetrical, or in symmetrically balanced pairs.

A sculptor can synthesize aggregates of single volumes along with other aggregates by mounting them on a single imaginary vertical axis, like chunks of meat and vegetable on a kabob. In African sculptures the chunks are usually symmetrical frontally across the axis, but they do not need to be symmetrical, as many of Brancusi's works show. Neither does the axis have to be straight; it may be curved, following the sculptor's invention. The artist may add varied ovoids and spindles to each other along an axis, converting them into undulant asymmetrical continuities.

Ovals with their implicit axes may be conveyed by convex surfaces or by a continuous linear surface, the undulations of which generate a series of underlying fruit volumes running into each other with as few breaks as possible, either in individual units or at the concave transitions between them. The contours of such a volume continuum may vary from different viewpoints, and the continuity of the overall surface may be verified by rotating the piece and checking the integrity of each stretch of contour. The sculptor needs to keep the intercuttings of such convexities clearly visible, usually as slight channels each with its own three-dimensional linear run, perhaps amplifying it into a concave-curved channel. Medieval Indian sculpture is composed almost entirely of such convexities laid out with their axes arranged at angles corresponding to the long bones of the human body in various postures. The only true concavities in these sculptures are the channels where convex surfaces meet. Most important for such volume aggregates is that the frontal faces they present directly to the visitor should themselves be three-dimensionally mobile and continuous.

A great deal of Western sculpture has used aggregates of internally faceted ovoid fruit volumes, aligned axially and intercut into each other transversely, then articulated by continuous undulant surfaces laid over them, to which they contribute their own convex and concave curvatures. This Western method treats the spatial content of its volumes as a kind of

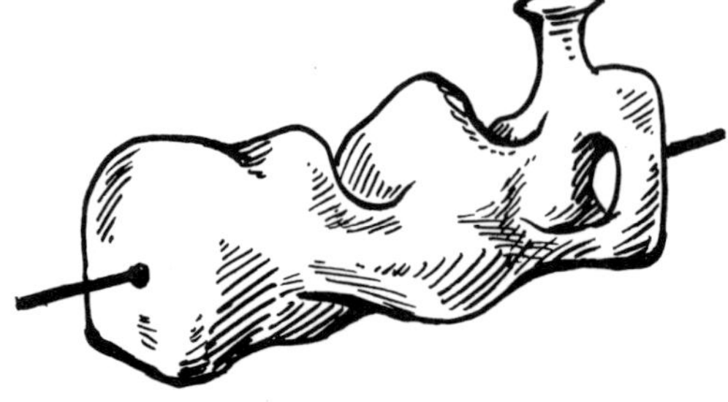

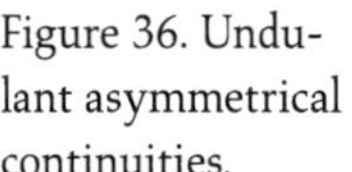

Figure 36. Undulant asymmetrical continuities.

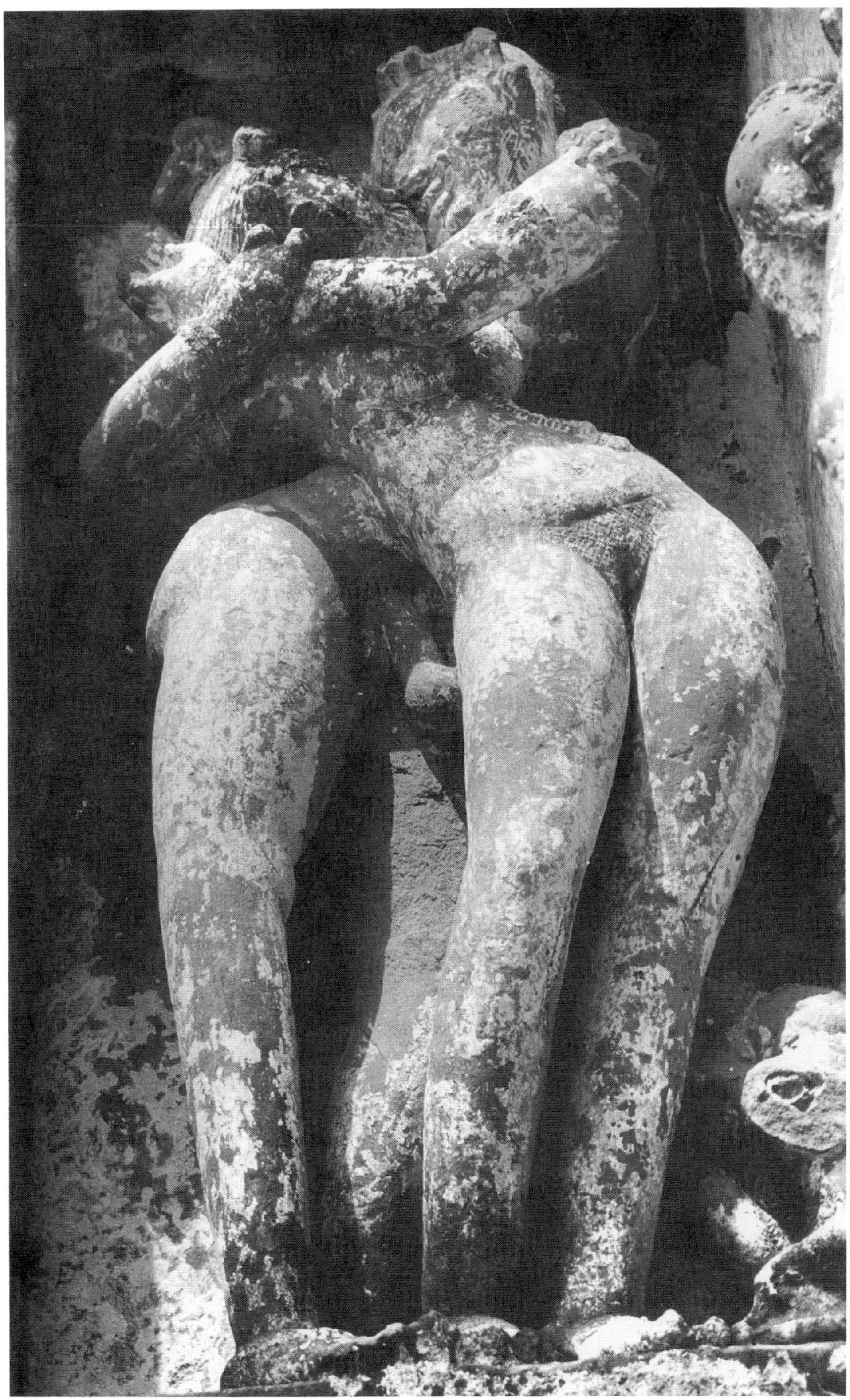

38. Heavenly couple, Khajuraho, Lakshmana Temple, Rajasthan, India, sandstone,
ca. 1000 A.D. The fullness of three-dimensional volume is defined by deeply convex
and continuously curving surfaces. (Private photograph.)

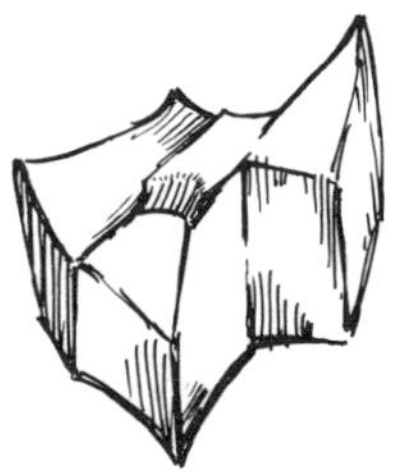

Figure 37.
Aggregate crystal
volumes.

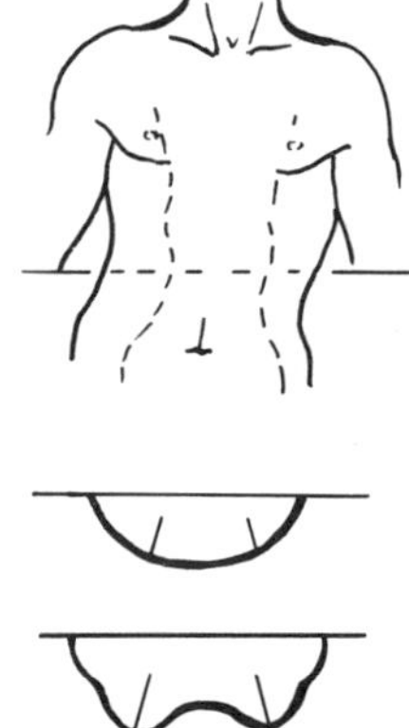

Figure 38.
Shed-lines over
the body. Top to
bottom: section
line; sections: shed-
lines suppressed
(banal), shed-lines
enhanced, *ronde
bosse.*

reality function or symbol for the being and presence of its body images. But it does not always avoid losing the faceted distinctness of its volumes' shapes and arriving at aggregates that resemble clusters of indifferent bubbles.

Crystal volumes at their most basic consist of flat facets meeting at a straight lattice of angular crests, the simplest and commonest of all being a mere box of some given proportions. The sculptor can extend and aggregate any of these volumes by developing both their surfaces and their crests along a three-dimensional twist or coil. The artist can define the limits of such extended volumes quite clearly and joint them at angles, or mark the meeting places of their surfaces with crests or channels.

One special technique for combining fruit volumes with crystal was developed in the European Classical tradition and survived well into the twentieth century in France and Germany (though not, it seems, in Italy, where it was submerged in the smooth finishing method already mentioned). This technique consists of interpreting the principal spatial content of, usually, the human body in terms of boxlike volumes, narrower across the front than across the back, so that the entire length of the receding side surfaces can be seen from the main viewpoints (as described in connection with *ronde bosse*). These two forward crests of the main volumes are connected into continuous "watershed" lines running in and out of the third dimension, which separate frontal from side surfaces. Either the summits of the shed-lines are rounded off, so that they remain fully present, or the crests are shaved off (at the risk of losing their value), or a row of varied ovoids whose curvatures are carried into the main surfaces as excavated hollows are laid along the crests, thus creating surfaces undulant in all directions.

In setting up all these aggregates, one final and paramount consideration is the positioning of the most prominent points of all surfaces and volumes in space relative to each other, to hollows, and to the most distant edges or background. The eye naturally assesses spatial depth and content in terms of degrees of relative prominence and distance from front to back, and the more strongly the artist establishes these relationships the more forceful the work will be. It is their extraordinary clarity in this regard that makes so many African sculptures powerful; it is also one of the elements of sculptural language that has been discounted in our times.

Rhythmic Aggregates

Rhythmic aggregates are a major resource for articulating sets of aggregates of other types. Certainly a sculptor can aggregate rhythms themselves together, as we saw earlier, in overlapping and interlinking series,

39. Jacopo della Quercia, *Creation of Eve*, Bologna, Istrian stone, 1430–34. All the figures, including the cloak of God, consist of volumes defined by clearly differentiated full and hollow surfaces. (San Petronio, Bologna; courtesy Alinari/Art Resource, New York.)

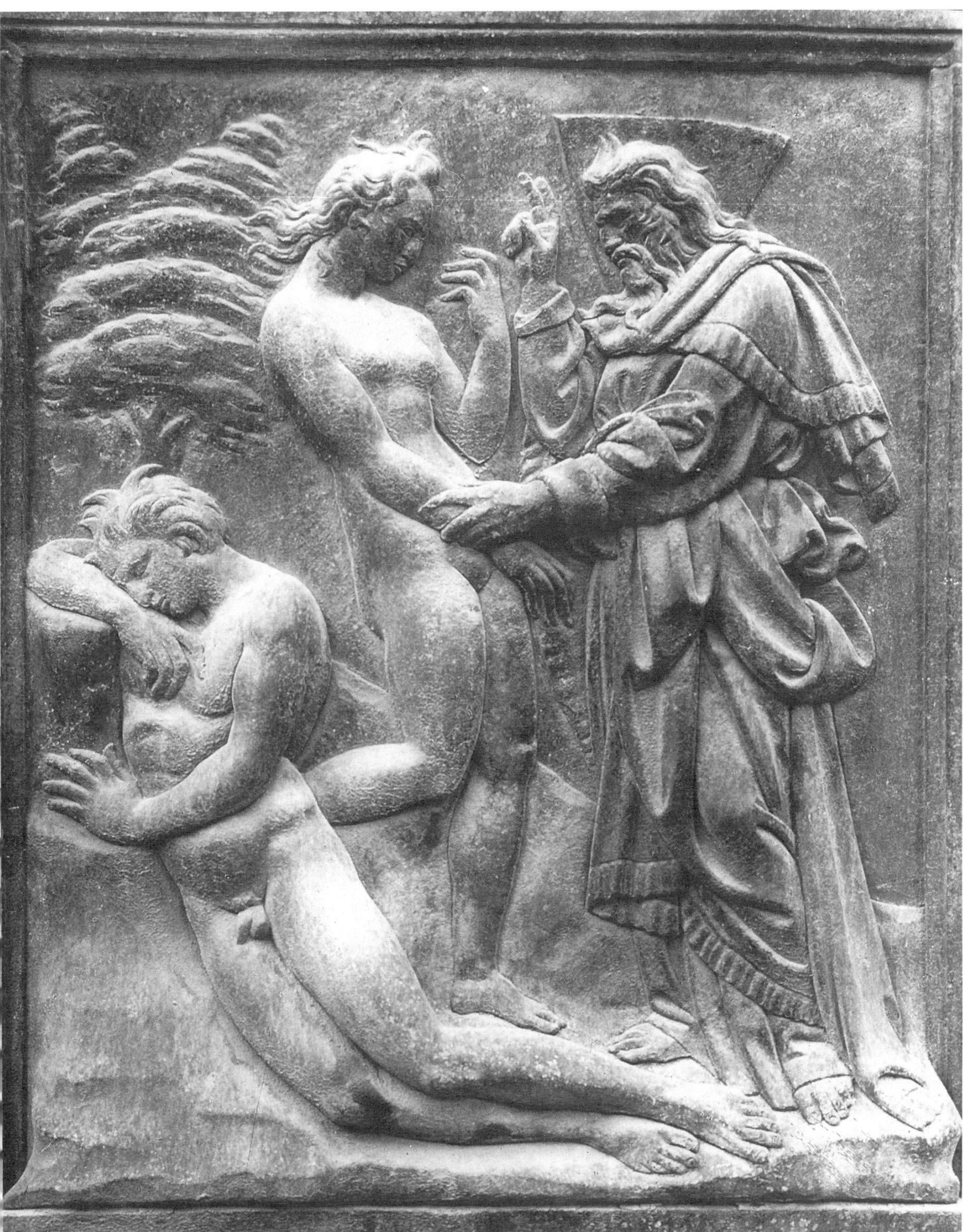

and subdivide or extend them by addition into longer spans. Since the nature of rhythmic aggregates is to lie spread through space, however, they work especially well through the entire structure of an image, unifying shapes of differing form as either virtual parallels or equal-angled fans, whose units may be multiplied or subdivided. For example, in Gothic sculptures the folds of drapery may carry emphatic transverse rhythms

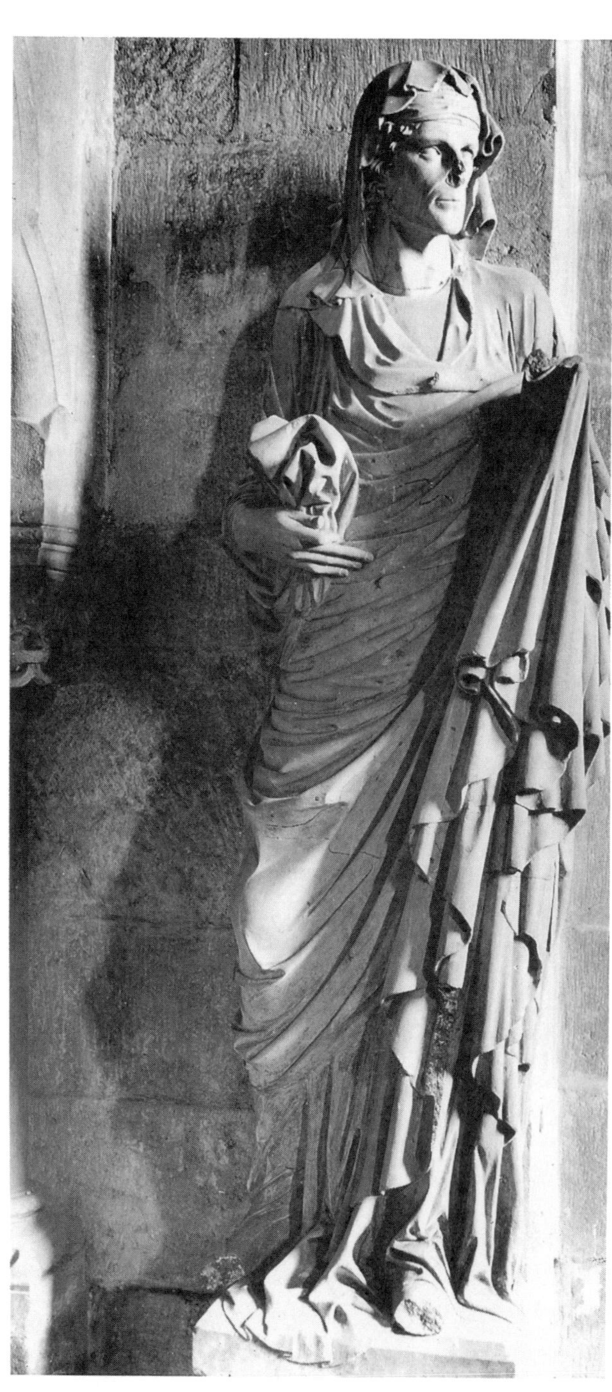

40. St. Elizabeth and the Virgin (the Visitation), facing across Bamberg Cathedral choir, sandstone, 1200–1230. The three-dimensional sculptural surfaces are all developed from a coherent mesh of vivid lines. (Courtesy Bildarchiv Foto Marburg.)

across their edges, which may be picked up by the splits between fingers of a hand but may seem to disappear over the surfaces of a face, though in fact they do not, simply recurring less obviously among their undulations. As well as operating internally over solid shapes, rhythmic aggregates can be effective in the contouring of negative, void areas, which define the spaces that impinge on and shape solid bodies.

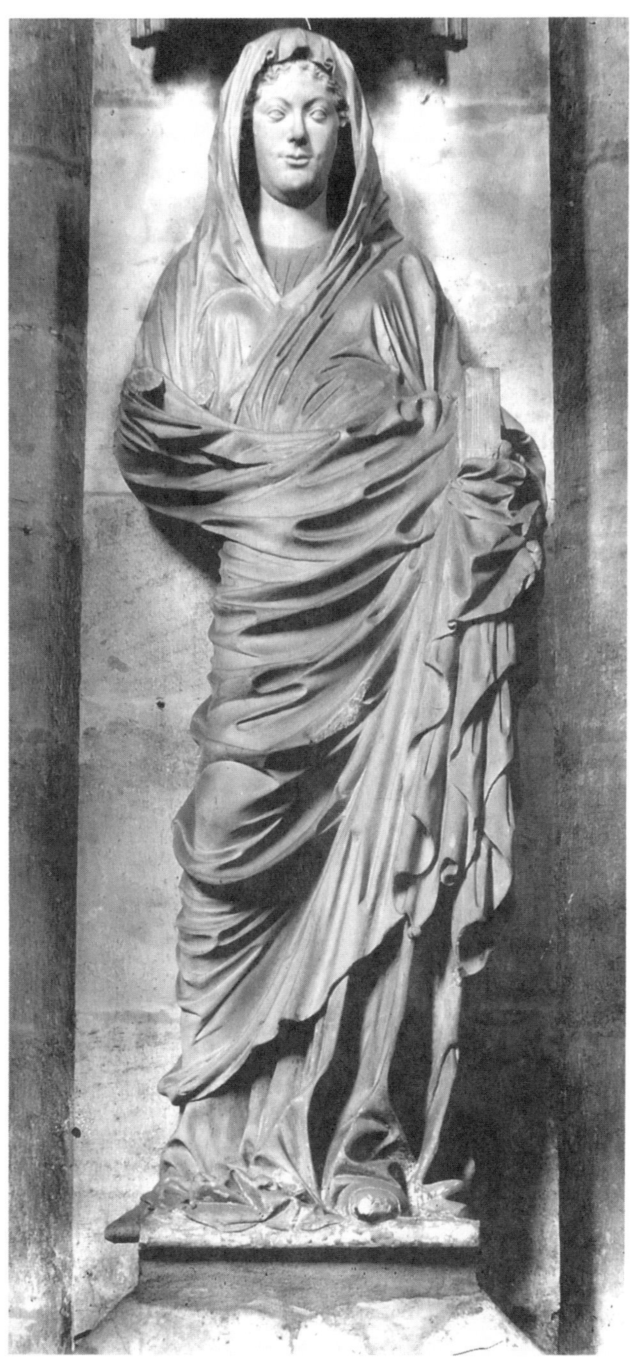

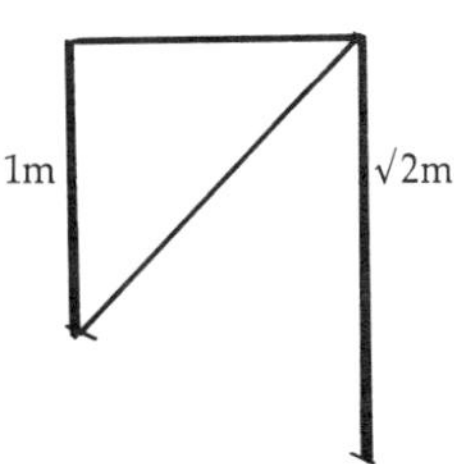

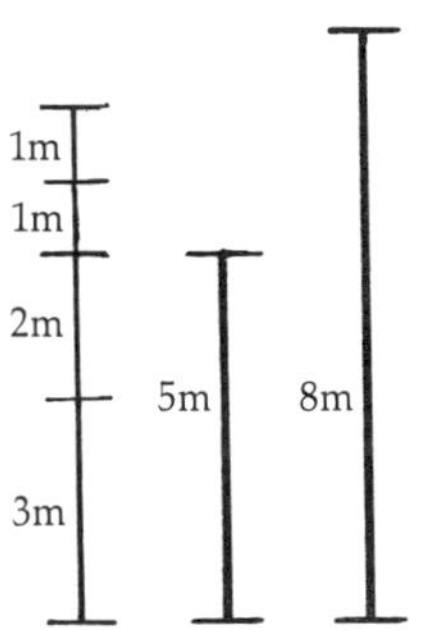

Figure 39. Proportions. Top to bottom: simple module (m); square root of 2m to 1m; golden section 8 : 5 m, derived from the Fibonacci series of numbers.

Proportion

We have considered rhythms so far as inventions introduced into sculpture at the level of basic shape, then built up into aggregates, but there is another process of rhythmic structuring, possibly more familiar to designers, which belongs especially to arts of space as limit. It helps to define them as such, and is sometimes easier for present-day Westerners to learn. It consists of subdividing the overall image according to a governing proportional scheme, and applying the scheme with its subdivisions to all the differing shapes and aggregates in the piece. This method may seem to have a prescriptive quality distasteful to artists who believe in total freedom of play, though without an awareness of its potential they risk falling into grossly banal rhythmic structuring without realizing it. The clearest and simplest but also most effective version of dividing space is the overall grid of squares or cubes. The grid may be either added or subdivided by two, four, or eight, or by three, five, or seven. The basic measures locate features of a piece that carry the main rhythmic stresses of its shaping, and the subdivisions count out the dimensions and placing of lesser features. A sculptor can play remarkably freely with such measures, as a means of articulating basic shapes and aggregates within the overall image.

The measures derived from such systems operate as basic modules (m) of rhythmic interval. Modules may be applied freely outside a grid system, intercutting them at right angles and diagonally. The powerful rhythmic effect of African and Mesoamerican sculptures depends on modular spacing, including simple grids, to articulate contours, major prominences, and channels as well as lesser components. Many twentieth-century artists have used more complex mathematical schemes, maybe without acknowledging them. Some have deliberately incorporated surds or wild measurements to break the regularity of a system and so produce a sense of uncertainty and unease—intercutting, for example, measures of eleven against two. The basic proportional systems include the "irrational" proportions of 1 : $\sqrt{2}$ or $\sqrt{3}$, and the famous golden section, based on the Fibonacci series of numbers 1, 1, 2, 3, 5, 8, 13, 21 . . . , which also generates a spiral when each numeral is squared. Other systematic proportions have been based on the side or diagonal of a square within a circle. All can be used as bases of artistic rhythms and treated quite freely with varied stress.

To conclude consideration of realized aggregates: rhythms and proportions can be used to unite even strongly contrasted basic shapes and aggregates, as well as the spaces that relate them. Such rhythms and proportions can make powerful contributions to the feeling of an overall image.

8
The Overall Image

Image as Focal Meaning

Let us return once more to Polanyi's illustration of focal meaning as being what we understand when we take an intuitive jump from subsidiary information that contributes to but does not already "contain" the whole. We can then interpret a sculpture's overall image as analogous to a focal meaning we intuit from its subsidiary aggregates and basic shapes, which similarly do not "contain" it. Thus the overall image of any individual work is in principle unidentifiable and indefinable in advance. A particular basic tenor may contribute a greater or lesser part according to the style and purpose of the piece. In the end, however, it is the topic working that gives rise to the overall image in the mind of the viewer. And this culminating image is what brings into focus and unifies all the visitor's analogical responses to the qualities of shape, aggregate, touch, and material the sculptor has produced. Even the sculptor of a major work may not be aware of the full extent of the meaning he or she has built into it. Nor should visitors, however deeply they explore their responses, ever expect to reach a final closed meaning. If they do think they have reached any such meaning, then either the work is shallow or they are deluding themselves.

During the first three decades of the twentieth century, when artists were deeply concerned with assimilating the lessons of so called "primitive" tribal works, many of the ideas that we now take for granted were first formulated. In 1918 the French poet Pierre Reverdy wrote, "The image is a pure creation of the mind. It cannot be born from a comparison but from a juxtaposition of two more or less distant realities. The more the relationship between the two juxtaposed realities is distant and true, the stronger the image will be—the greater its emotional power and poetic reality." This concept became a widely accepted definition among the Surrealists from its being quoted by André Breton in his first manifesto. It is still the basis of assemblage sculpture, and its great value for our era, which believes in the principles of total individuality, freedom, and novelty, is that its possibilities seem unlimited.

The Surrealist sculptor Arp wrote in 1950:

THE FORMS I CREATED
IN THE YEARS 1927–48
AND WHICH
I CALLED COSMIC FORMS
WERE VAST FORMS
WHICH WERE TO UNITE A MULTITUDE OF FORMS
LIKE THE EGG
THE BUD
THE HUMAN HEAD
BREASTS.

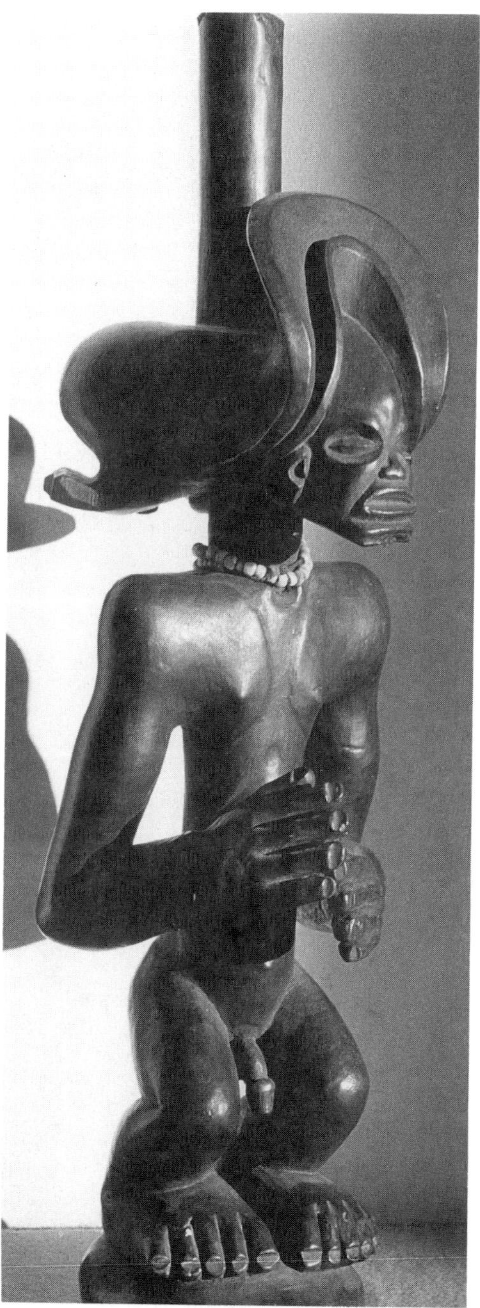

41. King image, Bajokwe, Gambia, wood (nineteenth century?). All the different shapes, developed to their maximum, symbolize the power and energy implied by kingship. (Courtesy Museum of the Civic Center, Philadelphia.)

Arp, however, did not simply juxtapose those forms in the shapes of his works; he ran them together into coherent bodylike images usually contained within a continuous skin. In effect he worked according to something not unlike the Indian sculptural technique described in Chapter 1, except that his total bodies did not follow an overall human pattern.

The idea of combining into single images references to remote orders of sense was widely discussed among poets all through the nineteenth century, especially the Symbolists, and had been long known to literature

42. Jean Arp, *Crown of Buds I*, stone, 1936. Embodies clear references to buds, breasts, and fruit, as described by the artist himself. (Peggy Guggenheim Collection, Venice; photograph by Carmelo Guadagno and David Heald, copyright © The Solomon R. Guggenheim Foundation, New York. Copyright © 1995 Artists Rights Society, New York/VG Bild-Kanst, Bonn.)

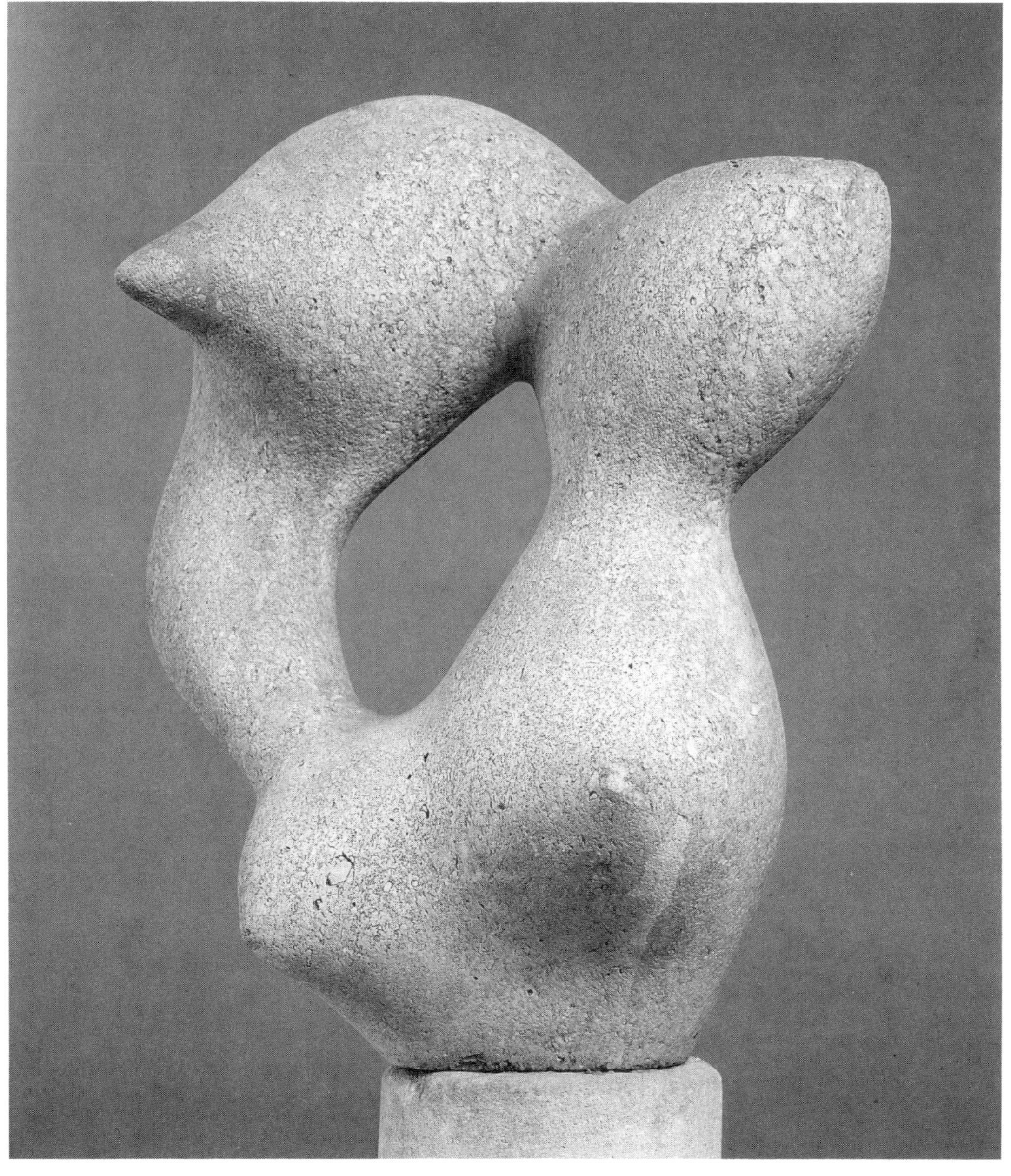

in the guise of simile and metaphor. Early in the nineteenth century the English Romantic poet Samuel Taylor Coleridge formulated the notion as a theory of the imagination (in his *Biographia Literaria*) in a way that covers both the figurative tenor aspect and the formal-analogical topic aspect of sculpture. He described the imagination as dual. The first imagination builds up our human images of everyday reality, enabling us to grasp pragmatic relationships and wholes, corresponding more or less with Polanyi's description of the meaning process. All that we mean by "reality" only exists for us as images anyway. The second imagination generates "emotional power and poetic reality" by dissolving, diffusing, and dissipating commonplace wholes in order to create fresh, unfamiliar ones not totally distinct from but wider-reaching than those of the first imagination. Since the Symbolist and Surrealist movements many twentieth-century artists have been especially concerned to dissolve, diffuse, and dissipate ordinary coherence as the prelude to juxtaposition or simple arrangement. However, they omit the correlative contained in Coleridge's concluding phase, the creation of fresh wholes, which major artists such as Arp, Picasso, Ernst, and Miró did not. In the last analysis, what matters for the overall image is its wholeness, articulating all its subsidiary elements without which there can be (as Theodor Adorno pointed out) no worthwhile and interesting whole.

Sculptures exist as enduring physical objects that combine a multitude of formal references to disparate regions of human experience. As well as the primary symbolic elements of basic shape and aggregate, sculpture needs, like any language, a symbolism of relationship and connection that aids the unification of parts into wholes. We now accept that we humans are animals who think by symbols and images. We recognize commonplace things and their interrelationships by matching them with images the first imagination has given us, confined within the conceptual limits of ordinary familiarity and use. We perceive every object—chair, tree, apartment block, automobile, mountain, cloud—through layers of other images acquired from our past experience of similars, and about which we have developed specific expectations. The sculptor's second imagination transcends these expectations by dissolving and recreating, not only fixing the recreations into permanent physical shapes but also superimposing matrixes from different symbolic orders and articulating them into otherwise inaccessible coherences.

This process exposes the fallacy according to which nonartists such as journalists, social historians, and some critics, who use art as material for their own purposes, assert that arts necessarily "express their time"— meaning by this the then-prevailing view of the world and reality. The poet and scholar Christopher Middleton has demonstrated with numerous examples that the exact opposite is the case with artists of the highest order: they work at variance with their time and may have to wait decades even to be recognized. Far from conforming to the conventional views prevailing in their societies, good artists are always striving to supersede them. Even when gestures of "mold breaking" have themselves become the aesthetic convention, these too have to be superseded. Some artists may certainly, in dispersing the rigidities of the first imagination, use their art to criticize overtly the follies of their time; so their work may be useful to the other disciplines. But sculpture, especially, amounts to an affirmation of positive values, using its presence as praise, and is never a species of reportage of supposed fact, mere grist to the mill of social history. It is true that all artists are bound to use as basic material for their symbolism what is available in their lifetime, including the demands of patrons, autobiography, and references to contemporary events, but the symbolism does not exist merely to record the raw material. It reaches into depths of analogy and correspondence—meanings beyond the text— far beyond the scope of outer description. The works of artists who see their role as executing historical instances in their medium seem pale and inadequate as expression, once a few years have passed.

Primacy of Overall Image

So far we have discussed the form-shape systems of the language of sculpture from the bottom levels up, from basic shapes to overall image. This is because the very idea of a language structure for sculpture is not familiar. As with spoken and written language, however, we learn to operate the structure by playing and practicing with it, by listening and reading, looking and studying, and formulating ever more coherent and meaningful utterances of our own. Then we start with what we want to say, shaping some demand or proposition that expresses the meaning we intend both in our words themselves and in the ways we utter them. So in sculpture we may start with the tenor or overall image and go on to embody it in an infrastructure of sculptural topic language.

As anyone who has composed seriously in any art form knows, in exploring the resources of a language to reach for intuited meaning we may find ourselves saying things we did not know we had ever thought. We may discover that the image we had at first intended to present emerges through the process with far more to it than we had imagined when we started. Although we may conceive what we think is a full-fledged sculptural image at the outset, we often end up with something deeper and wider reaching than our first idea. Not every sculptor works with or needs to invent completely original image ideas. Good or even great works have often been developed from other people's ideas. Ideas and preliminary sketches have been handed down by traditions, schools—even traded or stolen from artists' workshops.

This process of creative exploration during the execution of a work may seem to run counter to the notion artists often maintain, that rough sketches derived from playful experiment with the medium always have more "life" than a "finished" product. This may indeed be so, especially when the artist has few conscious resources of expression and relies on what is called (also in fields other than art) "fantasy technique." As Eugène Delacroix's journal shows, however, there is such a thing as inspired development work, which artists in other media such as music and theater have also described. The sheer physical demands of sculpture may seem to make such work appear less immediately available to a sculptor, but inspiration may take hold by returning to one's own previous work and seeing a vision of further reaches of implication within the structure that already exists.

There are three possible levels of syntactical integration in the overall image. First is the physical integrity of the piece or compilation. Second is the notional unity that may be given by some kind of tenor. Third is the set of relational symbols that the development of the topic incorporates. These levels of integration incorporate some notions we have already encountered.

Integration of Image

First is physical integrity, which needs little explanation. A sculpture clearly has to be a single object or a recognizably arranged collection of objects. A single piece poses no problem, nor does a group or groups united as continuous material, as features of a single structure (such as a temple or church), or on a single base or in a relief wall-frame. Problems may arise when the work consists of a collection of separate pieces meant to be read as a unity. An installation occupying the whole of a single spatial volume, such as a gallery room or walled space, may clearly be intended to be read as a mutually interacting set of components. But an assemblage that stands free of any encompassing space needs to be visibly distanced from its neighbors, either by open space around or by its distinctive formal coherence, or both.

The second level of integration of the overall image, the tenor, can be highly varied, depending on the ways it reflects the human interests of sculptor and viewer. Tenor is based broadly on the animate human or animal body image, its modifications and extensions into human contexts, as in still life, plus its intellectual, emotional, and mythic reflections. Our own bodies are the receivers, containers, and coordinators of our personal experiences and cultural inheritance; the overall three-dimensional image of a sculpture objectifies and articulates fields among these, which the sculptor particularly values for others to witness and assimilate. Such fields, of course, are by no means restricted to what is before the artist's eyes at some particular moment, but embrace phases of experience during his or her whole lifetime, which may not be consciously available to memory. Sculptural formulation changes their nature from a merely personal record to a statement of general significance.

Perhaps the most important fact about the body, and the most difficult to capture in sculpture, we know intimately: its "life" or "spirit." Without a symbolism of life, no sculpture succeeds. Generally speaking, this quality is carried by the basic shapes and aggregates; particular shapes —some appearing disconcertingly "unnatural"—which the sculptor attributes to specific parts and members of the body tenor are usually meant to symbolize characteristics of indwelling life. These may be the most difficult for members of other cultures to learn to recognize and accept.

It is the body image that acts as a channel for visitors to identify and assimilate the complex expression of a sculptural image. They do this both through normal human processes of sympathy and empathy with posture and gesture, and through the work's formally analogical topic language. Every icon a sculptor makes demands that visitors assimilate all of its image shapes internally to their own bodies. We can easily recognize how in different cultures, and in the hands of individual sculptors, the life and role of the body image may be differently expressed.

Imagery of Body Components

Traditional societies often have beliefs about the character and bodily locations of life energies and refer to these in their sculptural body images. Most peoples take the head and its main organs of sense and action, especially the eyes, as supremely important. As mentioned earlier, eyes are the principal emblem of the spirit, but the forehead and crown of the head are also widely considered as the vessels of spirit, intellect, and live creativity. They may be correspondingly emphasized, enlarged, and shaped to convey not only their importance but also the mythic value of their functions.

Some Congo masks are given enormous prominent eyes on snail-like stalks that assert vigorously the act of looking. Archaic Greek figures have high, arched, upper chests that indicate they are the container of the *thymos*, the dry and wakeful consciousness; their knees have strong shapes because these joints were considered the location of the essential strength of the foot warrior and were "loosed in death" (as Homer says). The later Classical Greeks loved not just abstractly but literally the beauty of the physical body with its smooth rounded volumes as an entire sensual presence, a presence revealed rather than hidden by drapery, which may partly account for their sculpture's popularity in officially body-hating societies of the Christian West. Some Gothic sculptures represent God the Father in the act of creation—thinking the forms of the world—with an enormous forehead. Peoples who take the body to be a mechanism may convey it with mathematical shapes, although sculptors like Michelangelo, who understood the anatomical mechanism well but felt it to be imbued with the life of the active soul, expressed that view in their topic working. Many Western sculptors have focused on the expressive lineaments of the face as revealing inspired personality. Others have concentrated on an image of the whole female body as an ultimately desirable source of life energy. To look seriously into these assumptions can lead us to explore and identify our personal assumptions about the symbolic values of our own body image.

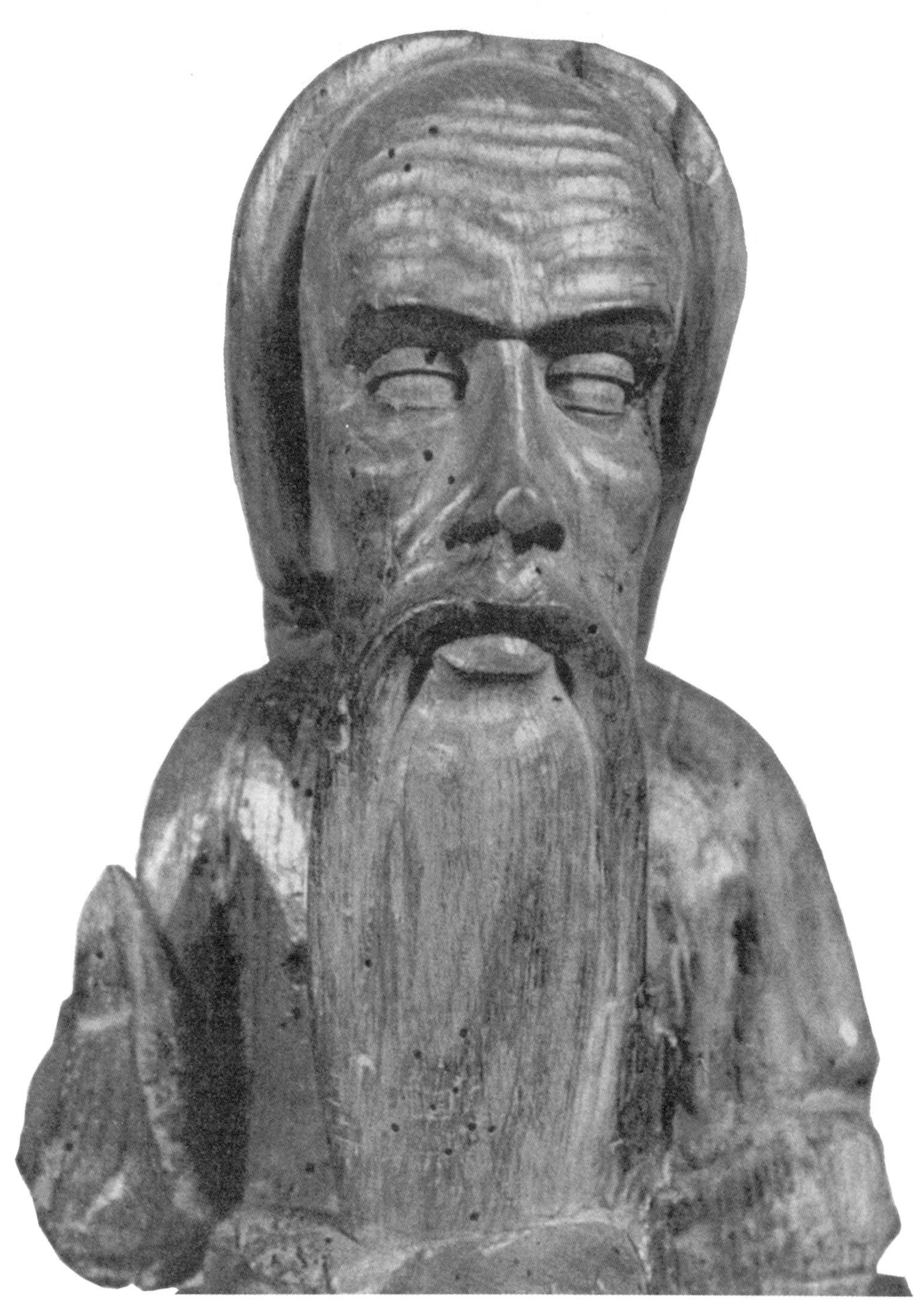

43. Meister der Riemer Altar, Mecklenburg, bust of God the Father, oak wood, ca. 1450. The exaggerated forehead symbolizes God's creative act as "thinking" the world into existence. (Courtesy Staatliches Museum, Schwerin, Germany.)

Body Qualities Amplified

The components of a body image may not resemble even superficially those of a human body, either because the image is aiming to compound a wholly symbolic body unit, as in some of Arp's or Moore's sculptures, or because it is precipitating into three-dimensional shapes the locuses of parts of the body as they move through space—arms, legs, garments. Locuses can be shaped as mobile surfaces, or even as solids. The kinetic acts of the live maker can be evoked by shapes such as concave scooping, dents, twists, pinches, or star-shatter impacts. The vigorous action of a body shape, such as toppling or stretching, is sometimes represented by an assembly of independent shapes occupying positions suggesting limbs, even bursting through a door frame so that they appear differently on each side, as Jean Ipoustéguy has done. Disjointed limb-shapes and torsos that are ragged and shredded or consist of crushed junk steel may evoke bodies subjected to violence.

Some sculptors appeal to inner bodily sensations by anticonventional subdivision, shaping, and size relations between parts: for example, perching a tiny, flame-haired "head" atop a long triangular "body" with enormous "feet," or setting a huge round "face" with bulging "eyes" on a little, raggedy, and schematic "body" with stiff "limbs." Twentieth-century Surrealist sculptors such as Ernst and Miró have made body images by juxtaposing incongruous objects (box, shoe, cowhorn, toaster), plastering their surfaces over, and casting them. The "body" makes its unnatural, evocative, and inanimate component shapes from alien orders of reality seem "animate" and hence threatening.

This procedure bears a relationship to one common in societies that do not adhere to strict canons of realism—finding and objectifying body images for imaginary beings that could never exist in reality. A prime example is the Chinese dragon, but many other sculptures follow the principle involved to a greater or lesser degree. Such images may have valid meanings, even though what they represent may not exist in that bodily shape. The thousands of sculptures of the Chinese dragon may depict a creature believed in by some people. But its extraordinary body, compounding lizard, goat, snake, fish, whirling water, and atmospheric vortexes, refers to tremendous phenomena of storm and cloud, with hundreds of miles of raging flood, that are desperately real experiences to many Chinese. This dragon body image was used by extension to refer to other kinds of irresistible power, such as the emperor's.

This example illustrates the essential and widespread principle that sculptured body images may be meant to identify the symbolic truth of complex nonbodily realities in terms that people can equate with their own bodily experience. To describe such phenomena in mere abstract terms, such as "energy" or "fertility," short-circuits and diminishes their effect. A similar approach is revealed in sculptural tenors that refer to inner human conditions without resembling the actual human body. They include, for example, physically energetic horses, rising and spiritually aspiring birds, crouching or attacking lions, and lonely, withered trees.

Object Tenors

Some tenors include inert objects for the sake of their human reference, such as early Buddhist sculpture's use of the cushion on a throne or a lone pair of footprints to indicate the presence of the Buddha at events in his earthly life, before he passed into Nirvana. In everyday life we may infer the presence of a business executive in a house from a briefcase by the door, or of a child from the bicycle in the hallway. They act as symbols by association. Likewise, we may infer the identity of saints from their normally associated emblems which we have learned of from literature: gridiron for St. Lawrence, or the lotus flower for Buddha-Vishnu. The overall image calls on all possible ways in which the mind can read its symbolic elements.

A comparable principle lies behind the imagery of landscapes and cityscapes, which reliefs may include as settings for figurative tenors that represent symbolic events. They may not simply depict "actual" places, however amply these may be developed from the artist's experience of actuality. In Christian art, for instance, the setting may signify the Holy Land or Jerusalem, in Buddhist art either North India in the fifth century B.C. or mythical hyperspace. We can best think of any of these as the necessary complement to any human-shaped being, for a body exists only as counterpart to the place and time at which it is present. This relationship also operates in reverse, to affect the actual-world settings in which we place sculptural body images. The latter become inevitable symbolic complements to the former, compelling the places that house them—temple or gallery—to participate symbolically in the overall image.

Some tenors that may seem to refer to pure external objects are sculpted only for the sake of their relevance to a human goal or desire. They may aid in "realizing" by ceremonial magic the spiritual identities of urgently needed physical counterparts, such as growing corn or the progeny of cattle among tribal people. In modern societies they may project fantasy images of the objects of human desires, ranging from sexually inviting persons (as in much advertising and Pop art) to horses, automobiles, and even industrial installations. As such they may work primarily as egotistic indulgence, and part of their appeal derives from how powerfully realistic they may seem.

Topic and Realism

In all sculpture "realism" has the function of persuading the person contemplating the work that its tenor either is or could be the case here and now at some level or has once been the case in the very shapes described. These shapes are themselves symbolic of those aspects of the world which the original consumers of the art normally accepted as "real." Realism of one kind or another has been a particular feature of Christian and secular western art, since the factuality of the Christian persons and narratives has been a cardinal feature of Christian doctrine.

How the artist handles the tenors and bodies in the overall image, how he or she treats them in the topic working, is of central importance to that image. It imbues the work with qualities of feeling that reveal the artist's attitudes and insights. Different kinds of topic expression appeal to and inevitably reveal the various temperaments among both artists and visitors, ranging from dedicated devotion and tenderness to complacency, scorn, savage hatred, and active butchery.

Icon and Iconography

We usually call the tenor subject matter of art its iconography. Iconography arises at the place where people encounter in their environment "the beyond" in some form as numinous or divine. This encounter constitutes a reciprocal relationship; just as child and mother define and identify each other mutually, so do created person and his or her creative "beyond." Sculptural imagery realizes the human mutuality of such an encounter. In religious terms an icon is felt effectively to contain as well as represent the most exalted human or spiritual pattern with which people may expect to identify, either through sustained disciplines of meditation or by contemplating with adoration both the teachings of which it is the focus and the significance of the forms and correspondences the icon arouses within them. So strong may be the feeling that the true icon is its numen that worshipers may touch it, kiss it, and scrape off and preserve bits of its surface in the expectation that it will work magically to their benefit. Icons may be large or small; large ones tend to be associated with dynastic dominance or wide social agreement, small ones may be the focus of purely personal adoration and prayer. The principle they embody, however, is neither large nor small. Powerful rulers have claimed to embody transcendent principles such as deities in their own persons, or at least to have exclusive access to major icons embodying the principle of rule. They then require that their state icons be invested with all the paraphernalia of crowns, robes, and jewels that symbolize their status, as well as the formal properties recognized at the time as conveying potency in more abstract terms.

The iconography an overall image conveys may be quite complex, based on elaborate compilations of tenor figures and objects which may refer to particular myths and legends that are themselves symbolic. It has often happened that a people takes possession of sculptures without knowing the original myths and legends behind their iconography. Then fresh myths are invented to match the image, a process called "iconotropy." All too often the array of common tenors, people, and things is treated as descriptive material for history without regard for their deeper symbolic references.

It is possible to misunderstand or change the meanings of iconography because it operates with recognizable objects, which, as objects, naturally mean different things to different people. For anyone to recognize amply the symbolic reference of any represented thing requires that he or she

44. Shiva in glory, Kailashanatha Temple, Ellora, India, rockcut, ca. 900 A.D. A huge aggregate of many different shapes, decorative in that they expand on and reinforce the glory of the central divine figure. (Private photograph.)

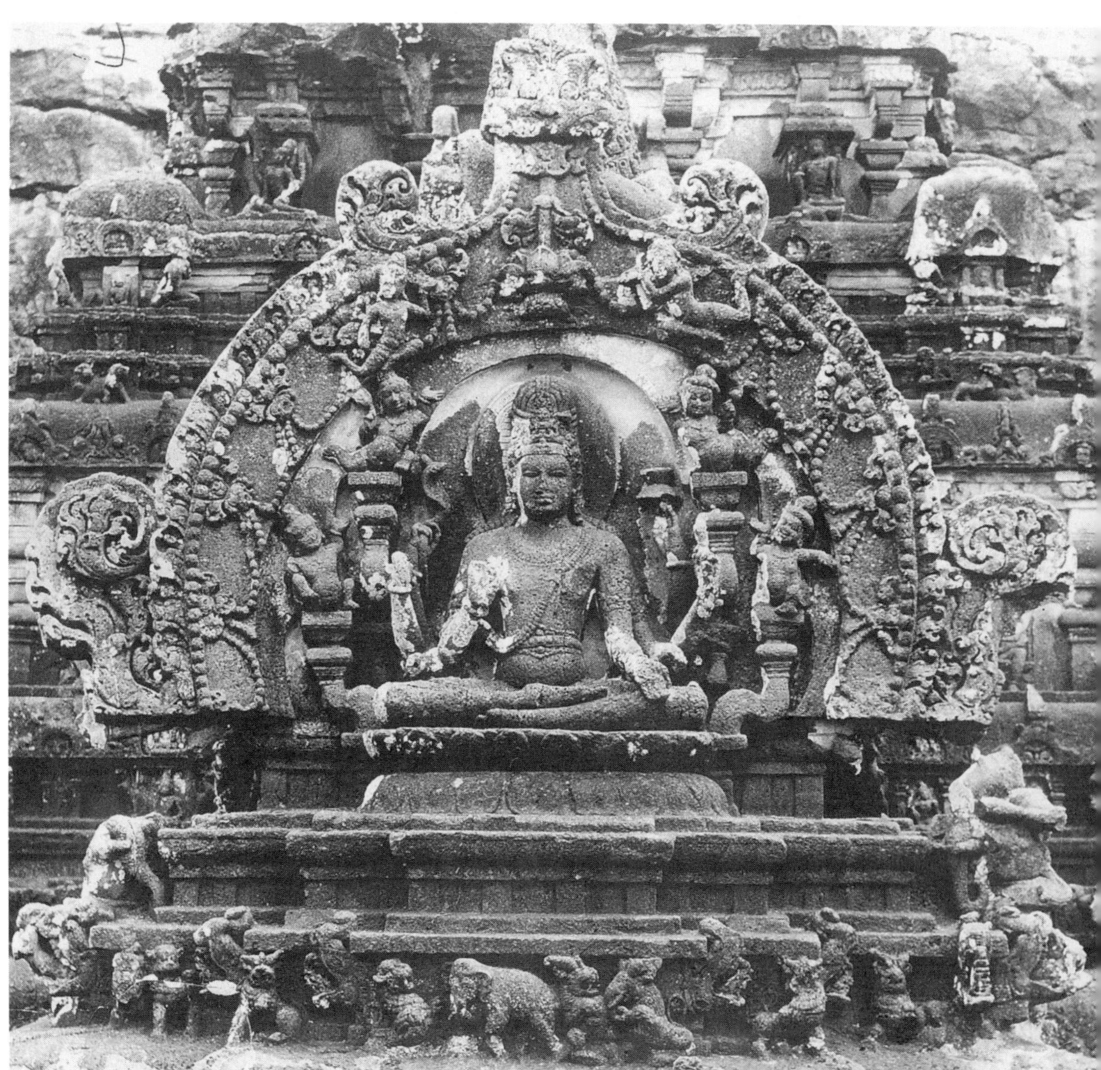

already have some idea of what that may be. Modern scholarship can help show us where to look. Art invests the "things" of iconography with form by topic working, to ensure that we do not read them as if they were everyday people and objects, but realize that they are symbols for something beyond what they would be in everyday reality. That identity is only a part—even if a major part—of the set of subsidiaries contributing to the overall meaning. A clear example is the female downward-pointing triangle referred to in Chapter 1. It does not refer to genitalia as such for their own sake; instead, its very formality shows that, even if it is placed on a sculpture in the correct anatomical position, it refers to genitalia as symbolic of something more than physical genitalia—usually in connection with female mythology. If genitalia were rendered with meticulous naturalism, the reference might stop at the plain fact.

Nonartists, including art historians, often fall into the trap of reading the identifiable people and objects in an already represented iconographic scheme in this literal way as if they referred to facts, not to a meaning beyond, which may be quite elusive and difficult to approach without misunderstanding. The iconography should be a vital area of creative invention. Most religious traditions have prescribed at least some part of the iconography of religious sculpture. Even so, a good artist's topic working, which we can think of as the iconography of form, always takes the meaning of the whole far beyond any prescribed basics. Some major late twentieth-century artists have developed their own iconographies, and since these are not commonly understood (perhaps even kept deliberately mysterious), they may be grasped only intuitively by visitors.

Groups and Address

Sculptors also combine tenor images into groups. How they position them in relation to each other and the visitor conveys an important part of the images' meaning, evoking responses rooted in our feeling for dramatic human interaction and address. Figure tenors that are side by side, facing front, may compel the visitor into one kind of response, such as being invited to identify with or even being cowed by them. Figures positioned face to face involved with each other invite the visitor to witness their interrelationship from outside. A composition of large groups resembling theatrical tableaux requires the artist to deploy an expressive language of bodily posture and gesture, and link up the shapes into meaningful sequences. Rodin was a master of this kind of expression.

The overall image may be extremely complex, involving far more than individual figures or simple groups. A cathedral or a temple covered with sculptured figures and decoration may constitute the overall image to which each individual figure contributes in its place, prescribed by the customs and doctrine of the religion it serves. Greek temples had figure compositions located high on the frontage in the pediment. Indian and Maya temples had humanoid and animal shapes "emerging" from their structures. Christian medieval cathedrals had many figures of prophets and saints placed along the doorjambs, images of doctrinal events such as the Last Judgment higher up, and saints and holy scenes in shrines and around the walls. All such figures were placed in their positions so as to address themselves to visitors in specific ways, especially from above down. This placement ensured that they would be experienced as more than commonly human—as potent spirits, gods, and inhabitants of the supernatural worlds, and in the case of Christianity, as figures who actually constituted "the Church." The point is that these figures address themselves in human terms intelligible to the human beings for whom they were made. The human modes in which they communicate are those that the people in each culture recognize and accept.

The French writer André Malraux described in his major work *The Metamorphosis of the Gods* how each traditional sculpture's early historical role as vehicle for images of the divine becomes progressively modulated and diluted, with periodic revivals. He stressed that sculptural images never represent or refer to simple things or persons as one might encounter them in the street, but refer always to the "trans-human," the more than actual. We might now say that the formal qualities of sculpture lift the images they embody to a level "out of this world." The designating forms in question, like the forms of all our arts, are not of the logical order of mental abstract generalities, abstracted from existing instances as a lowest common element, but point to concrete universals, which aim to comprehend all the possible variant relationships of the formal type.

If we recognize any all-embracing Whole of which all apparent separations and distinctions are functions—whether we call it a family of Gods, One God, Brahman, cosmic reality, the Absolute, the Will as thing-in-itself, or the Void—it must by definition also embrace all our varied thoughts and mathematical or philosophical ideas about it, all our investigative technology, and all our religious expressions. We must also recognize that none of our thoughts or ideas, however mathematically complex, can actually *be* it, escape outside it, or totally represent it: they are part of it. Throughout human history, including present history, people have tried nevertheless to face toward this Whole and imagine some forms through which they might reach, perhaps in stages, toward it. These forms have often been embodied in overall sculptured images, which by their scope and articulated wholeness, embracing both beauty and severity, serve as a numinous window onto something which the window itself cannot be. Temples and cathedrals work in this manner, and separate works of art whose tenors are the locus where the artist witnesses the maximum degree of Being can serve as stages on the way

45. *St. John the Beloved Asleep on the Bosom of Christ*, South German, wood, ca. 1310. This image expresses mystical love by its sequences of linear fold-shapes running across and uniting each figure with the other. (Courtesy Staatliche Museen zu Berlin.)

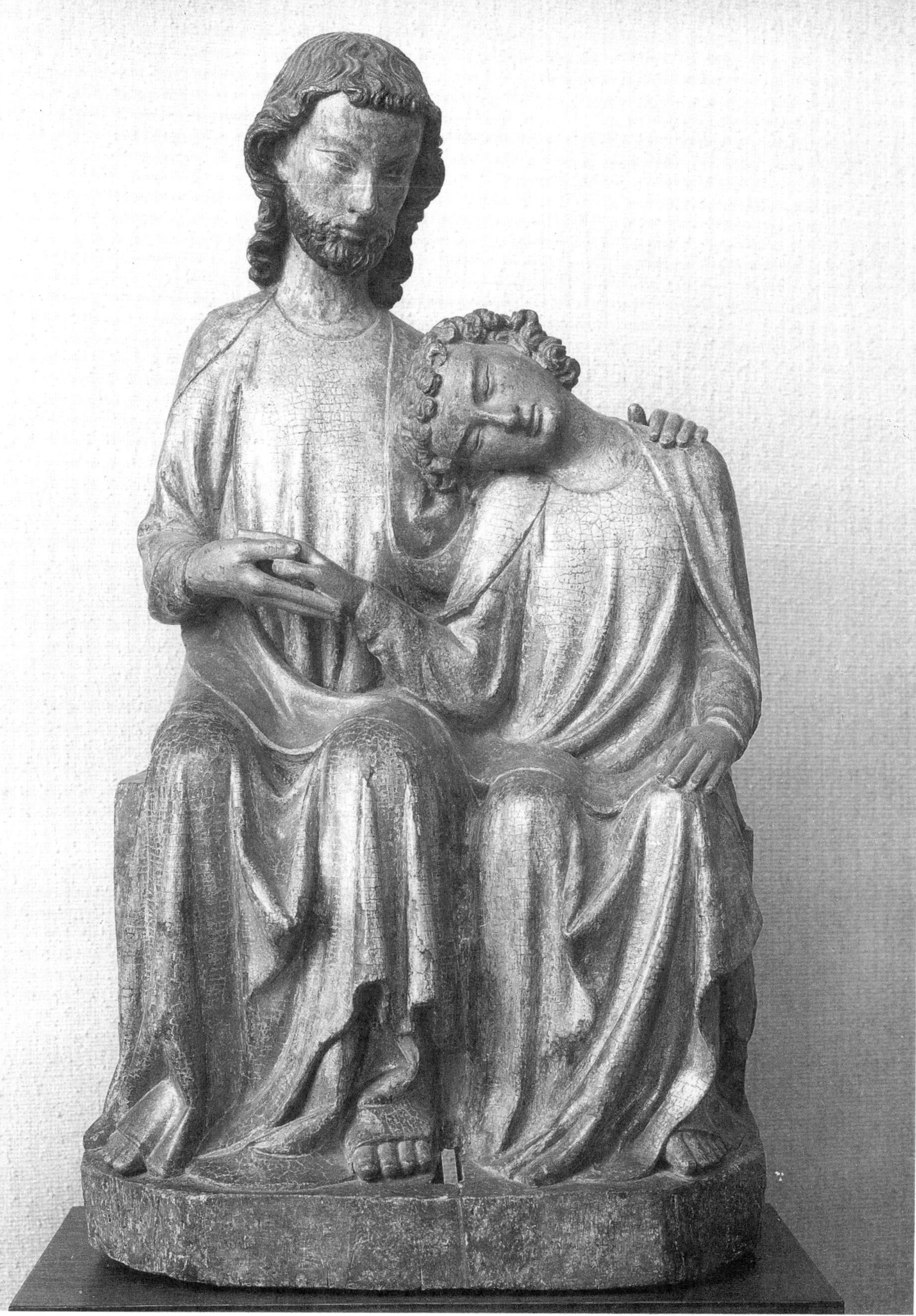

(which may be why some critics have called our museums of art our modern cathedrals). This notion provides a clear justification for the sculptor's continuous and endless search.

One characteristic of much recent and admired art, however, is the assumption that the only relevant level of reality is that of material object and external fact. Already existent physical objects, tangible, smellable, audible, tastable, and identifiable through first imagination concepts, have shapes that are all too often referred to in criticism as "forms," implying that *forms* are the same as *things*—a confusion this book specifically rejects. This confusion may be related to a need some artists recently have felt to take their places in the modern world as hard-nosed realists, rather than as the spiritualizers that some earlier twentieth-century artists, heirs of the Symbolist movement, undoubtedly were. In addition, contemporary arts are overwhelmingly concerned with "foreground objects," that is, objects close at hand rather than those suggesting deep space. Such an attitude seems to be historically conditioned rather than absolute, and possibly has been induced by modern city living. It contrasts sharply with attitudes familiar in other historical contexts where sculptors have consciously worked "for the eyes of God"—as for instance high on a cathedral fabric—intending their work to amount to an act of prayer and praise.

When we preserve fragments of great works of the past we may admire them for the power of their sculptural language, and we may supplement them with the help of art history and museological display techniques. But we would be wrong to imagine that we can do more than glimpse the shadow of their true overall images. Since the European Renaissance, we have installed fragments of sculpture in collections and museums: torsos, broken heads, even toes. Their very fragmentary quality can awaken in us feelings that are far more than mere nostalgia for a vanished past, playing on the pathos of vanquished kingdoms and our physical empathy for dismembered human forms, or on the enigma of objects whose signifying context has disappeared. Nineteenth- and twentieth-century sculptors have made works resembling damaged fragments of larger works that never existed, perhaps intending to attach these feelings to them, and so "authenticate" them by their reference (maybe ironical) to acknowledged "museum masterpieces." Some assemblage artists also make mock fragments to include in their compilations.

Image Articulation

Relational symbols for unity, which comprise the third level of integration in the overall image, can be based on schematic arrangements in space. Many Surrealist sculptors juxtapose—either side by side or one over the other, arrayed on a wall space or framed—components that are incongruous because they belong within orders of reality unconnected in the realm of the first imagination. A combination might be, for example, an eroded branch, monkey skull, light bulb, and torn magazine. These sculptors may set out their components in simple orders such as straight or curved rows, arranged on geometrical plans, on shelves or in tiered boxes, perhaps adding deliberately obscure or misleading titles or text. The artist may also use intuitive placing and deliberate mismatchings of weight and scale to contribute to the "dissolving, diffusing, and dissipating" of first imagination identities. This forces the visitor both to accept and to bypass such identities, searching deeper for second imagination correspondences. Many present-day sculptors still operate as latter-day Surrealists, perhaps because they feel there is no current iconography with symbolic depth to which they can subscribe.

The simplest juxtapositions can promote unexpected, often witty, formal images, such as Picasso's bicycle–bull's-head or Oldenburg's giant fabric cake and hamburger pieces (based on Salvador Dalí's earlier "soft watch" notion), or represent some part of the image in terms of another object—a nose as a thumb or penis, for example. But overall images that rely on nothing more than an arrangement in common space do not adequately symbolize the integrity and wholeness to which all aesthetic articulation ultimately refers, however strongly contrasted their basic shapes may be. Adorno pointed out that schematic arrangements amount to no more than ready-made commonplace wholes, already familiar, and that to use them short-circuits one of the main purposes of art, which is to discover fresh orders of wholeness. Radical shaping sculpture may be more likely to achieve this end.

Referring back to the two-dimensional tangram process, we can see how the overall image arises as an intrinsically static arrangement in and of three-dimensional space. The term *arrangement* implies elements to be arranged; these are the aggregates, which are themselves arrangements of basic shapes. The components of an assemblage function at both levels of arrangement. An arrangement works because the minds of both artist and visitor are able to identify between objective shapes formal connections that are not themselves recognized objects. The structure of the arrangement represents a kind of abstract summary of human experience of moving, acting, and changing, ordered and organized.

Just as there are many open possibilities for arranging the words of speech into extended passages of statement according to the relations implied by the matrixes of the given language, so too for sculptural language. The point of arrangement is not only to set out words or three-dimensional shapes in an abstract pattern but to connect up what they signify to the minds of both maker and receiver. In all languages, especially the visual arts, it is important to distinguish and identify elements to be arranged, the focal nexuses of relations, from the arrangement itself, so that the recipient can grasp the intended meaning.

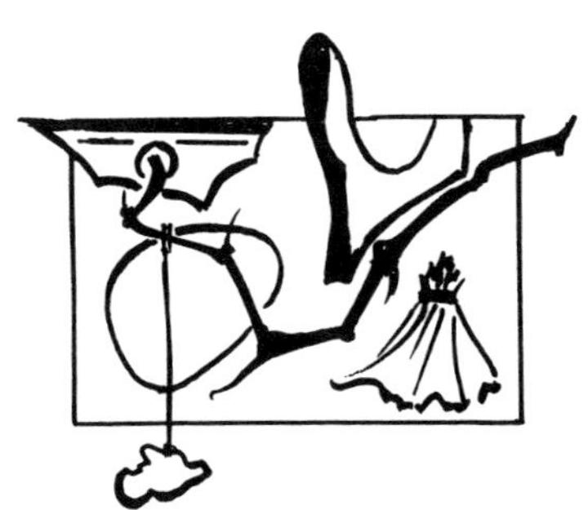
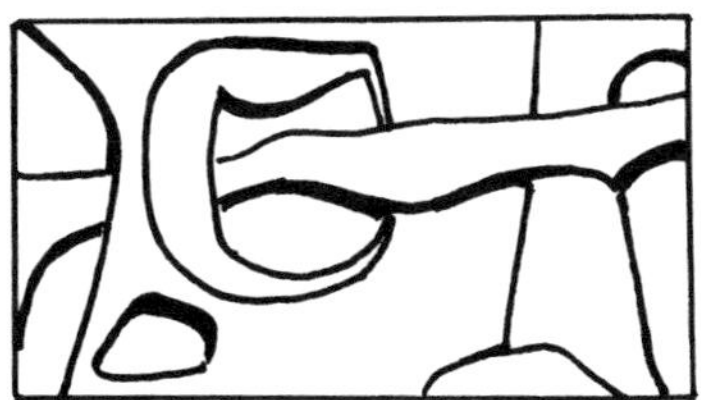

Figure 40.
Formal connections between shapes that are not themselves recognized objects.

Next I propose a few considerations basic to executing and laying out sculptural arrangements as overall images. They are suggestions, not rules.

Humanity and Order

The human being stands upright, surrounded, broadly speaking, by six directions he or she distinguishes in the environment of space: in front, behind, left, right, above, and below. These may be schematized according to the rectangular axes we apply to conceptualizing three-dimensional space, though in the direct and enormously complex human experience to which sculpture refers, we think of them far less rigidly and expect them to carry psychological implications. "Front," or "before," is the region to which we humans normally attend, where we feel alert and ready. "Back," or "behind," is invisible and dangerous, where we need protection. "Near" and "far," either of a whole sculpture or of relative positions of elements within one, can carry important implications. Any transitional moment from front to back or the reverse evokes responses colored by its direction. A frontal image "addresses" us with a specific emotive tonality. One we see from "behind" usually invites us to identify with it. Left and right define directions of transit across our field of attention. The physiology of the brain and consequent cultural adaptations differ between right- and left-handed people, and the usual direction of reading in literate societies also affects people's responses to and participation in directional moments.

We all experience "above" and "below" in relation to the pull of gravity. We naturally feel something "lying grounded" or heavy-based as being at rest, and something lofty as dominant if bulky, but rising or floating if less substantial. We use the terms *heaven* and *earth*, along with their connotations, to interpret our feelings about high and low. With the whole range of these direction-specific associations in mind, we can see that combinations of such directional moments embodied in particular shapes are capable of evoking a variety of more complex responses. A weighty sculptural feature rising and receding in space from the near lower left-hand side, on a diagonal course, will convey a certain expressive effect, depending on how we read its implied motion—another group of spatial and compositional elements will create a different impression. The underlying factor is that such meaning is derived in relation to our human scale and stance.

In creating a sculpture as an objective "other," we establish its sets of inner directions either as if they complete their interactions within the piece or as an environment into which we can physically enter. The former is normal with most (not all) radical shaping, the latter with environmental installation art.

Movement and Moment

Moments implying movement to the imagination play an overwhelmingly important part in the expression of all sculpture. Unless we are prepared to incorporate or respond to them with some degree of insight, we may have to remain content with generating or receiving relatively vague and weak responses. The actual movements that kinetic sculptors have so far been able to realize have been relatively limited, whereas the possibilities of implied moments have always been many and various. We interpret the expression of lines as analogous to verbs in speech referring to movement, action, and change, in terms of what we can call (following Matisse) arabesque functions: swoop, droop, sweep up or away, undulate from one side to another, move into or in from depth, reach, cross, spread, gather, hang, wheel, coil, enclose, and so on. Such movements may be carried by edges or surfaces, along, across, or through volumes. Complexes of these kinetic moments articulated and woven together among all the three-dimensional shapes composing an overall image generate its total effect.

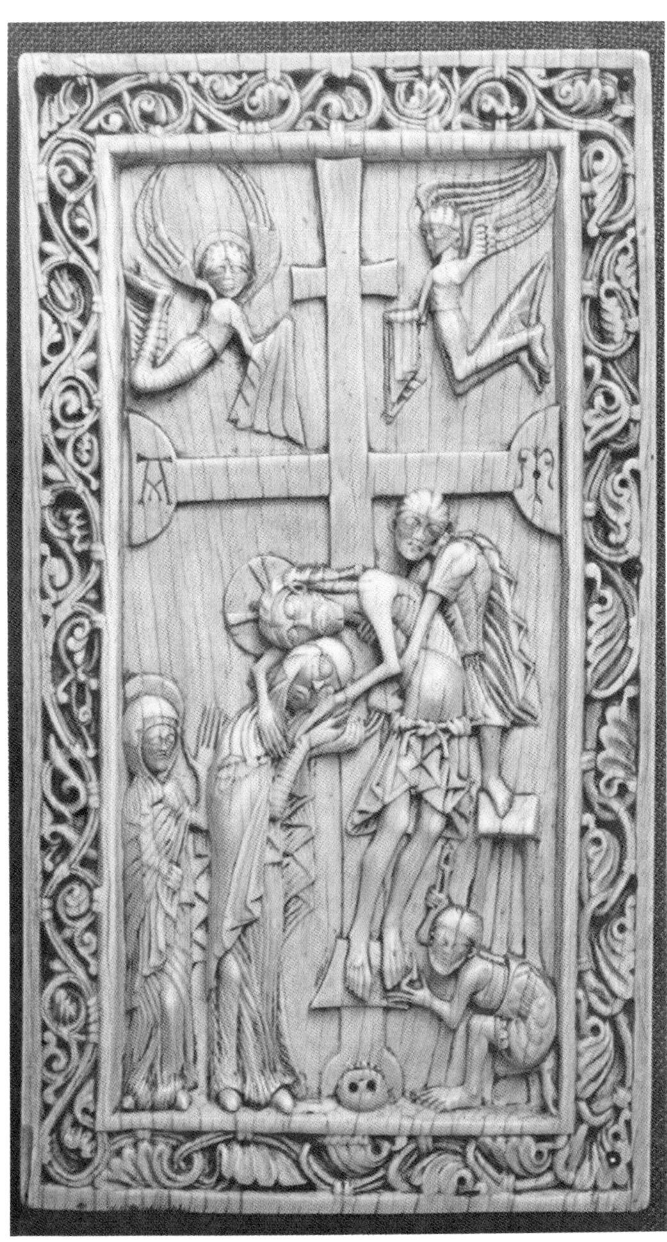

46. *The Deposition of Christ from the Cross*, English, ivory, ca. 1150. A tiny panel constructed as a dramatic sequence to be read from bottom left up through the heads and hands down to the crouching Magdalen at lower right; the angels signify ascent to Heaven. (By courtesy of the Board of Trustees of the Victoria and Albert Museum.)

Sequences

Implied moments may "interact" by being given specific kinds of connection to each other, which can be difficult to describe. A sculptor can, for example, give to some kind of linear vector carried along one direction of a surface either no teminus at all, so that it "floats" off free, or some definite and specified terminus in another shape which blocks it off or modifies its expression by linking it into a sequence of further shapes.

Connections between solids may also follow forms we have derived from encounters in the actual world or the world of art, such as the corresponding sections of an object broken by force, or the continuity between shapes where a slice seems to have been cut out, or the space between two end-walls which has a clearly defined negative volume. Other examples are ends that overlap, show identifiable stepped intervals, or participate in recognizable rhythmic sets. One special version of these kinds of junctions combines sequences of shapes that reach and bridge toward each other lengthwise, unsupported across open space. The purpose of all of these is to articulate the overall image and eliminate any feeling of repeated breaks and fresh starts, which can reflect or imply weak invention.

Variety of Size and Prominence

One general principle for composing overall images that we need to bear in mind (at the same time resisting any temptation to interpret it in alien sociopolitical terms as "antidemocratic") is purely visual-tactile in effect. Both Chinese painting theory and John Ruskin's writings on architecture pointed out independently that it is best to make all the elements of any composition accord with a set of distinct, varied, and consistent—but not deadly regular—scales of size and prominence. This means there should be a maximum and a minimum on the scales for both basic shapes and aggregates, and that a composition works best if at the upper ends of the scales there is only one or perhaps two principal and prominent features; around them, others lower down the scale toward the minimum may focus in increasing numbers. This meets the need for variation and eliminates the risk of involuntary dullness and repetition. All kinds of relationships between larger and smaller are possible; the larger may include and enclose the smaller features, hold a cluster of them together, or stand free among them. The sizes and densities of lower-scale elements may differ among the various aggregate regions of the piece.

A range of size and prominence challenges the sculptor's intuitions of balance. Indeed, establishing a sense of balance among the most widely differentiated and distributed elements of a scale is a major source of both unity and interest in an overall image, and marks an effective sculpture. The stronger the challenge, the more expressive the resolution. One of the outstanding characteristics of much recent art is excessive caution in restricting the range of types and sizes of elements included in a single piece.

Dance Masks

The tribal masks worn by dancers exploit actual movement and balance, which play significant roles in the overall images. We normally see the splendid masks made in Africa, Oceania, and the Pacific Northwest of America displayed stationary and isolated in showcases. Some masks have parts that the dancer could move independently, so we need to exercise our imaginations, perhaps with reference to documentary footage of the pieces in use, to sense what these sculptured pieces were meant to convey.

Order and Life

The overall image represents the final, overarching unity of a non-schematic order to which all the subsidiary basic shapes and aggregates contribute; we need to reach intuitively for what that unity might be. Just as we can think of a living organism as reducible to arrangements in space and time of cells and functional arrangements of cells into organs, which we recognize and interpret in terms of the organic whole, so too we can recognize the formed component material of sculpture in terms of its own kind of articulated whole. Even though a work may seem to be a simple, inert physical object, we have to recognize it as a construct in a human language, and appreciate both its meaning in human terms and consequently its metaphorical "life." The meaning of sculpture reaches far beyond the conventional utilitarian concepts and systems that govern our pragmatic activity and even our philosophies. It evokes levels of experience and order that may seem to have no pragmatic value whatever. Sculpture's value is that it offers its own intuitions of wholes as subsidiaries to a wider ultimate whole, which includes what we feel imaginatively as well as what we think we know factually. To intuit such wholes can lead to experiencing that which aesthetic theory in both the East and the West has recognized as in some sense the "sublime," a higher level of Being, a delight that cannot be described in alien languages whose concepts are circumscribed by their everyday, pragmatic and functionally predetermined systems.

9
Sculptural Drawing

Codes

It is impossible, of course, literally to transfer something three-dimensional—whether it be a motif in the actual world or an idea for a sculpture—onto the two-dimensional surface of a sheet of paper. Drawing operates through sets of codes we need to learn to use and read. Sculptural drawing tends to employ elements from these codes selectively. For example, since sculptures usually stand free in space, sculptural drawings are inclined to emphasize and shape especially carefully the outlines with which they enclose their tenors, so as to define them coherently in relation to their environment. Many sculptural drawings make no use at all of shading, and those that do may use it in special ways that do not refer directly to cast shadows.

In cultures where sculpture is the leading art, it is common for artists to begin by taking a formal grasp of the overall shapes constituting the entire tenor in terms of either defined enclosures or the extended linear contours of areas of surface. A sculptural drawing thus tends to confront and define all the component parts of the image equally.

Graphic Aspects of Three-Dimensional Working

Drawings are made with some kind of pointed implement that leaves traces of its movement over the surface. The beholder scans these traces to read their rhythmic changes of direction, thickness, and speed. The point can be of any thickness, ranging from a pen or pencil to a bunch of straw or cloth. A narrower point, however, is better for sculptural drawing because it defines the limits of shapes less ambiguously, although it may therefore lack some of the expressive qualities a looser point can impart. In this respect there is a distinct relationship between specifically sculptural drawing and writing; the earliest forms of hieroglyphic writing (for example Egyptian and Mesoamerican) refer to conceptually enclosed and contained objects in neutral space.

It is likely that drawing and sculpture have always had some kind of relationship, since we have seen how the surfaces of fully three-dimensional works are functional derivatives of mobile scanning traces through space. Early drawing probably developed more complex sequences of shape across its notional space than sculpture across its actual space, though

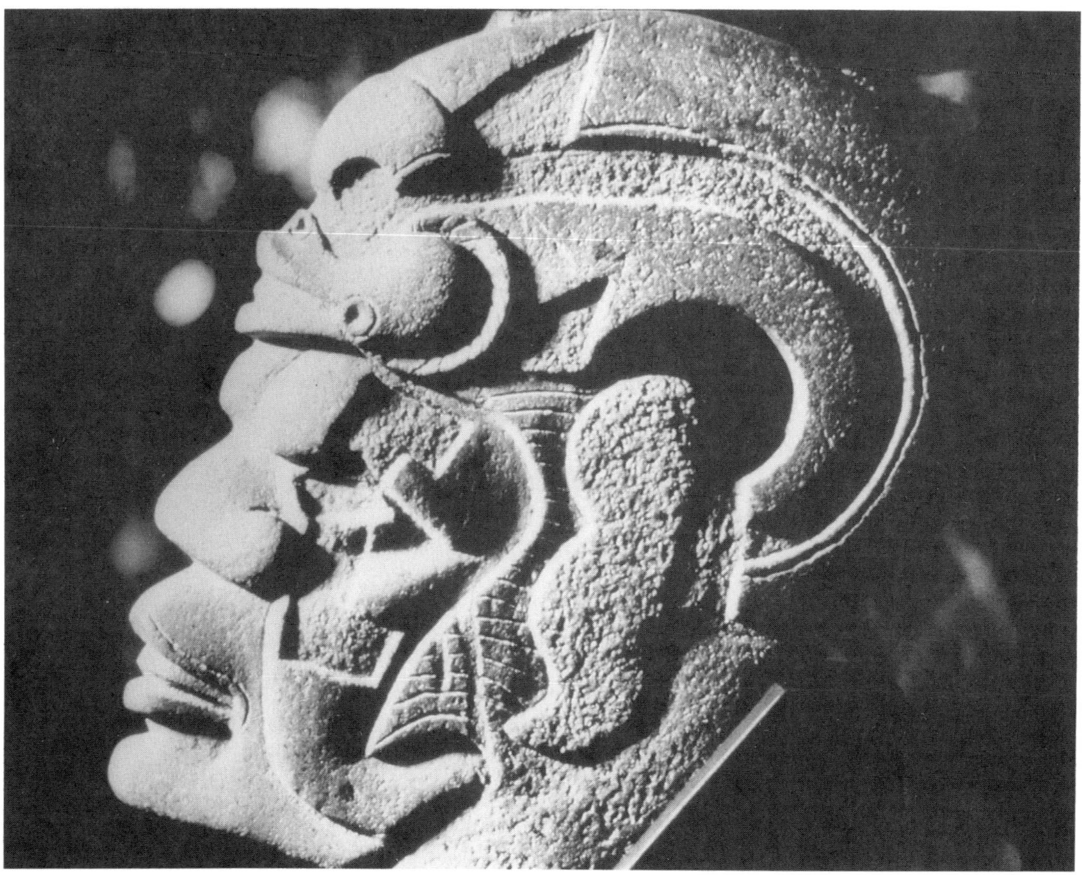

47. Axe, Vera Cruz, Mexico, basalt, classical period of Vera Cruz. Flat, linear, stylized gesture-shapes imbue the ritual implement with its supernatural power. (Courtesy Instituto Nacional de Antropología e Historia, Mexico.)

good sculpture develops its own kinds of three-dimensional linear complexity; we can talk in a real sense of "drawing in space." Sculptors' drawings reveal how they conceive their three-dimensional works as transverse spreads of body across a notional, void ground, which, so to speak, stands up vertically in relation to the viewer. This notional void gives our visual field its extent across our sight lines, and seems to be vital to our three-dimensional spatial perceptions, as was discussed earlier. Among sculptors, even highly skilled draftspersons depict relatively few foreshortenings.

During prehistoric Magdalenian times, the artists who modeled the clay relief of mating bisons in the Tuc d'Audoubert cave in France, and who carved the cavewall relief of the Venus of Laussel in the region of Aquitaine, were laying out and raising their images according to linear outlines conceived originally in two dimensions. Even the famous little Paleolithic stone carving called the "Venus of Willendorf" has a distinctly graphic frontal aspect. These works exemplify the notion explained earlier of the "presentation face." If we study one of the major Paleolithic wall paintings of an animal, we can see how the artist obviously worked at a slow pace, constantly checking across the surface of rock being outlined (in effect a presentation face) to match what he or she was immediately doing to previous stages in the work.

In the earliest great phases of sculpture in the Middle East, in Egypt and Mesopotamia during the third and second millennia B.C., the major powerfully three-dimensional sculptures, and even the smaller hand-modeled clay pieces, followed originally graphic, frontally conceived designs. These designs were orthographic projections, in which every part is viewed as if from a sight line at right angles to it, following the plan of the writing line and using the basic formal repertoire that the written script schematizes. Even now it can be interesting to consider the relationship between a sculptor's handwriting and the formal repertoire he or she uses in major art work.

Orthographic Projection and the Cone of Vision

We do not have any sculptors' designs from the Classical Greek and Roman periods, but such two-dimensional art as we do have suggests that the mode of orthographic projection continued through the Archaic and early Roman periods, and was probably only modified late in the first century A.D. Orthographic projection is a natural design approach for sculptors who are carving largish images — nearly life-size or over — squared off in advance, sometimes only roughly. They then confront each area as they work it at the comfortable level of working, more or less at right angles, and cut back around the contours from the front at first and incorporate the side faces similarly. Many carvers do this still and draw accordingly.

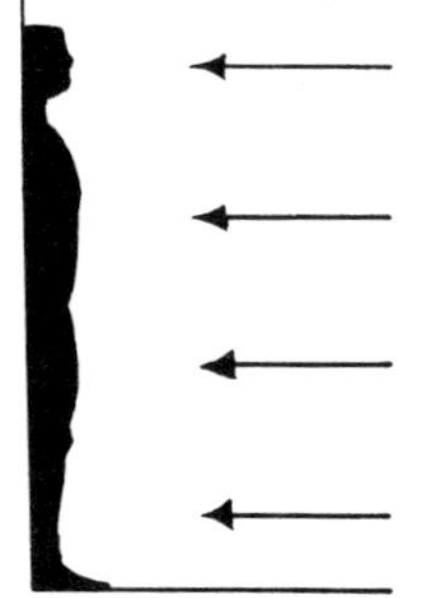

Another approach that can be important, especially for smaller-scale pieces, is based on the natural "cone of vision" which comes fully into effect at short viewing distances. A viewer (not a toucher) looks down onto the tops of lower shapes and either slightly down on or level with upper shapes. A sculptor who is accustomed to working at such scales tends naturally to draw "cone of vision" images, with the topsides of their lower elements seen more extensively than those of higher elements. This approach to the drawn image belongs to the era of "optical veracity" perspective art, after about 1480 in the West until twentieth-century "post-tribal" sculpture arrived. It is associated with developments in painting and the growth of the practice among sculptors of drawing for viewers besides members of their own studio.

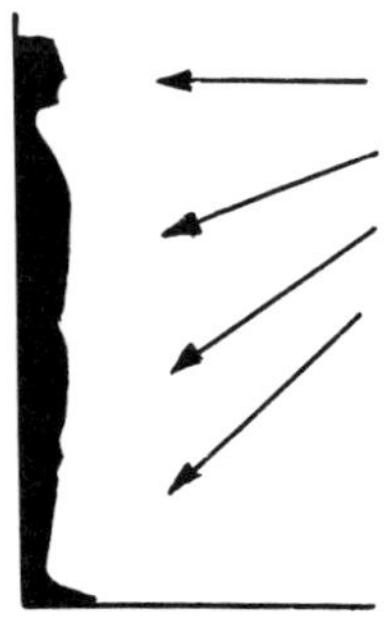

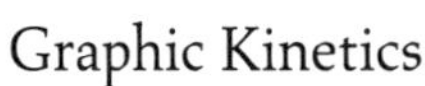
Figure 41. Orthographic approach (above) and cone-of-vision approach (below).

Graphic Kinetics

An important aspect of the relationship between drawing and sculpture is the way in which sculptors seem to adopt into their material shapes the hand's kinetic sweeps, curves, and undulations natural to pen or brush drawing of their time. For example, in some Romanesque stone reliefs we can see imitations of the pen squiggles we recognize from manuscript drawings along the bottom edges of draperies. The sustained convex curves of the brush contours we know on Greek vase paintings surely reflect the carefully continuous surfaces of sculptures contemporary with them.

Even more compelling is the parallel between the long, deeply curved and undulant wiry lines of Far Eastern drawing and the contours and surfaces that the contemporary sculptors developed from them. This effect may have resulted from the custom, widespread especially among Buddhist icon sculptors who wished to stay as faithful as possible to sacred old prototypes, of keeping and passing on from master to pupil collections of pattern drawings from which they worked, and which might have been themselves in a relatively archaic version of the current drawing style. There is thus a literal reason for thinking of sculpture as "drawing in space," especially for the way in which it invites the imagination to participate in the experience of the hand's movement.

Sculptors and Drawing

In many great sculptural traditions—for example, African and some Mesoamerican—sculptors probably did not draw their images in advance, perhaps not even laying them out graphically on the block. They simply followed the routines of their learned craft. A German woodcut of the mid-sixteenth century depicts a late Gothic carver chopping a figure out of a tree trunk with a large axe, directly from an unwilling live model who is being firmly held in position. Until relatively recently, sculptors may not have needed to draw, unless they also worked in two-dimensional media.

Sculptors' drawings fall into two principal types. First is the class of mere mnemonic notes, usually no more than schematic outlines of overall ideas or proportional schemes in basic linear technique. (Keeping parts of a large image in proportion when cutting material away can be particularly demanding.) Second is the class of drawings that set out to emulate the three-dimensional effects of worked sculptural shape. This category includes painters' drawings handed to craftspeople for them to carry out in three dimensions, as Picasso and Miró did. Some modern sculptors have adopted the drawing-board methods of the technical draftsperson to design pieces they intend either to execute themselves or to employ others to execute.

The first class has been used in nearly every culture, especially where it has been important to pass on accurately the layout and proportions of sacred images for religious reasons. Among the earliest examples surviving are probably the fifth-century-A.D. Buddhist drawings preserved in China and Japan, which record image patterns invented thousands of miles away and centuries earlier. In Europe famous examples are those in the sketchbook of the thirteenth-century master mason Villard de

Honnecourt, many of which record designs of both buildings and sculpture he studied on his extensive travels. This class depends on the executive skill of the sculptural craftsperson for realization in three dimensions. In practice, however, many earlier sculptures must have been based on initial graphic images, though not necessarily made by the sculptor, only handed on to him or her from an ecclesiastical authority. Some Romanesque reliefs on architecture are obviously based on drawings in styles familiar in monastic miniature paintings (complete with those pen-squiggles defining the edges of drapery). Many surviving Anglo-Saxon and French Romanesque outline drawings could well have served as patterns for sculpture—particularly reliefs, which depend on graphic invention.

The second class of drawing developed in fourteenth-century Italy, so far as we know, as a consequence of the collaboration between sculptors such as Giovanni Pisano and Andrea Pisano and painters such as Giotto, who had studied ancient Roman sarcophagus sculptures. Giotto is supposed to have introduced into painting and drawing certain techniques of tonal modeling intended to produce the effect of plastic relief. These were developed during the next two centuries to include the intensification of dark color tone outward from the centers of volumes toward the contours where the surface is supposed to turn away into depth. Although this technique was superseded in Renaissance Italy by other methods, it was revived in more recent times by sculptors such as Maillol and Renoir to emphasize the tactile roundness of their volumes.

During most of the Gothic period in Europe, the ecclesiastical patrons of major sculpture approved in advance the iconographical designs of religious sculptures they were commissioning. For this purpose the sculptors had to submit detailed drawings called *modelli*. Whereas painters were able to execute their own such drawings, sculptors were often obliged to hire two-dimensional artists with graphic skills; when they did make their own, the drawing was usually naive.

Drawing and the Frontal Face

Most sculptural drawing of the second class firmly delineates shapes that are known to be present, rather than formulating an optical field of darks with veils of shadow and uncertainties both as to where one three-dimensional shape ends and another begins, and as to the three-dimensional inflection of the frontal faces. Sculptural drawing normally establishes the silhouette contours of shapes clearly, thus defining the inflection of side surfaces, and adopts or invents devices for conveying the inflection of frontal faces.

These devices are extremely important. It is possible that their loss from modern techniques of drawing in favor of planar two-dimensional edge-dominant design is partly responsible for the twentieth-century loss of attention to inflecting the frontal faces of three-dimensional inventions.

In ancient Classical times the main volumes of bodies had been stated as clearly shaped, flat enclosures articulated by long lines running over them to indicate continuous channels subdividing the surface into lesser volumes. Relief was defined by channel lines overlapping in series. In the first century A.D., Roman artists developed techniques of pure shadow modeling of plastic volumes.

The Gothic period evolved the technique of developing the contours of shapes inward, tracking with a multitude of short strokes the principal longitudinal run of each surface. This approach matched the Gothic emphasis on distinctively linear invention. After about 1490, Albrecht Dürer invented "bracelet shading" in his drawings and engravings to match his emphasis on the rounded oval volumes in terms of which he conceived his bodies; artists and engravers all over Europe took up this method. The individually distinct strokes used as shading follow the rounded volumes, fully revealing the envisaged run of the surface, and so resemble a series of bracelets, as might be worn on an arm. Leonardo da Vinci, who had labored for years on a massive equestrian figure in clay, drew the outlines of its opulent curved volumes over and over using elaborate and subtly modulated shadow modeling and contour tone, rubbed and hatched, in combination with bracelets. Michelangelo combined convex and concave bracelets into long sequences running diagonally across the front faces of his figures as if they were runs of claw-chisel strokes, combining them with broken and end-overlapping contours and shadow modeling.

In the Baroque era Gianlorenzo Bernini contributed an extension to the shadow tone repertoire by concentrating his darks into strong pools of shadow where in one of his sculptures there would be a deeply cut hollow. This development, and probably the earlier ones as well, were due to the growing interest during the sixteenth century among collectors and other artists in drawing as an independent art.

The foregoing list of devices for developing the inflections of the frontal surfaces is virtually complete. Later sculptors, such as Barlach and Brancusi, have in effect made personal adaptations of one or more of them, using brusque strokes or varied dots.

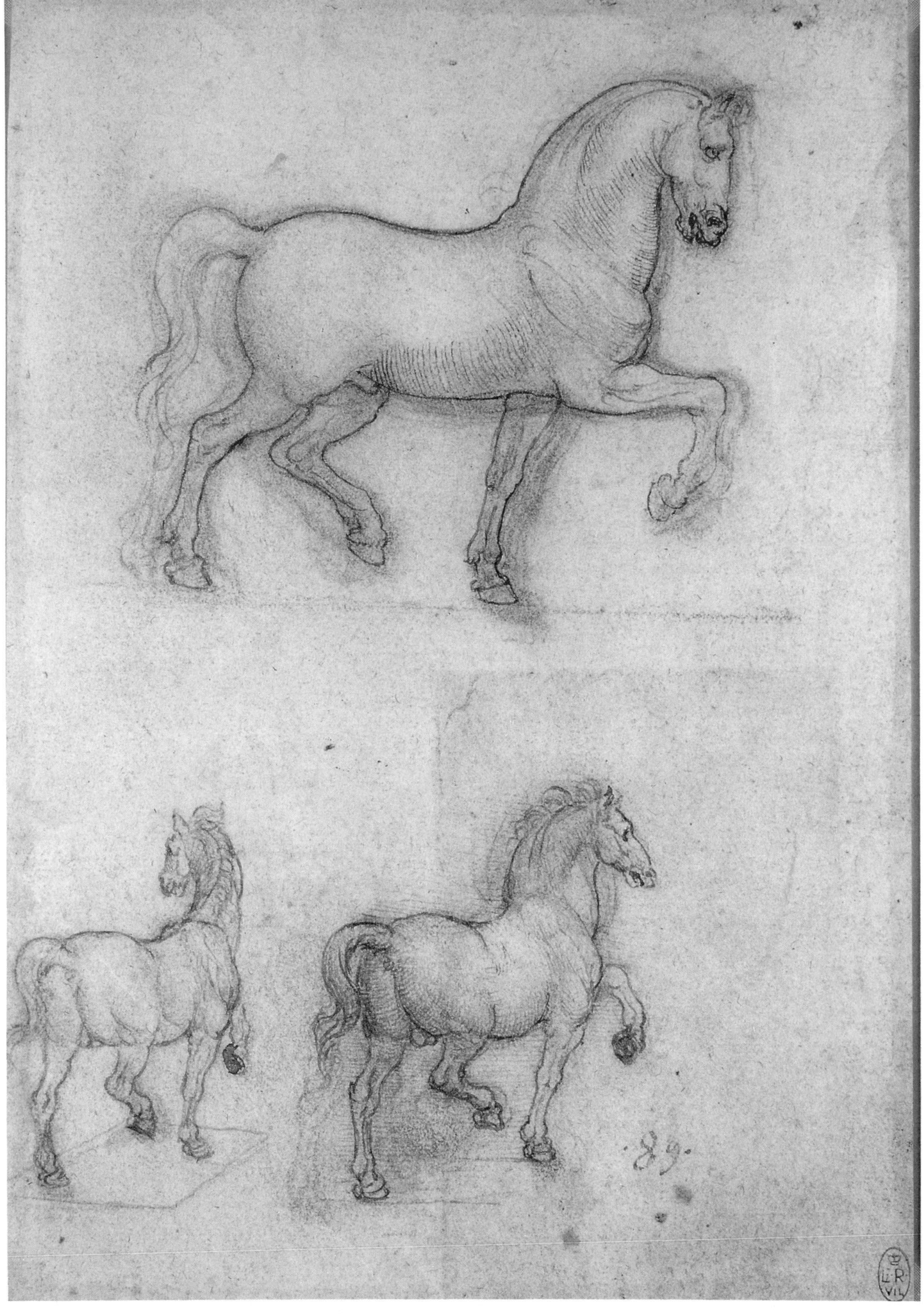

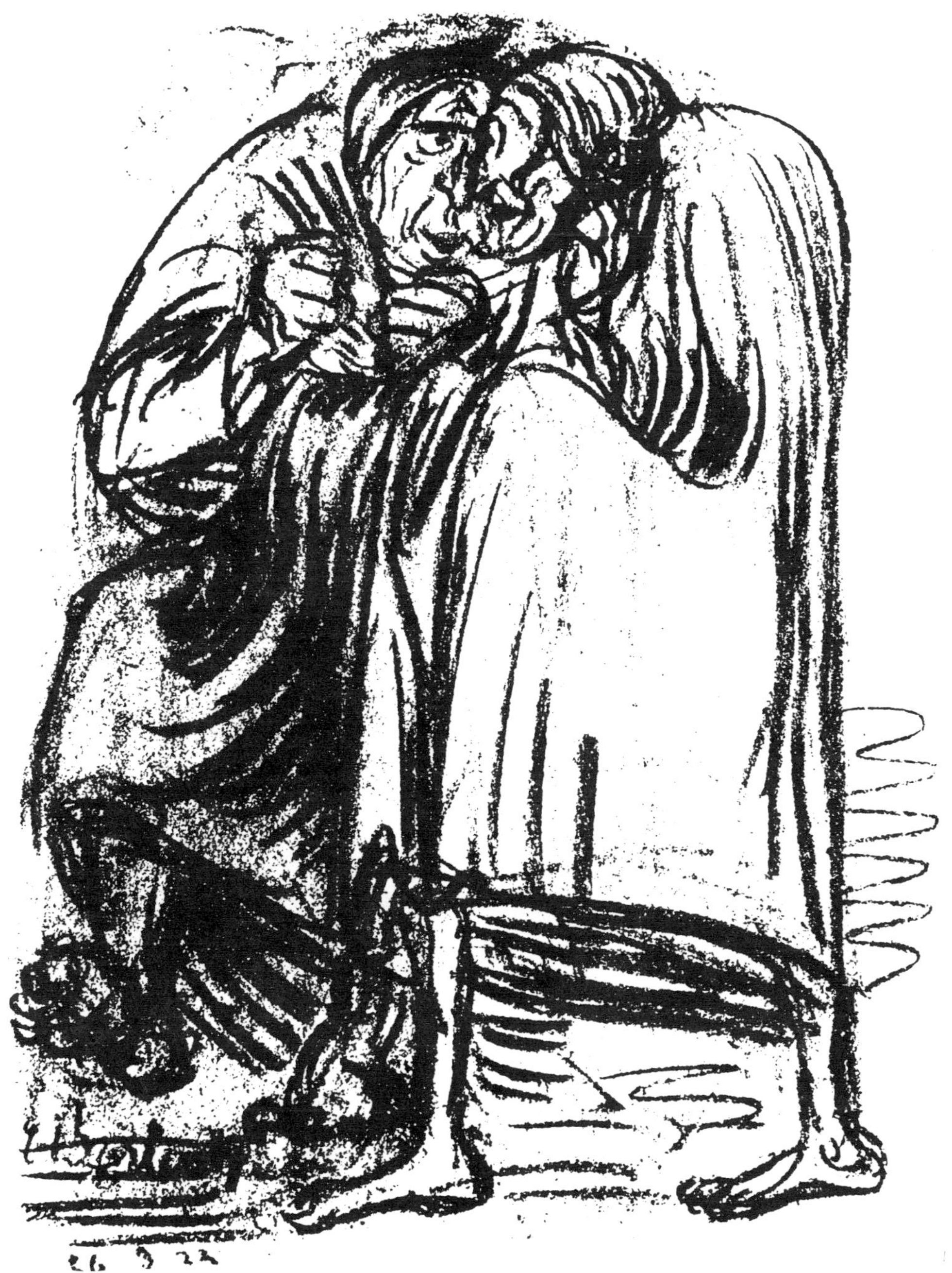

49. (above) Ernst Barlach, *Pair of Furies*, charcoal drawing, 1922. The spatial movement of the facing surfaces is roughly indicated. (Ernst und Hans Barlach Lizenzverwaltung, Ratzeburg.)

48. (left) Leonardo da Vinci, three studies for an equestrian monument, drawings in pen and ink over black chalk, ca. 1493. The artist has delineated the deeply rounded volumes not only by contours but also by "bracelets" reaching around front-facing surfaces. (Courtesy The Royal Collection, copyright © 1994, and the gracious permission of Her Majesty Queen Elizabeth II.)

Conclusion

In identifying and defining the elements of sculpture that make the art form a sophisticated human language of communication that operates across boundaries of time and culture, this book offers fresh lines of investigation for contemporary sculptors and a new and flexible critical-aesthetic framework for all who wish to gain deeper insight into the medium. We have seen that the material and technical aspects of physical making carry their own cultural and metaphorical implications, but that the richest resources for sculptural expression exist at a level of formal imaginative technique, comparable to the application of linguistic structures in spoken language and note-scale-composition structures in music.

Meaning in sculpture is generated through an inner dialogue between the representation of the subject (the tenor) and expression via formal practices and structures (the topic). This basic truth and an awareness of the range of formal-expressive techniques that can be deployed by the sculptor have previously been viewed or intuited largely in isolation, if considered at all. But it is precisely by reaching an integrated vision of these different processes at work that we, as sculptors and viewers, may move toward a richer, more complete experience and understanding of three-dimensional art. The formal-sculptural concepts introduced here are intended to extend the symbolic and formal language resources and make available, in sculptural terms, new grammatical or syntactical possibilities through their varied combination. This foundation allows us also to approach more complex issues to do with the referential range that derives from formal articulation, and with the immanent spiritual and poetical qualities investing sculptural "manifestation" in real space.

Why should all of this be so important? Put crudely, it may help restore the dignity of art's content, as against its marketing presentation; equally, it demonstrates that sculptural thought need not be a slave to those layers of meaning inherent in whichever technical practices are adopted. But above all, it provides a key to our reception of sculptural imagery, and elucidates how the "meaning beyond the text," as it is expressed within the *overall image*, achieves its final and unique resolution in the analogical response of the individual viewer.

Index

About the Author

In parallel with a distinguished academic and publishing career, which spanned Western, tribal, and Asian arts, Philip Rawson practiced as a sculptor all his life. Thus *Sculpture*, completing a trilogy with his *Drawing* and *Ceramics*, genuinely stands as the fulfillment of a life's work.

PHILIP RAWSON (1924–1995)